ISIS

THE

UNIVERSAL GODDESS

Goddess of Love and Great Mother—these are the best-known of Isis' aspects. But those are just two of her many faces. This book introduces you to Isis, the Goddess of Healing and Magic; Isis, the Sun and Moon Goddess; and Isis, the Goddess of the Stars and the Earth. Isis in *all* Her aspects is thoroughly explored in this comprehensive book, which includes the history of Her worship, ancient and modern rites, spells, and festivals that honor this world goddess. deTraci Regula, a Priestess of Isis, also presents rare and ancient texts on Isis in an accessible form for you, the modern reader, to ground you in the foundations of Isis worship today.

The few other books about Isis that are available treat Her as an entirely Egyptian goddess. However, *The Mysteries of Isis* presents Isis in Her full glory as a universal goddess, present throughout history in all places and times. Explore Her fascinating associations with gods and goddesses of the Egyptian, Asian, Greek, Roman, Celtic, Scandinavian, and even Christian pantheons. Most of all, you will gain an enormous amount of practical information and many simple techniques to create your own unique relationship with this Goddess of all Goddesses.

Isis has endured—and so has the yearning in human hearts for the divine touch of this goddess. With her abundant array of aspects and faces, Isis offers a rich focus for worship, magic, and spiritual growth.

ABOUT THE AUTHOR

deTraci Regula has been a Priestess of Isis with the Fellowship of Isis since 1983 and is a priestess in other magical traditions as well. With David Harrington, she is the co-author of the upcoming biography of their friend Scott Cunningham, *Whispers of the Moon*. In addition to work in the animation industry on such secular epics as the animated version of *Attack of the Killer Tomatoes*, she also produced and directed the video programs *Herb Magic* with Scott Cunningham and *Witchcraft: Yesterday and Today* with Raymond Buckland.

When not writing, deTraci Regula practices Taoist painting and exploring the family genealogy. Accidentally named for her ancestor William deTraci who was one of the four knights who rather messily assassinated Thomas a Becket in Canterbury Cathedral, deTraci Regula comes from a long line of pagans and freethinkers. Another of her ancestors was chastised by the local bishop for "consorting magically with the horses," though what that means exactly has been mysteriously excised from the family histories. A third ancestor, a Protestant during the reign of the Catholic Queen, "Bloody" Mary, was dug up and burned as a heretic after his death because of certain comments he made in his last will and testament. Although a European Black Virgin statue known as "Our Lady of Regula" may have originally been a depiction of Isis, Ms. Regula can unfortunately find no evidence that would support her claiming the site and statue as personal family property.

TO WRITE TO THE AUTHOR

If you wish to contact the author, please write to her in care of Llewellyn Worldwide, and we will forward your request. The author and the publisher appreciate hearing from you and learning of your enjoyment of this book and how it has helped you. Llewellyn Worldwide cannot guarantee that every letter written to the authors can be answered, but all will be forwarded. Please write to:

deTraci Regula
c/o Llewellyn Worldwide
P.O. Box 64383-K560-6, St. Paul, MN 55164-0383, U.S.A.

Please enclose a self-addressed, stamped envelope or $1.00 to cover costs.
If outside the U.S.A., enclose international postal reply coupon.

FREE CATALOG FROM LLEWELLYN

For more than 90 years Llewellyn has brought its readers knowledge in the fields of metaphysics and human potential. Learn about the newest books in spiritual guidance, natural healing, astrology, occult philosophy, and more. Enjoy book reviews, new age articles, a calendar of events, plus current advertised products and services. To get your free copy of *Llewellyn's New Worlds of Mind and Spirit*, send your name and address to:

Llewellyn's New Worlds of Mind and Spirit
P.O. Box 64383-K560-6, St. Paul, MN 55164-0383, U.S.A.

Llewellyn's World Religion and Magick Series

THE
MYSTERIES
OF
ISIS

Her Worship and Magick

deTraci Regula

1995
Llewellyn Publications
St. Paul, Minnesota 55164-0383

FIRST EDITION
First Printing, 1995

Cover design: Anne Marie Garrison
Cover painting: Moon Deer
Book design, editing, and layout: Susan Van Sant
Art research and editing assistance: Maggie Sullivan
Photographs: Paula Morgan
Rider-Waite Tarot card illustrations reproduced from the designs by Pamela Colman
     Smith in the 1922 reprint of the original 1910 edition of the *Pictorial Key to the Tarot*
     by Arthur Edward Waite, William Rider & Son, Ltd., London.

Grateful acknowlegement is made to E.J. Brill Publishing Company, Leiden, The
     Netherlands, for permission to use an excerpt from Apuleius of Madaura's *The Isis
     Book* (*Metamorphoses, Book XI*), translated and with a commentary by J. Gwyn Griffiths.

Library of Congress Cataloging-in-Publication Data
Regula, deTraci
          The mysteries of Isis : her worship and magick / deTraci Regula. — 1st ed.
          p.   cm.   — (Llewellyn's world religion & magic series)
          Includes bibliographical references and index.
          ISBN 1-56718-560-6 (trade pbk. : alk paper)
          1. Isis (Egyptian deity)—Cult—Miscellanea.   2. Magic
     I. Title.   II. Series.
     BL2450.I7R44   1995
     299—dc20   95-20520
                                                                             CIP

Llewellyn Publications
A Division of Llewellyn Worldwide, Ltd.
P.O. 64383, St. Paul, MN 55164-0383

Printed in United States of America

ABOUT LLEWELLYN'S WORLD RELIGION AND MAGICK SERIES

AT THE CORE OF every religion, at the foundation of every culture, there is Magick.

Magick sees the world as alive, as the home which humanity shares with beings and powers both visible and invisible with whom and which we can interface to either our advantage or disadvantage—depending upon our awareness and intention.

Religious worship and communion is one kind of magick, and just as there are many religions in the world, so are there many magickal systems. Religion, and magick, are ways of seeing and relating to the creative powers, the living energies, the all-pervading spirit, the underlying intelligence that is the universe within which we and all else exist.

Neither religion nor magick conflict with science. All share the same goals and the same limitations: always seeking truth, forever haunted by human limitations in perceiving that truth. Magick is "technology" based upon experience and extrasensory insight, providing its practitioners with methods of greater influence and control over the world of the invisible before it impinges on the world of the visible.

The study of world magick not only enhances your understanding of the world in which you live, and hence your ability to live better, but brings you into touch with the inner essence of your long evolutionary heritage and most particularly—as in the case of the magickal system identified most closely with your genetic inheritance—with the archetypal images and forces most alive in your whole consciousness.

OTHER TITLES BY THE AUTHOR

Forthcoming Books

Whispers of the Moon. A biography of Scott Cunningham coauthored with David Harrington.

The Animal Companionary. An unfinished work by Scott Cunningham being completed by David Harrington and deTraci Regula.

Videos

Herb Magic. Scott Cunningham, produced and directed by deTraci Regula.

Witchcraft: Yesterday and Today. Ray Buckland, produced and directed by deTraci Regula.

Lo, I am with you, Lucius, moved by your prayers, I who am the mother of the universe, the mistress of all the elements, the first offspring of time, the highest of deities, the queen of the dead, foremost of heavenly beings, the single form that fuses all gods and goddesses; I who order by my will the starry heights of heaven, the health-giving breezes of the sea, and the awful silences of those in the underworld: my single godhead is adored by the whole world in varied forms, in differing rites and with many diverse names.

Isis to her worshipper Lucius, in Apuleius' *Metamorphoses*.

To Scott Cunningham

Without you much of this book
and much of this writer
would not have been possible.

TABLE OF CONTENTS

Preface — xiii

Chapter One: The First Hour of Daylight
AWAKENING ISIS — 1

Morning Rite to Isis • Morning Rite to Osiris

Chapter Two: The Second Hour of Daylight
PURIFICATIONS FOR RITES OF ISIS — 11

Washing Rites • The Physical Effects of Spiritual Cleansing • Natron • Baths for Purification • Anointing •
Cleansing with Light • Cleansing Ritual Objects, Stones, and Crystals

Chapter Three: The Third Hour of Daylight
ISIS THE UNIVERSAL GODDESS — 21

Isis in Egypt

Chapter Four: The Fourth Hour of Daylight
VISITING THE HOLY HOUSE OF ISIS — 27

Going to the Temple of Isis • Inside an Egyptian Temple • Inside a Greco-Roman Temple • A Few Major
Temple Sites of Isis • Temples of Isis Removed from Egypt • Creating Your Own Temple •
Dedicating a Shrine or Altar

Chapter Five: The Fifth Hour of Daylight
GARBING FOR THE GODDESS — 43

Sacred Clothing • The Knot of Isis • Jewelry and Amulets • Symbols, Signs, and Correspondences of Isis •
The Spectrum of Isis in Ritual Garb

Chapter Six: The Sixth Hour of Daylight
EXALTING ISIS — 67

Praisesongs and Invocations • Goddess of Ten Thousand Names • Personal Names of Priestesses, Priests,
and Devotees • Self-Naming Rite

Chapter Seven: The Seventh Hour of Daylight
THE NOONTIME RITE — 81

Isis and the Sun God Ra • Noontime Greeting • Solar Eclipse Greeting •
The Meditation of the Sun

Chapter Eight: The Eighth Hour of Daylight
ISIS AS A GODDESS OF WAR — 89

Cleopatra the Seventh • Cleopatra Selene—Reflecting Her Mother's Glory • Zenobia, Queen of the Nabataeans, Conqueratrix of Egypt • Queen Serpot and Prince Pedikhons—Battle of Death and Love • Isis Victrix Rite for Protection and Defense

Chapter Nine: The Ninth Hour of Daylight
ISIS AS SEA GODDESS — 97

Invocation to Isis • The Ploiaphesia Festival • Isis as Goddess of Travellers • Meditation of the Waters

Chapter Ten: The Tenth Hour of Daylight
FESTIVALS OF ISIS — 101

The Beautiful Wandering Starry Year: Several Calendars of Egypt • The Egyptian Year • Birthdays of the Gods and Goddesses • Monthly Observations and Daily Associations • The New Year's Celebration • The Going-Forth of Isis: Going-Forth Rite • The Sacred Rites of Koiak—The Osirian Mystery • Ploiaphesia—the Festival of Navigation • Night of the Tear Drop of Isis • Eve of the Epagomenal Days • Isis In Modern Festivals

Chapter Eleven: The Eleventh Hour of Daylight
ISIS THE GREAT PHYSICIAN — 115

Dream Incubation • Diseases and Healing • Manifesting Healing Energy • Ancient Healing Prayers • Isian World Healing Rite • Isis and Modern Diseases

Chapter Twelve: The Twelfth Hour of Daylight
ISIS AND OTHER DEITIES — 127

Isis and Egyptian Deities • Isis and Asian Deities • Isis and Greco-Roman Deities • Isis and Celtic-Scandinavian Deities • Isis and Christian Deities:

Chapter Thirteen: The First Hour of Night
THE EVENING RITE — 149

Nepthys Meditation • The Lunar Meditation • Lunar Energy Exercise

Chapter Fourteen: The Second Hour of Night
IN THE KITCHENS AND GARDENS OF ISIS — 155

Sacred Foods of Isis and Osiris • A Lunar Feast Menu • Miscellaneous Recipes • In the Garden of Isis

Chapter Fifteen: The Third Hour of Night
ISIS THE DANCING GODDESS — 167

The Visit of the Goddesses • Magic Mirror Dance • Isis and Modern Dance • Music in the Temple • Purification with Sound and Motion

Chapter Sixteen: The Fourth Hour of Night
ISIS AS LOVE GODDESS — 177

Isis and Love Spells • The Story of Eros and Psyche • Isis and Early Romance Novels •
Polarity Development Exercise • Into the Coils of the Labyrinth

Chapter Seventeen: The Fifth Hour of Night
ISIS AS DIVINE MIDWIFE AND MOTHER — 187

A Rite for Protection of Children • Parenting Dedication • An Isian Lullabye

Chapter Eighteen: The Sixth Hour of Night
ISIS AND ALCHEMY — 191

Isis and the Angel Amnael • Everyday Alchemy • Scents Sacred to Isis

Chapter Nineteen: The Seventh Hour of Night
RITE OF NIGHT — 197

Midnight Rite • Meditation on the Midnight Isis • The Black Rite

Chapter Twenty: The Eighth Hour of Night
ISIS IN THE STARS — 203

Prayer to Inanna • The Stellar Meditation—Isis of the Heavens

Chapter Twenty-One: The Ninth Hour of Night
ISIS AND THE WORSHIP OF THE HANDS — 209

Sacred Scarabs • Palm Divination Strips • Sistrums • A Traditional Isian Festival Decoration

Chapter Twenty-Two: The Tenth Hour of Night
THE ORACLES OF ISIS — 219

Isian Interpretations of the Major Arcana • The Lotus Reading • Egyptian Runestones •
Divination with Scarabs

Chapter Twenty-Three: The Eleventh Hour of Night
ISIS AND DREAMING — 243

The Journal of the Dreamtime • Dream Diary Entry Format • Learning to Dream • Dreaming Exercises •
Posture for the Temple Sleep • Banishing Rite for Nightmares • An Oneirocrit's Handbook •
Basic Dream Analysis • Dream Interpretations

Chapter Twenty-Four: The Last Hour of Night
MYSTERIES OF ISIS — 253

Mysteries of Isis, Ancient and Modern • The Origins of Isis • Ancient Practices •
Isis and Initiations • Guided Initiations • Recognizing Initiation • Ordination

Appendix A
PLUTARCH'S ACCOUNT OF THE STORY OF ISIS AND OSIRIS — 267

Appendix B
PLUTARCH'S ACCOUNT OF THE ORIGIN OF SARAPIS — 273

Appendix C
APULEIUS' ACCOUNT OF THE PLOIAPHESIA — 275

Appendix D
RESOURCES — 281

ENDNOTES — 284

BIBLIOGRAPHY — 289

INDEX — 294

PREFACE

IFTEEN YEARS AGO, ON a winter's night in Laguna Beach I found on a shelf in the Fahrenheit 451 bookstore two novels by Dion Fortune. These books, *Moon Magic* and *The Sea Priestess*, had a profound impact on my life in that it was within those pages I was first consciously introduced to the living Power of Isis. Through the years that followed I returned to them many times, always drawing new insight, and after several years, I realized that I had found my spiritual path for this lifetime. The rites of Isis resonated for me in a way that no others did. Gradually, I found myself talking to others of this glorious Goddess and of my relationship with Her. I began guiding others, informally, offering what I had discovered and sharing the same books.

Every once in a while, someone wanted more historical information, simpler rites, or additional guidance than the novels alone provided. The seeds of this book were in those requests.

While studying biology at the University of California at Irvine, I discovered in the library dozens of rarely seen books exploring various aspects of the worship of Isis and other deities. In particular, I found R. E. Witt's *Isis in the Greco-Roman World*, and discovered that the history of the worship of Isis was even richer and more varied that I had discovered in my other researches. Many things I had long felt about the Isis faith, but could not confirm, were verified at last in Professor Witt's delightful book. My faith and understanding grew from finding that work.

A lucky chance brought me in contact with the Hon. Olivia Robertson and the Fellowship of Isis, and I was ordained as a Priestess of Isis in 1981. Though the benevolent influence of the Fellowship enlightens every page of this book, this is not an "official" publication and the opinions and information reflect my own point of view and experience, and, of course, any errors are my own.

I hope that the volume in your hands helps you to further explore this sparkling Goddess and find Her meanings for your own life.

May Isis bless!

June 7, 1994
San Diego

ACKNOWLEDGEMENTS

The writing of this book has occupied half a decade and more. During that time, I have been blessed with the influence of many individuals. While some of these persons may be surprised that they had an impact on this volume,there are pages or paragraphs and even chapters that would not exist had their paths not crossed mine.

To all of you, and the many others not listed here, I give my thanks.

For encouragement, inspiration, insightful comments, and great food, my mother, Lorna McGaw.

For providing information, challenges, and/or opportunities for insight, Pediusiri, Jacques Gautreaux, Blair

Knepher, and Dr. Barry Sandrew are all thanked.

For asking all those questions, (especially "So, is the book done yet?") my friends and colleagues Kim Conaway (who modeled the hand positions in the photographs for the Magic Mirror Dance in Chapter Fifiteen), Robert Silva, Rachel Amov, Paula Morgan and Doug Foley and their sons Christopher and Douglas, the late Robert Rike, and the elusive Jana Galadriel Beeman. Morgan MacGregor, who took on the onerous task of pencilling through a manuscript in the presence of the cranky author is to be commended. The friendship and support of David Harrington is also gratefully acknowledged.

For helping to make the completion of this work and others possible, Rick Barker.

No writer is independent of the works that have gone before. The authors are acknowledged in the Preface and in the Bibliography, but here I wish to acknowledge the help and support I have received from the booksellers. Among these, Judi Wilkins, priestess/proprietor of The Better World bookstore, who painstakingly tracked down rare texts for me and shared her joyful energy on so many occasions. And to Jeff Bohannon, proprietor of the Safari Bookstore, who once opened his store in the middle of the night when I realized I absolutely had to have that antique volume with the engraving of the Temple of Isis at Philae right now! and who, along with the other excellent booksellers on Adams Avenue, brought to my hands many obscure and necessary volumes.

Mrs. Mattie Kuiper's kind permission on behalf of E.J. Brill to include exerpts from J. Gwyn Griffith's outstanding translation of Apuleius' *Metamorphoses* on behalf of E.J. Brill is gratefully acknowledged, as is my gratitude to the publisher M.J. Vermaseren that such a fine series of scholarly Isis-oriented materials exists.

And finally, to the persons who had the most impact on the very existence of this volume. I thank Carl and Sandra Weschcke of Llewellyn Publications for the opportunity to join the Llewellyn family of authors and see this work in print. Without the contributions of my editor Nancy Mostad, who guided me and encouraged me to complete this work during a very difficult time, this book would be in a very different and, I believe, much less satisfying form.

I am also grateful to the other members of the Llewellyn team who made this book possible. I'd like to thank Susan Van Sant for her book design and final editing; Anne Marie Garrison, Maria Mazzara, and Tom Grewe for their work on the cover, illustrations, and other artwork; Maggie Sullivan for her art research and proofreading; and Lynne Menturweck and Marilyn Matheny for overseeing this work to its completion.

I acknowledge and thank Isis Herself for what I have perceived as her guidance and many blessings, not least of which was the many years of friendship and inspiration I was blessed to receive from the late Scott Cunningham. Isis, please watch over his rest, and let us know him again.

Again, you all have my gratitude.

——— Why Isis? ———

IF YOU ARE READING this book, chances are that you have felt a resonance with Isis. You may have felt curiosity, a sense of security, or a warm brush of energy when you have encountered a mention of Her. Or you may already be actively participating in the worship of Isis but want to know more of the ancient paths and modern practices.

This book is a day in the Temple of Isis. Its chapters are hours, its pages minutes. We begin with the jubilation of a morning rite, and end with mysteries revealed only while the stars are bright in the sky.

The air is cool as the dawn breezes rise. The sky is lightening in the east. Isis, Goddess of the Rosy Dawn, awaits.

Come.

Morning Prayer to Isis.

Chapter One
The First Hour of Daylight

AWAKENING ISIS

Awake in peace, O Lady of Peace ...
Goddess of Life, Beautiful in Heaven ...

—Padiusiri, from the "Hymn to
Awaken Isis in Her Shrine at Dawn"

A<small>T THE DESERT EDGE</small>, along the banks of the Nile, a distant chanting is heard as dawn streaks the sky.

High on a seaside cliff, a lonely marble temple rings with an early orison to Isis that competes with the birdsong in the trees.

By the marketplace in Rome, a tavern-keeper shakes his head, knowing he is opening his doors late because the Rites of Isis are already underway.

Not far away, the Emperor of Rome hears the Morning Rite begin and decides that yes, it would be wise for him politically and spiritually to dedicate a new temple to this powerful Goddess.

In England, a half-Celt, half-Roman woman thrills to the shaking of a sistrum as a robed priestess begins the ritual.

In a lonely caravanserai on the Silk Road leading to Asia, a travelling priest looks to the globe of the sun rising orange through the desert dust, and yearns for the high carved pillars decorated with gemstones in the magnificent temples of his Goddess, now a thousand miles away.

In the midst of the Nile on the island queendom of Meroe, Her Majesty the Candake shakes a sistrum in unison with the chanting, praying that her Goddess will smile upon her efforts this day in war.

In a ship on a stormy sea, the captain calls upon Isis to save his craft and crew, while a passenger dedicated to a new faith hears their prayers and wonders if this supposed Goddess can ever be conquered, so pervasive is Her influence.

In a barbarian encampment deep in the dark forests of Europe, a returning chieftain announces that his son will be renamed to honor Serapis, the consort of Isis, whose worship he has come to know among the "civilized" world.

In the hills of India, a king of the lineage of royalty enthroned by Alexander the Great in his conquest of the East pauses by a glowingly beautiful statue of Isis and nods in agreement as a priest sings Her praises with half-forgotten verses.

A young girl, dedicated to Isis until her marriage day, daydreams of her beloved and hurriedly runs to the temple where she hopes to see him among the congregation.

In the long hallways of the Library of Alexandria, a lone scholar whispers the words of the morning litany as he pores over an ancient scroll before blowing out his oil lamp and letting the dawnlight enliven the faded words on the page before him.

MORNING RITE TO ISIS

In the many diverse Temples of Isis, the morning litany to awaken Her was chanted each dawn. Though the words differed from temple to temple and changed to suit the unique natures of Isis' manifestations, the meaning and purpose of the opening ritual remained unchanged.

After the night hours passed, the image of Isis, a spark of whose divine essence enlivened the temple, was now awakened, refreshed, anointed, dressed, and presented with offerings. Although often the hours of the night were mythologically very busy for the gods and goddesses, and the nighttime hours possessed their own rituals and rites,

Isis, Queen of the Underworld, gives water to the Heart-soul.

Statue of Anubis lying on plinth with beads. From the collection of the author.

still the loving awakening of the gods and goddesses took place each dawn. The rite was performed unfailingly, whether by a sole priestess in an obscure country shrine, or by a procession of priests and priestesses, chanters and singers, crowding a temple's dim chambers.

For Isis, the morning awakening must have brought a smile to Her lips because Her many aspects and diverse functions would seem to preclude any chance for sleep and divine dreaming. As Queen of the Underworld, sleep and the dreams and astral travels they bring are Her particular domain, aided by Her companion, colleague, and nephew, the jackal-headed Anubis. And as the protectress of Osiris, several of the night hours are Her special post when She must stand ready to defend against the demons of the night who would seek to do harm to

the dead and sleeping souls under Her care.

As Lady of Light and Flame, Isis is Mistress of the Dawn, and the pink glow preceding sunrise is Her smile welcoming the day to come. As both a sun goddess and a goddess of the moon, She is present in both the setting moon and the rising sun, and as a goddess of the air, the morning breezes, especially those from the cooling north, also carry Her essence. The Lady of the Green Plants spends some of the night hours coaxing seeds to sprout and leaves to unfurl; the flowers of the morning open to the touch of Her fingertips.

No need, then, for eternally-vigilant Isis to be brought awake. But now, so that Her priestesses, priests, and temples can be spiritu-ally awakened and reminded that with this new day She again abides with and within them, the Goddess

Isis multiplies Her presence to fill each of Her temples and permit Her Awakening.

Prayer of Awakening

Awake, awake, awake,
Awake in peace,
Lady of peace,
Rise thou in peace,
Rise thou in beauty,
Goddess of Life
Beautiful in heaven.
Heaven is in peace
Earth is in peace
O Goddess,
Daughter of Nut
Daughter of Geb
Beloved of Osiris
Goddess rich in names!
All praise to You
All praise to You,
I adore You
I adore You
Lady Isis!

(Egyptian version)

Nehes, nehes, nehes
Nehes em hotep
Nehes em neferu
Nebet hotepet
Weben em hotep
Weben em neferu
Nutjert en Ankh,
Nefer em pet!
Pet em hotep
Ta em hotep
Nutjert sat Nut
Sat Geb, Merit Ausar,
Nutjert asha renu!
Anekh hrak
Anekh hrak
Tu a atu
Tu a atu
Nebet Aset![1]

Anyone can perform this rite. The shaking of a sistrum can be added to open and close your observance. Although best suited for morning, this rite can be performed anywhere under any conditions. It can also be used whenever and wherever you need to awaken yourself to the presence of the divine. If you have a special sacred space already set aside, you may wish to perform the rite there. If you have a statue or drawing of Isis, or simply a propped-open book containing an image of Isis, light a candle in front of the image and recite the rite.

After the prayer is recited, stand in silence for a moment. If you can, leave the candle burning for a time. When you do extinguish it, wait until the tip of the wick has ceased glowing and the last wisp of smoke has dissipated. This shows respect for the Goddess and provides an ending for your rite. You may also choose to waft the smoke from the extinguished wick up over your head in a purification and blessing.

It is said that all true sanctuaries of the gods and goddesses maintain a perpetual altar fire. In fact, this is one way that an astral vision can be tested, because a genuinely contacted temple will have its altar light burning, while unconsecrated areas which resemble temples may not. You may want to maintain the altar fire by visualizing a glowing sphere emanating from the candle and enclosing it. Although a physical flame is very satisfying to our senses, this mental flame will serve the same function of keeping the temple space active if circumstances do not permit you to maintain a physical flame.

In doing this rite, always remember that you are not worshipping the image but the intangible, omnipotent, yet personal force which you have chosen to be reminded of in the lines of the representation before you. Images, whether drawn, carved, painted, or written, are lenses that transmit and color the divine energy. Over time, as you draw divine energy through them, some physical images take on a spirit of their own, in close alliance with the deity whose essence the image has absorbed. But this is not precisely identical with the vast reservoir of divine energy behind the image itself.

When performing the Morning Rite, you may prefer to recite the Egyptian version or the English version. I enjoy using the Egyptian as an acknowledgement of Isis' ancient roots, but any language is acceptable. Remember that the object of prayer and ritual is to move you into the right frame of mind and soul to communicate with your deity. The true gods are always ready to listen and wholly multilingual. *We're* the ones who need to be adjusted and brought into harmony.

This Morning Rite, as with any type of daily rite regularly performed, can help you become and stay in tune with the energies of Isis. Feel free to alter the wording to suit your own preferences. For example, some people are uncomfortable using the archaic term "thou." If this creates a stumbling point in your prayer, change it or leave it out. Or you may prefer to write an entirely new version of the Awakening. A new rite or hymn is an excellent and traditional offering to the Goddess Isis, and can also be

helpful in preparing for initiation into Her mysteries.

If you find, as I often do, that any commitment to a daily ritual, whether it's taking vitamins or praying to Isis, encounters an obstinate resistance in your soul, you may be interested in my own experiences with performing this prayer.

Of the thousands of times I have presented the morning ritual, I have sometimes said it hastily, sometimes

Cleopatra VII depicted as the goddess Isis.

slowly, other times reverently, or with boredom, with doubt, with faith, with gratitude, with joy or choked with tears. I've said it clearly, pouring into it all the power I can muster, and I've said it—many times—slurred with sleep. I have said it perfectly a hundred times in a row, only to confuse it with the words of a nighttime ritual on the hundred and first. I have said it in darkness, when the sun is a secret behind the moonlight, and I have said it when the day is so late that the summer sun-beetles are out flying in the heat of the day. I have said it many times in the hour of grey light when the promise of yellow sunlight seems an unlikely dream. And in the pink half-hour

Isis with solar disk, staff, and ankh.

which matches the hour of sunset on the opposite side of the day I have said it.

One morning I said it right.

I was still in bed, just rising up out of dream. Dawnlight was touching the curtains of the window behind my bed. As I rose into consciousness, the words of the hymn were already tingling in my throat. It was as if these words echoed on eternally from some primal utterance, and I was only receiving and transmitting them through one more passage, giving one more voice to a dawn-hymn created each morning by the tides of the cosmos. For a blissful instant, I was in epiphany, at one with the Goddess and what is beyond all gods and goddesses, at one with the universe I inhabit, at one with myself.

That morning was my initiation into why the repeated daily rites and rituals are important. I had unknowingly prepared for the moment by learning the hymn by heart, and repeating it under all conditions, while thinking vaguely that I was showing reverence for Isis and achieving a little resonance with the old temples.

However, by the grace of the Gods and of Isis in particular, I was richly rewarded for even this haphazard devotion.

☽·☉·☾

Though simply saying the prayer aloud or in your mind is sufficient, you may want to expand this rite to more nearly match the ancient ritual. Most temples possessed small statues of the gods and goddesses, which were kept in small shrine rooms.

A Pharaoh making offerings.

In these rooms stood the *naos,* or shrine box, which was a decorated cabinet of appropriate size for the statue. During the last ritual of the night, at about midnight, the officiating priest would reverently shut the doors and seal the shrine, usually binding the door handles with cord and then placing a wax or clay seal over the knot. Some versions of this rite identify the clay seal as the "Flesh of Isis," followed immediately by a declaration that though the clay will be broken, it is not the goddess which will be destroyed, but only clay.

In the morning, when the dawn rite was performed, the officiants would approach singing and chanting while incense would fumigate the air. The highest-ranking priest or priestess would approach the shrine and open it. Lamps were lit and old offerings cleared away. A special box, the "meryt" box, held the oils and other necessities for the awakening of the statue. These boxes were oblong with ostrich feathers, symbol of Ma'at, the personification of justice and truth, facing inward on each corner.

The statue was then washed, anointed, and dressed. With large statues, this might involve actual clothing, often donated as offerings by wealthy worshippers, or created by temple weavers. Smaller statues would receive a change of ritual jewelry or be draped about the shoulders with shawls of fine fabric.

In Egypt at Abydos, a very early sacred site dedicated to the worship of Osiris, the husband and brother of Isis, the officiating initiate would first undergo purifications, usually a ritual cleansing with water, and would then offer incense in the outer hall outside of the room

Nineteenth-century engraving of the Temple of Abydos.

where the shrine was kept. As the officiant did so, the following prayer to Osiris was recited.

MORNING RITE TO OSIRIS

I come into Your presence, O Great One, after I have been made pure.
As I passed by the goddess Tefnut, She made me pure.
I am a priest, and the child of a priest of this temple.
I am a priest, and I come to do what must be done.

The officiant then went to the shrine of Osiris and opened the clay seal, saying:

The clay is broken
And the seal is loosed
That this door may be opened

And all that is evil in me
I throw on the ground
Like this broken clay.

After additional minor ceremonies, the priest approached the statue of Osiris and delivered the Awakening, part of which is quoted here.

Peace to you, God,
Peace to you, God,
The Living Soul
Conquering His enemies
Your Soul is with me,
Your image is near me,
I am purified in Your presence.

Offerings of foods, milk, beer, or wine were then presented to the statue. In rich temples, only a symbolic fraction of the many offerings provided by the worshippers or produced by the temple lands would be presented. Even these, after a few hours in front of the statue or at the time of the next rite, would be removed and distributed to the poor or consumed by the priests, students, patients, and others who were dependent on the temple for sustenance.

If you are accustomed to starting your day with coffee, breakfast, or merely by taking your vitamins with water, these things can be offered and sanctified by raising them with both hands before the altar and holding them there for a moment. A small wand or scepter can be used as the *khereb*, a tool which is waved over offerings to consecrate them. If you are concerned that your cold morning cereal may not be ritually appropriate, remember that foods, beverages, and all things that sustain life are sacred to Isis.

For many, the initial lighting of the candle and the reciting of the Awakening should precede any other morning activity, since this way will take advantage of the mild post-sleep trance many of us experience in the early morning.

When at all possible, the use of alarm clocks should be avoided, though modern schedules make this difficult. The sudden jolt to semiconsciousness chases away memories of dreams which are often at their most vivid and meaningful in the early morning hours. Radio alarms, when they bring up music rather than voices, are preferable to standard alarms, since they can help maintain the light morning trance state.

However, a true morning-person may prefer to begin with a purifying shower or bath. Suggested instructions for this are found in the following chapter, "Purifications for Rites of Isis."

Depending on the amount of time you can allow for the Morning Rite, and on the presence of others nearby, you may want to light incense as an offering. For a Morning Rite a spicy rather than a sweet fragrance is preferable. A resiny incense with strong solar connotations, such as frankincense or myrrh, is very good. See Chapter Eighteen, "Isis and Alchemy," for further suggestions.

If incense is not appropriate, a drop of essential oil placed on a crystal to evaporate is a pleasant, smoke-free alternative.

Above all, be joyous in the performance of the Morning Rite. A new day has come, full of potentials beyond our imaginings but easily within reach of the Goddess and those to whom She extends Her help and love.

*A nineteenth-century depiction of Murchison Waterfall on the Upper Nile.
Water from the Nile was especially venerated for purification and cleansing.*

Chapter Two
The Second Hour of Daylight

— PURIFICATIONS FOR —
RITES OF ISIS

TO BE IN A state of spiritual purity is a primary goal for the priests, priestesses, and worshippers of Isis. Though life in ancient times, in most cases, was lived at a much slower pace, with more contact with natural and human-designed beauty, rites of spiritual cleansing were constantly performed. Purification rites were required before entering sacred enclosures, before praying, before invoking the divine Power to heal.

We who follow the temple paths today live in a world where it is all too easy to be contaminated. Today we take it for granted that our physical environment is unclean and unhealthy and we count ourselves lucky if this onslaught of misplaced matter is within "safe" levels of contamination. In today's world, with its noise, ceaseless and sometimes senseless activity, it is even more crucial and wise to retreat and grant ourselves the blessing of purification.

Purification rites are in essence simply a conscious cleansing of the spirit as well as the body. They are a form of blessing where positive "pure" energy draws or drives out negativity and contamination. A well-performed purification is equivalent to preventive psychic healing and can also enhance the benefits of both modern medicine and spiritual therapy.

WASHING RITES

Members of the clergy of Isis were well known for their physical and spiritual purity, and their frequent ritual washings earned one class of priesthood the nickname "the *ueb*" or "the washed ones." Open-minded Christian writers praised the cleanliness of Isian priests and priestesses while deploring the filthy habits of early ascetics and holy hermits bent on "mortifying" or killing off their own flesh and the fleshy urges contained within themselves. Against these scruffy monks, the clean beauty of many of the Isian rites and clergy stood in bright contrast.

Water plays a critical role in purification ceremonies around the

world, and it was especially important in the purification rites associated with the temples of Isis. Many temples of Isis and of Serapis possessed large basins for purification rituals, and a ritual asperging, or sprinkling, of water sometimes greeted members of the congregation at the daily public rites of Isis. Daily purification of the temple by fire (either a torch or incense) and water (an asperging or sprinkling) was essential, in addition to the purification rites of the clergy themselves.

Robert Wild, in his *Water in the Cultic Worship of Isis and Sarapis*, suggests that the priests and priestesses paid special attention to washing the head and hands prior to entering the temple or participating in the rites. This is consistent with ancient Egyptian depictions of purification of an individual standing under crossed streams of water emanating from vessels held by deities, usually Thoth and Horus. Sometimes a steady stream of small ankhs, symbols of ever-fresh life, were depicted instead of water.

The emphasis on purifying the head, the junction of spiritual and material aspirations, underlined the belief that mere physical purity is not enough—the spirit and the mind must also be cleansed and purified.

Water from the Nile was particularly venerated for its powers of purification and healing. Pilgrimages to obtain Nile water for temple use were frequently undertaken by devotees.

In Roman times, one priestess was said to be unsatisfied merely bringing back water from the mouth of the Nile where it poured into the Mediterranean; instead she travelled

Pyramid in Lake Moerus. Water, in the form of sacred pools or lakes, was often an essential element in the design of temple grounds.

far up the river to the island queendom of Meroe, which was considered to be near the ultimate source of the Nile. Other pilgrimages, though not so extensive, were recorded for devout adherents of the worship of both Isis and Osiris, who was sometimes represented by a vessel filled with Nile water, and who promised his followers an abundance of "cool water" in the afterlife.[1]

A modern day priestess of Isis, Dorothy Eady (Omm Sety) lived for many decades near the remains of the sacred Osireion at Abydos. For healing, she used Nile water which welled up into pools among the stones of the temple.

Large sacred pools, really small artificial lakes, often were part of Egyptian temple-grounds and were used for ritual ablutions as well as serving as staging areas for the water-borne battles of the festivals of Osiris.

THE PHYSICAL EFFECTS OF SPIRITUAL CLEANSING

Purification rites have much more than a merely psychological effect, though that component is very important. Spiritual effects aside, there is also a physiological effect in simple washing.

Our moods and experiences during a day cause our skin to exude various substances. Some of these simply evaporate, but others linger on the skin and will gradually be reabsorbed, often after they have fermented or have become rancid. Chemical traces of anger or stress need to be washed away; otherwise, the body will be chemically reminded of its original distress and may keep reexperiencing the negative responses. This is a genuine barrier to spiritual experience and balance, but one which can be easily conquered with simple cleansing. For this reason, it is also important to separate physical cleansing from the spiritual blessing which is contained in the ritual bath, washing, or anointing.

Since the priestesses and priests were often the most highly-trained physicians of their time and place, it should not surprise us that many spiritually cleansing substances and methods have undeniably potent physical effects.

Aside from the general benefits of cleaning the skin of the traces of the day's experiences, many of the

Shores of the Nile.

A purification bath is best taken in an unhurried, meditative state.

materials used for purifications have documented antiseptic, antiviral, and even antibiotic properties.

Constantly in contact with physical and mental illness, the purification rites provided the temple staff an advantage in resisting disease, allowing them to minister to others without succumbing themselves.

NATRON

Sodium-based natron water was used widely in Egypt as a purifying wash for the body and for the mouth. A modern version of natron can be created by mixing together baking soda with purified water.

To awake their spiritually cleansing qualities, both the water and the baking soda can be blessed and charged separately and then stirred together. The simplest method of doing this is to place the soda into a small, clean bowl. Call healing energy into your hands (see the section entitled "Manifesting Healing Energy" in Chapter Eleven, "Isis the Great Physician") and pick up the bowl, saying the

following or a prayer of similar meaning:

Isis, glorious Goddess,
Holy one, make pure this substance
Let it partake of Your divine unity
and purity.

Fill the bowl with healing power and as it crests, set it down and clap your hands away from it. Raise healing energy again for the water, and once more while you mix the baking soda and water together. Swab the natron water over your body during your shower or bath, and rinse your mouth out with it as well.

BATHS FOR PURIFICATION

The simplest purification bath is simply a hot tub into which a couple of tablespoons of table salt, baking soda, or earth salt have been added. Earth salts which have been mined rather than extracted from seawater are especially good for this purpose.

You may prefer to use sea salt and honor Isis as Goddess of the Sea as you do so, but many Egyptians regarded sea water as related to Set and impure, truer now in this age of pollution than ever before.

Consecrating any of these salts for use in a purification bath follows the same procedure as that of creating the natron water. It can be as simple as calling up the healing energy into your hands and saying "Isis, please bless this salt."

In preparing any purification bath it helps if you can attain a peaceful state of mind before entering the bath itself, so that the bath can work on deeper spiritual contamination instead of first needing to calm you. Usually, you will want to bathe or shower with soap and water before submitting yourself to the bath of purification. As you make your preparations, be calm. Take your time. It is rare that conditions would be so drastic that you would have to hurry into a purification bath.

Using hyssop or other purifying herbs, shake out a healthy handful of the herb into the palm of your hand and add it to about a pint of water in an enamel pan. Stir with a wooden spoon to moisten the leaves. As the leaves swirl, they spiral into a trance-inducing kalei-doscope of greens. Gaze on the leaves and inhale their fragrance as the water heats. This will help purify you internally as well. If you like, draw the sacred symbol of the ankh or the Throne of Isis into the water as you stir.

At the first hint of small bubbles forming around the sides of the pan, turn down the heat. Let the tea rest for a moment, and then strain the liquid into your bath, using a non-metal strainer if possible. (You can, of course, let the leaves remain in the liquid which is poured into the bathtub, but this generally does not have a very purifying effect on the plumbing.) As an alternative you can sew herbs up into clean cloth and place that directly in the bath, but the resulting water is generally less potent than using the tea method described here.

As you pour the liquid into the tub, you may choose to say the following:

Isis, glorious Goddess,
Lady of green herbs
Cleanse me of all impurities
Wash me with Your light
Free me of the clutter that clings to me
Make me pure to walk Your paths.

Follow the tea into the tub and soak. Since this is a purification, it is preferable that you cover yourself completely with the water, either by dipping your head briefly or by pouring a cupful of the bath water over your head. If you have a medical condition that doesn't allow you to submerge yourself, simply pour some of the bath water over your head.

Purification baths are enhanced by sunlight or candlelight, particu-larly if you have the time and incli-nation to pursue meditation in addition to the basic purification. Do not rush a purification bath; like most herbs, hyssop and the other purification herbs have a slow but thorough action and should not be forced along. Avoid the temptation to compress the purification bath into a brief shower. Although even a quick purification rite is better than none, the benefits are not as complete.

Some herbs, particularly hyssop, tend to be drying to the skin, so after the bath you may wish to use oil or lotion to remoisten the skin. This is also an excellent time to perform an anointing which will help to seal the effects of the purification bath.

Hyssop Bath

Perhaps the most potent of purifying herbs, hyssop has been used for millennia. Scott Cunningham's *Encyclopedia of Magical Herbalism* gives older versions of the name hyssop as "Yssop" or "Isopo," both of which may derive from the medieval memory of Isis as "Ysis, Ladye of Herbs," as She was depicted in an early manuscript by Christine de Pisan.[2]

As a purification herb, hyssop has been used in Jewish and Christian rites, and it is still used by Jewish worshippers in the ritual mickva bath for spiritual cleansing.

Fragrant and clean, hyssop imparts an unmistakable quality to the water which can be felt as a subtle, almost effervescent tingling. Whenever you are feeling too cluttered spiritually by the demands of the world or are reeling from emotional upheavals, a hyssop bath can help restore inner balance. It is also ideal before important rites or festivals, or before important secular events in your life.

When buying, gathering, or growing herbs for purification purposes, insist on the finest quality, free of pesticides or roadside pollution. Loose hyssop tea is a woody herb consisting of some leaves with many small stems. Depending on the time of year, it may be flecked with bits of purple, pink, or blue flowers.

ANOINTING

Anointing with oil is one of the most ancient forms of blessing and purification. It is simple, quick, can be done anywhere, and is very effective. In its simplest form, anointing is accomplished by placing a fingertip moistened with consecrated oil onto the forehead and uttering a word or two, such as "Isis Bless!" or "Goddess bless Your worshipper."

Many different oils can be used for anointing. However, in general, avoid synthetic blends. These are not as potent as genuine substances which have endured the challenges of surviving within the plant kingdom. Sanctify any oil before use by charging it with healing energy in the Name of Isis.

For a more elaborate anointing, touch the oil to your forehead, throat, heart, stomach, groin, knees, and feet. Being nude for this is more convenient, but not essential. If absolutely necessary, anointing can be done through clothing and still confer a positive effect.

An Anointing Rite

Anointing the body with charged or sacred oil is a way of drawing power into the anointed area, power which drives out misplaced or negative energy, or confers special abilities, such as the oils still used in some modern coronation rites. Sacred oils and unguents have been used in many cultures, and were common in the ancient world.

A simple anointing rite can be created by bringing down the divine energy into your body, part by part, and asking for a blessing or insight for each area, as in the chant models provided in Chapter Six, "Exalting Isis." This is a very flexible rite which can be changed with each performance. It can be as detailed as you like—if you want to individually anoint each of your vertebrae, or every joint of your toes, go ahead. This thorough anointing is especially healing in cases of injury or chronic pain.

Stand and breathe deeply until you are aware of energy filling your body and flowing around you. Pause and wait until these energies stabilize. Charge your hands with healing energy. A candle or other light source should be present during this rite, which can also be performed in front of a sunny window or outside if conditions permit. Avoid fluorescent lighting or any light which you find unpleasant. Incandescent or heating lamps provide a pleasant spectrum of light for this rite.

Greet Isis. This can be a spoken, formal hailing, such as "All glory to You, Isis, be with me in this rite," or simply a silent acknowledgement or visualization of a favorite image of Isis. As you say the words, anoint yourself with the first two fingers of your dominant hand, dipped into or dabbed with the oil. It is easiest to anoint yourself from a small bowl of oil placed near you about waist-high.

I stand pure in the light of Isis
Your light flows within me and
through me.
The light of Isis touches my head;
may I unite with the divine.
The light of Isis flows to my forehead;
let my mind be cleared.

The light of Isis flows within my
throat; let my voice be true.
The light of Isis flows within my
heart; let my soul be loving.
The light of Isis flows within my
stomach; let my instincts be right.
The light of Isis flows within my loins;
let my desires be holy.
The light of Isis flows within my legs;
let my travels be blessed.
The light of Isis flows within my feet;
may my placement be just, and my
footsteps forever welcome in the holy
places.
The light of Isis flows within my
hands; may my works be pleasing to
You, Isis.
Abide with me, Isis; let me live within
the glory of Your light
Forever and ever.

Remain still until the energy begins to soften. This rite of anointing can also be used with the following techniques of cleansing and healing with light.

CLEANSING WITH LIGHT

Lying on green grass, on a soft sandy beach, or even on hard, bare earth bathed in moonlight or sunlight provides a double cleansing. The planet below you will automatically "earth" negativity, drawing off any clinging energies not actively generated by you. The light above you will cleanse, purify, and refill you with energy.

This type of cleansing and charging is particularly useful when you are exploring the solar, lunar, or stellar aspects of the worship of Isis. It can also be incorporated into a meditation rite or other ritual. Ideally this should be done nude, but this is not essential and may be

unwise, depending on your location. If the outdoors is not accessible, even lying on the floor in front of a window can help ground your energies and clear your aura, the web of subtle physical and spiritual energies which encompasses all beings.

Cleansing with Colored Light

Colored light can also cleanse and heal. Stained glass windows provide a wonderful source of multi-colored light. Depending on your needs, different colors of light may be more effective than others.

A healing technique used by Mexican shamans is to fill colored glass bottles with water, leave the bottles in the sun, and then use the light-charged water for healing and purification, prescribing different colored light-charged water for different conditions. Green is used for healing, red for emotional conditions, yellow for intellectual concerns, and blue for anxiety.

CLEANSING RITUAL OBJECTS, STONES, AND CRYSTALS

Objects which you obtain for spiritual work need to be physically and psychically cleansed when you receive them or purchase them, unless they have been specially charged for you by the person giving them to you and you wish to retain that person's energy on the object. In this case, merely physically cleaning the object will not delete the intentional charge. Items, especially crystals, that have been sitting in a shop for any period of time are usually in need of a good physical and psychic cleaning.

Before using any psychic clearing method, start with a phys-ical cleansing. Use your judgement and experience; don't take sandpaper to a delicate antique wooden candlestick. Some stones with a sandy structure, such as lepidolite or sandstone, may start to dissolve in water. These can usually be wiped off with a slightly damp cloth.

Cleansing objects spiritually can be done in a variety of ways. Here are several techniques.

Light

Stones can be purified by exposure to sunlight, moonlight, or both.

You may prefer to leave clear quartz, which is most easily aligned with lunar energy, exposed to moonlight during the three nights of the full moon. To intensify the lunar influence, move the crystal before the rays of the sun strike the area. This method cleans the crystal and simultaneously charges it with lunar power. The lunar cleansing and charging is especially appropriate when you are exploring the Lunar Goddess aspect of Isis.

Generally, objects made of wood or metal will not be easily purified using light alone. They may need to be left out longer (in which case night-moisture or sun damage needs to be considered) or may need an additional censing or charging. Even then, older objects and articles which have been repeatedly charged by another person may never be completely freed of prior influences.

Censing

Censing stones and other objects in order to cleanse or charge them has been practiced by many cultures around the world.

For an Egyptian-influenced cleansing, use frankincense or

myrrh burned on charcoal. Copal, a New World resin, can also be used because of its similarities to ancient incense trees, some of which are now extinct. Opopanax resin was also used in temples of Isis and may be used here.

Kyphi incense can be used to clean objects, if you prefer. However, kyphi is a complex incense comprised of many ingredients.

Cleaning is best accomplished using simple, pure ingredients. For the same reason, stick or cone incenses should be avoided since they are often comprised of many ingredients, some natural, some artificial, and also contain chemical contaminants to encourage steady burning.

Washing

Crystals enjoy an extended bath now and then. If you are fortunate enough to have a fountain, stream, or waterfall accessible to you, place the stone where water will fall onto it. If you live in an area where drought is not a concern, you can leave a crystal under a slowly dripping faucet.

A salt water soak, while not as beneficial as a cleansing under running water, is fine for most purposes. If a stone or crystal just doesn't feel right to you, you may need to select another stone rather than try to cleanse one which is simply not compatible with you.

꠫·ꞝ·꠫

An illustration of Isis with accompanying text (note "various names of Isis" in left column) on a page from Athanasius Kircher's Oedipus Aegyptiacus, *Rome, 1652, shows that even at this late date She was not forgotten.*

Chapter Three
The Third Hour of Daylight

⸻ Isis the Universal ⸻
Goddess

THE HISTORY OF THE worship of Isis is long and complex; this brief overview provides an indication of its scope until this past century.

Ancient and beloved, Isis nurtured Her native Egypt as Goddess of the Throne, Goddess of Love and Magic, the Great Sorceress Who Heals. Ever present, Her worship under the name of Isis is documented in the Pyramid texts of the Fourth Dynasty (circa 2600 B.C.E.) and probably stretches back into pre-dynastic times. Worshipped alone, with Her husband Osiris, or the others said to be mated with Her, Isis' rites were kept throughout Egypt, from little shrines in farmers' houses to temples staffed with princess-priestesses.

As Egyptian sailors travelled the Mediterranean, and as foreign seafarers

A hall in the Library of Alexandria.

reached Egypt, Her worship also travelled across the face of the Western world. A goddess of a complex and complicated nature, many paradoxes—some would call them mysteries—arose within Her faith. On one side, Her clergy were admired because of their wisdom and purity; on another, worshipers of Isis embraced Her as a goddess of erotic and romantic love.

Her followers in past times were emperors and commoners, freed-women and slaves, merchants and seafarers. Then, as now, all races were admitted to Her temples and to the ranks of Her priestesses and priests. Turning away none, Isis has been revered since classical times as

the one deity above fate, who can rewrite the stars' forebodings.

Artists and craftsmen invoked Her as the ultimate muse, while early scientists felt Her presence among their alembics and crucibles, and texts on alchemy were written in Her name.

Along with Serapis, a dynamic aspect of Her dying and resur-recting husband Osiris, Isis presided over the magnificent Library of Alexandria and its School of Medi-cine, which set the standard for the education of ancient physicians. At the same time, many of Her followers were cured of their ailments merely by spending a night in Her temple in the hope of

Nineteenth-century engraving of the temple ruins on the island of Philae.

receiving a healing dream or a vision of the Goddess.

As the Roman Legions traveled, so did the worship of Isis. She was worshipped in ancient London and at many places in France and Germany. Throughout the Middle East and on the islands of the Aegean Sea Her temples are common, though now mostly reduced to ruins.

When the temples of other gods and goddesses were burned and broken during the turbulent birth of another faith, Pagan priests and priestesses fled to the walls of the sanctuaries of Isis and were welcomed to worship their fallen deities within the sanctuary of Her temples, sometimes alongside Christian heretics seeking similar refuge.

Hers was the last Pagan temple to hold worshippers, on the sacred island of Philae in Upper Egypt. But in 595 C.E., centuries after the official banning of the Pagan faiths

by the Roman Emperor Constantine in 383, this last sanctuary was closed by force and its priests destroyed or dispersed.

Isis then became Isis Amenti, the Hidden Goddess, and draped Her worship in disguise. Many of Her titles were applied to the increasingly popular Virgin Mary, and statues of Isis nursing Her son Horus were renamed and placed in churches, many of which were built over the remains of the ancient Iseums.

Even after Philae fell, the worship of Isis persisted. As late as 756 in France, a Christian cleric bewailed the fact that there still were those who went up the slopes of Mount Anzin to worship Isis and other deities. A portion of Her rites may have persisted until the tenth century at Harran in Arabia, and may also have been celebrated in Western China during the T'ang Dynasty. A medieval manuscript preserves the name of Isis, mentioning an "Ysis, Ladye of Herbes," showing that Isis' consummate healing skills were still not forgotten after the Dark Ages had lifted.

In more modern times, Isis makes Her presence felt in Masonic and Theosophic philosophy, in the rites of ceremonial magicians, as a Goddess of some traditions' Wiccan celebrations, and as the answerer of prayers of the numberless individuals who have turned to Her.

There are as many ways to Isis as there are individuals. The path will be different for everyone, as Isis takes an active and personal interest in all aspects of the existence of Her followers.

ISIS IN EGYPT

Khemi, the Black Land. *Tamera*, the Land of the Sun. These were the names the inhabitants of Egypt claimed for their country. Desert cradling a thin strand of rich soil, Egypt rose up, a miracle of the sacred Nile.

Dramatic and powerful, each year heralded by the rising of the blazingly bright star Sothis, this ancient land was blessed by the unwavering rhythm of the flood and the abundance that followed in its wake. Yoked to the benevolent tyranny of the river, it seems that it was easy for the Egyptians to yoke themselves to the gods as well, and a religious path that remained startlingly unchanged for nearly three thousand years.

The Egyptian people, while united by the Nile, were diverse in their religious beliefs. Different gods and goddesses, while sometimes recognized as emanations of a single source of divine power, were worshipped in different places. Their rites generally followed the same pattern wherever they were performed, regardless of the deity presiding over a particular temple or shrine. Only a few of these myriad entities achieved universal reverence

Osiris, brother and mate of Isis.

*Isis suckling Horus in the papyrus swamps. On the left, Thoth gives Isis the
emblem of magical protection, while on the right Ra presents Her
with an ankh (symbol of life).*

throughout Egypt. Both Isis and
Her husband Osiris received veneration throughout Egypt.

Isis and Osiris appear to have
enjoyed separate veneration before
they became a "married" couple in
the Egyptian pantheon. Traces of
either Isis or Osiris before the fourth
dynasty are slim. What indications of
their worship remain are ambiguous
and controversial. In earliest times,
the throne symbol of Isis was para-
mount and apparently unique to
Her; She was the possessor of the
throne, or the throne itself, who
determined what pharaoh was
worthy to sit on Her lap.

The origins of Osiris are if
anything even more shadowy. Some
ancient writers believed that Isis
and Osiris were human beings, a
king and queen of Egypt, who
through their good works and
personal tragedy became deified by
their followers. The litany of benefits that they were said to have
brought to their people certainly
would have earned them deification: agriculture, writing, medicine,
an end to cannibalism, foundation
of religion, weaving, the art of
embalming ... the list includes
virtually every aspect of human
endeavor.

Although the story of Isis and Osiris is well-known by students of Egyptology and mythology today, the Egyptians themselves did not emphasize it. The only nearly-complete version of the story that still exists is what the Greek writer Plutarch compiled and presented to a priestess of Isis and Osiris, Klea. There are also many variants existing in fragments in Egyptian writings.

Setting aside the deeper religious and mythological associations, the basic story of Isis and Osiris is that of a benevolent royal couple attempting to further the cause of civilization. While Osiris travels the world to bring Egyptian culture to adjacent nations, Isis rules alone.

However, their success and love for each other incites the jealousy of Set, their brother, who succeeds in murdering Osiris and plans to force the right of kingship from Isis, who confers the power of the throne on whomever She takes as Her husband. Isis discovers that She is pregnant by Osiris, and, with the help of Her advisor Thoth, escapes to the concealing swamplands to bear and raise Her son alone. Using the knowledge She has obtained during Her years of rulership, She instructs Horus in the arts of politics and war so that he may avenge his father and reclaim his throne.

Through many conflicts complicated by Set's treachery and shrewd political maneuvering, Horus nonetheless triumphs repeatedly with Isis fighting at his side and negotiating on his behalf. Finally, the issue of succession is settled in their favor and Horus becomes Pharaoh, restoring order and harmony to the land. Now it is Isis' turn to travel the world beyond Egypt's borders.

Chapter Four
The Fourth Hour of Daylight

VISITING THE HOLY HOUSE OF ISIS

T HE HOUSES OF THE gods have always been places of pilgrimage, drawing worshippers from near and far to dwell for a few moments or a few days in the glow of religious insight and power. Even within the temples, the initiates proceeded from grade to grade, gaining admittance to the inner courtyards only after proving themselves worthy of entrance through many mental and emotional trials. The Sacred House is a challenging haven, a protective but unyielding envelope wrapping around an initiate like the tough sac encompassing a developing baby.

When exploring religious alternatives which take us away from the present religion of our near relatives, many people

find themselves following a faith related to their religious or national ancestry. For example, the resurgence of interest in Wicca and other nature-oriented religions practiced in Western Europe is mainly confined to those who draw ancestry from that area. Part of this is, unfortunately, due to racial or cultural biases which may cause exclusion of others of sharply different ancestry, but most of it is due to the human yearning to "really belong" and to take advantage of the trails of genetic memory when reincarnational memory is absent or lacking.

When we look at ancient religions today, particularly those of Egypt, they may seem exotic, mysterious, very different. Few persons claim Egyptian ancestors and fewer still, except for some of the modern Egyptians themselves, can verify such claims. For many people, it may seem that there is no personal genetic trail to follow back to the temples of Isis.

Isis with sistrum.

But the faith of Isis so took the ancient world by a life-giving storm that virtually everyone drawing ancestry from Europe, the Middle East, Africa, and the British Isles may well have had a many-times-great grandmother or grandfather worshipping at a Temple of Isis. From the Berkshire downs to the shores of the Black Sea, from Ethiopia and Nubia to Paris and Cologne, temples of Isis thrived for hundreds, sometimes thousands, of years.

Finding a memory of an ancient temple that can be partially or fully verified is a wonderfully empowering experience, especially if your memory seems to be unlikely compared to what you may have heard about the ancient temples. Several times I had a "memory" of a temple, the features of which seemed so utterly impossible that I expected my mind was just doodling and randomly combining bits and pieces of what I had read. But in each case, as I found new references, these surprising aspects of the temples have proven to be true of at least one temple at a specific time in history.

Because of this, before "contaminating" your possible memories with the selection of information that follows, try the following meditation exercise. If you are not accustomed to visualization, you may want to try this exercise several times. The best time to attempt this exercise is late at night, when you can fall asleep afterward, but any quiet, undisturbed time will do.

GOING TO THE TEMPLE OF ISIS

For this exercise you should be in a comfortable place with as few irritants in the environment as possible. These may include noise, temperature, the presence of others nearby, insects if outdoors, etc. Pets are sometimes highly alarmed at any quiet or light trance work, and may attempt to "bring you back" by licking you or standing on your chest. They may also be protesting that you did not choose to take them with you on an interesting mental journey. Other pets may intuitively understand what you are doing and settle down nearby for some meditational work of their own.

If the environment allows, you may wish to be naked. In any case, make sure your clothing is non-restrictive and of a neutral texture. As you calm the mind to look within, minor irritants are intensified on your way to relaxed meditation. Eventually, it becomes possible to meditate in any circumstance despite distractions, but in the beginning it is important to give yourself as many advantages as possible.

Have ready at hand a notebook and several pens and pencils. It is also pleasant to have prepared a light snack to help you ground yourself after the temple exploration. If you do prepare food, make sure that the smell of it is thoroughly washed from your hands; otherwise, this may be distracting.

Once you are certain that the nearby environment is as free of distractions as possible, lie down. You may want to spread a towel or other material over the carpet or ground first. Do not use a pillow. If this is too uncomfortable, you may want to roll up a washcloth or other small towel and place it under your

neck or the small of your back. Stretch out and breathe deeply.

You may wish to invoke the guide of Isis and guardian of otherworld journeys, Anubis, to help you on your temple quest. Anubis may initially be present to you in the form of a big, friendly dog, often black in color. His name in Egyptian is *Anpu* or *Anupu*. You may also visualize or "feel" the presence of his other form, a jackal- or dog-masked priest, bare of chest and kilted in the ancient Egyptian manner. Often he will be holding a Set-headed scepter to indicate his

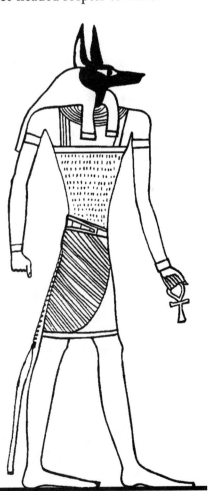

Anubis, God of the Dead and guardian of otherworld journeys.

Rectangular halls separated by pylon gates comprise a typical Egyptian temple, as seen in this illustration.

dominance over the disruptive forces of his uncle.

As with any rite, you can make this invocation or prayer for guidance as complicated as your prefer, but essentially all that you need to do is verbally or mentally ask for *Anupu's* guidance. If you prefer, you may wish to directly ask for the guidance of Isis Herself. Remember that a request to either of these deities for more guidance can be made at any time during your mental explorations.

Prayer for Guidance from *Anupu*

Anupu
Wise herald and guide
Guide me in the ancient ways
Where I have walked before
Lead me to walk again.
Anupu
Be with me on my journey.

Now, let your mind be calm. See where your thoughts want to go. If your mind tries to fill with mundanities, gently dismiss these intrusions. Focus lightly on any temple image you like. Wonder to yourself if you

ever were in a similar temple, and if the answer seems to be "No," try to think how your experiences may have been different.

Keep bringing up the seed-image of a temple or other ancient building or sacred site, such as a grove or tumulus. The outer appearance of the sacred spot is often not as important as what you find inside. Note the physical features of the area. Is it near the sea, high on a mountainside, set against low hills, or in the middle of a desert oasis? If these details are unclear, try to lift up your perspective for an aerial view, as if you were flying over the site. Check the condition of the temple. Is it new and perfect, or falling into ruins? If you do see a ruined temple, try to heal the image into a complete one. Remember there is a vast choice of time periods possible to visit—and every temple was once brand-new.

Also, notice if the temple is wholly one style or substance. You may visualize a temple primarily of stone, but the outbuildings may be of a more temporary material such as mudbrick or wood. Is the temple decorated? Are there people in it, and, if so, are they all priestesses and priests, or are there ordinary people present as workers or worshippers? What do the people look like? Do they notice you?

If there seems to be a festival or special celebration underway, try to sense what the focus of the festival is. Later, you may want to check the Isis Calendar for celebrations that might fall near the date you are performing the meditation. Bear in mind, however, that no rules of time apply in these meditations and that you may just as likely encounter a springtime celebration while a snowstorm is pounding the windows of your present-time home.

Walk through the temple, continuing to notice your impressions. What path do you take? Faced with a choice of direction, where do you naturally want to go? Are there places that seem forbidden to you, or places where you feel you belong? If you encounter a block in your path—a blank wall, a door that will not open

to you, or if the images become harder and harder to maintain, mentally turn around and retrace your steps. You may find that the temple has changed. Continue to note your impressions.

It is important that you try to come back out the way you went in and that you make a solid decision to end the vision. Otherwise, you may find yourself still seeing fleeting images for some time after the exercise. This can be interesting, but it is best to keep all vision work separate from everyday life. If you do note additional information after the formal end of the exercise, write it down but restate your intention that the temple visit is over for the time being. Like any thoughts which strongly occupy your mind, remnants of a meditation can be distracting. It is also very wearing to be functioning on two modes of consciousness at the same time. This is why it is ideal to perform this exercise shortly before sleeping.

A nineteenth-century illustration of the propylaea (temple entrance) on the Island of Philae.

Nineteenth-century illustration of sphinxes along sacred road.

INSIDE AN EGYPTIAN TEMPLE

Near most of the Egyptian temples was a sacred lake or large pool which was used for purification purposes and also as a staging area for the boat battles of the Osirian mystery plays. There would also be an encircling wall protecting the various buildings of the temple complex, as well as the temple itself. These walls were often of mudbrick, so few traces of them remain.

A typical Egyptian temple was usually approached by a paved road lined with sphinxes on each side. One or more great gate-walls, called pylons, would stand in front of the temple itself. These were possibly originally protective in nature, but later temples incorporated them into the temple layout itself, where their function was not physically but spiritually defensive. Usually, they would be covered with decorative reliefs painted in bright colors.

At their simplest, Egyptian temples consisted of a series of three rectangular areas with a series of doorways piercing through the middle. Each area was separated from the others by a high wall, usually inscribed or painted. Usually the sacred areas would diminish in size as a participant approached through the temple rooms. Steps often joined the different court-yards.

After the pylon was the great, or outer, court, surrounded by a colon-nade of massive pillars. These pillars could be capped with an image of the deity of the temple, as they are at Denderah, where the columns are Hathor-headed. They might take other decorative forms, being carved to represent bundles of papyrus or lotus stalks.

The next area encountered would be the hypostyle hall, a room forested with pillars. This was the end of the areas commonly acces-

Hathor-headed columns at the Temple of Denderah.

Chapter
Four

*Visiting
the
Holy House
of Isis*

33

sible to all during the festivals. Beyond the hypostyle hall were the actual sanctuary rooms of the deity, usually three, with the central one occupied by the chief deity of the temple and the adjacent chapels assigned to the deity's husband or wife, child, or other crucial deities.

The inner, most venerated sacred space was called the Holy of Holies. At some temples additional rooms would be located behind the Holy of Holies. In the case of Osiris, who had a chapel or suite of rooms in almost all the temples of Egypt, sometimes several rooms would be linked with his sacred chapel. These rooms were used for the enactment of the mysteries of his resurrection.

Inside these chapels was a gilded wooden shrine containing the statue of the deity honored. In front of this shrine stood the sacred processional boat used to carry the shrine outside on procession days.

The temples were the precinct of the priesthood, with the common people allowed only into the outer courtyard during festivals. Some temples found unusual ways of preserving the sanctity of the temple while allowing the public spiritual access to the most sacred areas. At the Iseum at the Hathor temple complex of Denderah, the space on the outside wall directly behind the sacred cult statue was marked with a false door where persons not permitted inside the inner sanctuary could still place offerings close to the Goddess, material walls no barrier to Her power.

A similar feature was found at the larger temple of Hathor, which

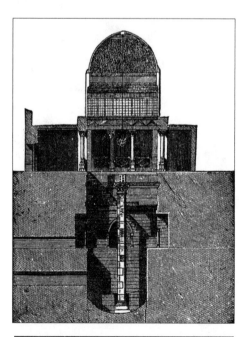

A Nilometer. The waters would flow into the bottom of the chamber and be measured against marks on the walls or columns.

also included several rooftop chambers devoted to the Osirian resurrection mysteries. At this complex stood two mammisseums, or birthhouses, where the mysteries of the birth of the gods were enacted. One was wholly Egyptian, while the other was erected during Roman times. These buildings were also used in rites pertaining to the birth of Horus.

Shrines and temples both grew with the strength of the worship of a deity in a specific area. A small or single-roomed shrine might eventually be surrounded with additional chapels and courtyards as the needs of the religious services grew.

INSIDE A GRECO-ROMAN TEMPLE

Greco-Roman temples to the Egyptian gods took many varied forms, but in general were smaller than their Egyptian counterparts. Temples of Isis outside of Egypt were frequently simple square buildings fronted with four columns. Often, the building itself would be of stone, but associated buildings might be of less permanent materials. Frequently, the temple area was enclosed by a wall. The cult statue of Isis generally was in the rear of the temple facing the entrance. Where several deities were worshipped, usually the chief deity would be placed to the left, with associated deities such as Anubis, Serapis, or Harpocrates taking subsidiary positions to the right of the primary statue.

Temples of Isis were often found in the area near the town theater, and in some cases a temple would even share a wall with a theater. Many temples, especially in early times, were placed in less desirable locations since the ruling Roman aristocracy still had questions about the propriety of the foreign goddess.

A tavern jug found in the Thames indicates that the tavern itself could be found right next to the Temple of Isis, and, so far, is our primary indication that a temple existed in London.

Subterranean rooms were often built into Greco-Roman temples, and in some cases could be flooded with water for initiations or as local "Nilometers" imitating the life-giving rise of the Nile flood far away in Egypt. Temples dedicated to healing would usually have a long hall for patients to sleep in dormitory-style while waiting for a healing dream to be granted to them.

The most crucial difference between Greco-Roman temples of Isis and Egyptian temples is that in the Greco-Roman world, temples of Isis were much more accessible to the general public. Although temples of other Greek and Roman deities were not as a rule accessible to the people on a daily basis, Isian temples (or Iseums, as they were often called) held daily rites open to the faithful. The public could even attend the early morning opening ceremonies when the statue of the Goddess was revealed by the opening of the curtain, a practice which had replaced or augmented the Egyptian rites which centered around the sacred shrine box. Dining halls were also attached to temples, and temple revenues were increased by the dues paid by dining-clubs to use the temple facilities for their gatherings.

As with other ancient temples from the Greek and Roman periods, the original buildings were often brightly painted, not the pale marble ghosts centuries of rain and wind have left to us.

A FEW MAJOR TEMPLE SITES OF ISIS

Isis possessed hundreds of temples and shrines. She shared many more with Osiris, Serapis, and other deities. Only a few of the places which held Her sanctuaries are given here. Perhaps one of these will stimulate a long-forgotten memory for you.

Abydos

The mysterious temple of Osiris at Abydos may pre-date the pyramids. The monolithic style of the inner chambers is similar to the construction of the Sphinx, and may date from before the historical Egyptian civilization.

Abydos was one of a handful of temples that recreated the primeval mound of creation. Inside the temple, an earthen mound rose from the center of a long pool. In it, Osiris was said to be buried.

The sacred decorations at Abydos are possibly the best preserved in all of Egypt. Although dedicated to Osiris, this spot is clearly Isis' territory, with many beautiful representations of the Goddess on the walls.

Abydos is the site where Omm Sety, a priestess of Isis, unofficially served for several decades.

Alexandria

Isis had a number of temples in this sparkling city of gypsum-plastered buildings. Alexandria was regarded as Her special city in later times,

Chapter
Four

*Visiting
the
Holy House
of Isis*

35

and Her consort Serapis was also widely worshipped here. One of the temples to Isis in Alexandria appears to have been within a sea cave under the isle of the Pharos, where the famous tall lighthouse, one of the seven wonders of the ancient world, guided seafarers for many hundreds of years.

The Museum and Library at Alexandria was the foremost university of ancient times, and was considered to be under the special patronage of Isis and Osiris.

Coptos

Isis was worshipped here in the temple of the ever-erect Min, god of fertility. One account of the death of Osiris states that Isis was at Coptos when She heard the news, and that She immediately cut off a swath of Her hair as a sign of mourning.

At Coptos, in the forecourt of Her sanctuary, there was a statue of a deceased scribe with a text that offered the services of the individual depicted as an intermediary of Isis. "I am the messenger of the Mistress of the Sky. I belong to Her outer court. Tell me your petitions so that I can report them to the Mistress of the Two Lands, for She hears my supplications."

There may have been a rite of *hieros gamos* (sacred marriage, celebrated either symbolically or physically between a priest and priestess of the wedding divinities) performed for Isis and Min at Coptos.

London (Londinium)

Although the exact site has yet to be found, Roman London had at least one temple to Isis. Other British sites which have yielded Isian objects are York and Silchester, among others. Several burial sites of members of the Isian clergy in England have yielded miniature sistrums, sometimes of silver.

Menouthis

This temple of Isis was renowned as a place of healing. After the physical temple was destroyed by fanatical adherents of the new cult which spread through the Middle East during the early centuries of this era, the priests and priestesses continued the worship in private homes for the next fifty years, until they were finally betrayed after an ostensibly Christian couple journeyed to see the priestess of Isis in the hopes that She could end their infertility.

This unnamed priestess, perhaps only too aware of the threats to her life and worship, gave the childless couple her own infant. They returned to their home village, filled with praises of the Goddess Isis, which attracted the attention of the clerics in Menouthis. The underground temple was betrayed by a brother of a monk, a man who had been refused entry into the higher mysteries of Isis.

We do not know what happened to the priestess who gave up her own child, but we do know from Christian records that a priest of the temple was made to stand by and identify each of the many statues of the gods before they were destroyed in front of him. After the cataloguing of the deities had finished, the priest was subject to death, though the author omits whether or not he was executed immediately.

The betrayer of the Isian temple was doubtless honored greatly by his associates because the maxim at the time was that a "demon who heals is a thousand times more dangerous than one who curses," since the demonstrated healing powers would find sympathy among the desperate, especially if recourse to the new religion had failed.

Paris

The Church of Notre Dame incorporates an Isian altar into its stonework, and it is likely that this church was built at least partially over an Isian shrine.

Some writers have attempted to draw Egyptian origins for the name "Paris" and the tribe, the Parisii, who inhabited the area. "Per-Isi" could be translated as the Egyptian term meaning "Temple of Isis." The validity of this hypothesis lies in the fact that some purely Egyptian objects found in the area may pre-date the later spread of the worship of Isis through Greek and Roman sources.

The Egyptophile Napoleon believed in this derivation of the name Paris, and for a time Isian symbolism was incorporated into the seal of Paris. As late as the sixteenth century, a woman was punished for offering veneration to a statue of Isis preserved in Notre Dame. Unfortunately, after this stalwart priestess suggested to the priest that the true spiritual center of the church was located within the statue of Isis, the priest ordered the image smashed into dust. The fate of the worshipper is not recorded.

Petra

Petra, the city carved from rock, is entered through a narrow cleft in the rocks called the Siq. At the end of the Siq, at certain hours, sunlight blazes against the lovely rock-hewn, pink temple structure called the "Pharaoh's Treasury." This structure has been considered by some writers to be a temple of Isis and may well have been served by Her priests and priestesses. A standing goddess-image carved from the rock may represent Isis, but is worn by wind and by gunshots. An unfortunate legend indicated that the stone vessel at the top of the structure was filled with gold, and in modern times nomadic tribesmen have practiced their marksmanship on it.

More certain is the identification of Isis with the Nabataean goddess Al-Uzza, whose temple lies farther up the canyon. Tiny Isian headdresses crown the surreal carved images of the goddess Al-Uzza, who was also identified with Aphrodite. Incidentally, the sacred stone of the Ka'aba at Mecca, now an Islamic shrine, was originally a temple of Al-Uzza.

A Gallic statue of Isis.

Ruins of the temple of Isis on the Island of Philae.

At least one inscription identifies a priest of Isis working in Petra, though it is not clear which, if either, temple site he attended.

Petra lies hidden in a deep crack in the desert and was, for a time, the capital of the Nabataean nation discussed in Chapter Eight, "Isis as a Goddess of War."[1]

Philae

The island temple of Philae still haunts us with its delicate beauty. Subject to a relocation to a nearby island so that the temple would be removed from the dissolving waters of the Aswan-dammed Nile, this temple was the last to cease its worship of Isis, enduring until the late 500s C.E. Local tribes, the Blemmyes and the Nobatae, negotiated with the Romans to assure that they retained access to the island for worship of Isis on festival days and that a statue would be lent to them each year for their festivals. For a time, Christian and Isian rites were celebrated here simultaneously, but after the expiration of the hundred-year treaty between the Roman Empire and the native tribes, the rites of Isis were finally forbidden and abandoned.

For many decades a "red hawk," apparently a type of parrot, was worshipped at Philae as a representation of Horus.

Pompeii

The worship of Isis was very active in Pompeii and Her temple is among the better-preserved buildings. Small in size, the number of worshippers at the temple appears to have been relatively large. The remains of the last priest's meals were found in its ruins. Some scholars believe the paintings at the "Villa of the Mysteries" represent Isian initiation rites.

TEMPLES OF ISIS REMOVED FROM EGYPT

During the rescue of the monuments of Upper Egypt prior to the filling up of Lake Nasser behind the new Aswan High Dam, a number of small temples were offered as incentives to various museums and organizations. If a nation provided funding or other support for the hurried removal of the major temple sites to other locations in Egypt, they could take home a smaller temple for free. Since the worship of Isis was very prevalent in the Nubian region where the dam was placed, several of these displaced temples are temples of Isis, or temples where She was worshipped along with another deity native to the region.

A number of nations took advantage of this "Bonus-Temple-With-Donation" policy. Both the worship of Isis and Her physical temples seem to travel easily around the world. In ancient times, sometimes inscribed blocks from a tumbled temple would be sent to another temple location, and statues and other objects travelled between temples. However, even the most ardent worshipper of Isis, such as the Roman priestess who travelled all the way up the Nile to Meroe in search of pure water for temple use, never considered bringing back an entire temple, at least as far as we know.

More information on these temples removed from Egypt may be found in *Temples and Tombs of Ancient Nubia: The International Rescue Campaign at Abu Simbel, Philae, and Other Sites*, edited by Torgny Save-Soderbergh.

Temple of Debod — Madrid, Municipal Park, Spain.

This third-century B.C.E. temple was decorated, and possibly built, by a Meroitic king, Azekheramun. There are also Ptolemaic portions of the temple, which was dedicated to Amun in some inscriptions and to Isis in others.

The Temple of Debod was a station, or resting place, on the annual journey of a statue of Isis through the northern part of Lower Nubia to give blessings to the land.

Temple of Dendur — New York Metropolitan Museum of Art.

This small shrine was once staffed by priests from the Temple of Isis at Philae. Consisting of only three rooms, it was built against a cliff which contained a tomb of two brothers, Pedesi and Pehor, sons of a Nubian ally of Rome whom the emperor wished to appear to honor by constructing the small temple and dedicating it to their memory.

The public is not allowed to enter the frail sandstone temple itself, but can view the outside of the structure and see some of the decorated interior through the doorways. It is said to be best viewed at night, when the lighting is most dramatic.

Temple of Taffa — Leiden, Museum of Antiquities, Netherlands.

This charming temple watched over the turbulent waters of the Nile on whose banks it stood. Dedicated to Isis, this temple has survived the ravages of time, a haphazard restoration attempt at the turn of the century, and an unintended dismantling when it was struck by a ship.

In addition to this temple of Isis, the Leiden Museum houses one of the best Egyptian collections in the

Chapter
Four

*Visiting
the
Holy House
of Isis*

39

world. Leiden is also home to E.J. Brill, a publishing company which produces many scholarly books on Isis and related subjects (see Apppendix D, "Resources").

CREATING YOUR OWN TEMPLE

As you attune with the worship of Isis, you will find that your physical surroundings become your temple. While few of us can afford to dedicate an entire residence or even an entire room to worship and magical work, your home will nonetheless become a temple to you.

As a general rule, cleanliness, neatness, order, and beauty are essential to the efficient operation of a home-temple. However, had perfect housekeeping been an absolute requirement for entering the clergy of Isis, I would never have been accepted. My temple is very much still under construction!

Before you dedicate your home as a temple, you will probably begin to gather together objects that mean Isis to you. Shrines and altars will start growing up around your house, seemingly without your intention. A picture or statue or piece of jewelry with the image of Isis or another deity will suddenly place themselves together, and then someone will come along with a candleholder or oil lamp, an altar cloth will find itself beneath the other objects, and a collection of stones and herbs will artfully arrange themselves nearby.

For worship of Isis, nothing is needed other than a mind and heart that desires to worship Her. Most of us gather helpful objects to tune our minds in the direction of the Goddess.

A simple altar to Isis consists of an image of Her, equipment for burning incense, and a source of light. This can be a candle or oil lamp; if circumstances such as pets, small children, or fear of fire is a concern, use a small, pretty electric lamp as your main altar light. Asian stores sometimes have small lotus-shaped lamps with colored bulbs. These can work well for the worship of Isis. (For rites where you are constantly present, you will probably prefer oil lamps or candles, but an electric lamp can burn as the "eternal flame" without fear.) The light source can be placed in front of the image, or a pair of light sources can be placed on either side.

Much of current magical or Wiccan practice places altars low to the floor, so that worshippers need to kneel or bend to reach articles on the altar. This is awkward and unnecessary for the rites of Isis, which traditionally use waist-high altars placed either in the center of the working area or against a wall.

The top of a bookcase or a shelf attached to the wall both work well. Two wooden storage cubes, usually available at home improvement stores, can be stacked together to form a square altar of a height that works for many people. From the same source, one can invest in a single marble tile to place on the altar top. The altar side surfaces can be decorated with images.

You can also decorate the top of the altar, though a plain surface is less distracting. The Bembine Table of Isis, or *Mensa Isiaca*, is believed to have been the top of an altar to Isis, and is a perfect example of just how complex such an altar design can be.

If you do decide to decorate, altar cloths can be used to change the background surface to accommodate the needs of your rites. These cloths can be plain, patterned, or embroidered.

Shrines in Egypt normally consisted of the shrine box, a cabinet built to receive the statue of the god or goddess, and a boat-stand on which the shrine box was placed. In procession, the box and boat would be carried out among the populace, with the doors on the shrine open so that all could gaze on the empowered statue of the deity.

Usually, the altar or shrine would be placed in the east, the direction where the sun rises. However, this can be changed to accommodate the room where the shrine is placed. Even in Egypt, temple complexes sometimes would be oriented to the local flow of the Nile, rather than to the path of the sun. The Nile was considered to be a more important source of life for the temple. In addition, some temples would be in alignment with other stars, and this would affect the direction of the temple structure as well.

Temples in the Greco-Roman sites often took their placement from natural features in the landscape, rather than by strict adherence to directions. Allow yourself flexibility in this area.

DEDICATING A SHRINE OR ALTAR

No matter how your shrine or altar evolves, either by intent or merely by collection, at some point you will want to formally dedicate it to the Goddess. This can be by simply stating mentally, "This (area, table, shelf, etc.) is my (shrine/altar) of Isis; Goddess teach me the ability to feel Your Power in this place."

You may also purify and consecrate each altar object individually, dedicating each one to the service of Isis, and then dedicating the whole altar or shrine as well. For the dedication, make an offering of flowers and incense. You may also want to keep fresh flowers on the altar daily.

Shrine Dedication

*Come to Your house, Great Isis,
    come to Your house.*
*Your sacred objects are prepared
    and await You here,
    in Your house,
    the Holy House of Isis.*
*Come to Your house, Holy Isis,
    come to Your house,
    the shrine doors are open,
    I await Your presence in Your
    shrine,
    the Holy Shrine of Isis.*
*Come to Your house, Great Lady,
    come to Your house, Great Goddess!
    Your Priest/ess calls to You,
    come to Your house!*
(repeat until the energy is tangible)

The Glory of Isis is present.
The Power of Isis is present.
The Love of Isis is present.
The House of Isis lives!
*May Your Priest/ess always find You
    here, here, in the House of Isis.*
*May Your Priest/ess always know You
    abide, here, in the House of Isis.*
*May Your Shrine always glow with
    Your Glory.*
*May Your Shrine always sing with
    Your Energy.*
*May Your Shrine always emanate
    Your great Love,*

Chapter
Four

*Visiting
the
Holy House
of Isis*

41

Here, in the Shrine of Isis.
Here, in the Shrine tended by Your
  Priest/ess.
Here, in the House of Isis!

Abide in Your House, Isis!
Abide in Your House!
(repeat verses to raise power, if necessary)

☽ · ◌ · ☾

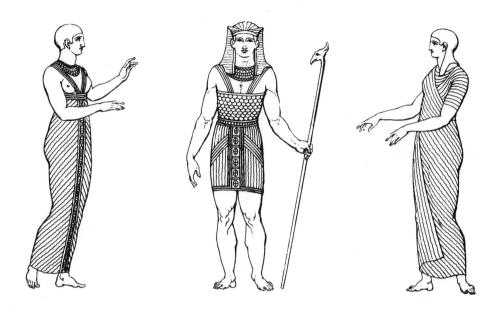

Chapter Five
The Fifth Hour of Daylight

GARBING FOR THE GODDESS

I N EGYPTIAN AND GRECO-ROMAN temples the ritual washing, anointing, and dressing of the sacred statues were crucial to the temple rites. Depending on the wealth and the size of the temple, and the extent of its weaving workshops, the statue of the Goddess might be garbed in different clothing daily or several times a week. In other temples, the sacred image would receive a new robing only once or twice a year at major festival times, or at the New Year.

The "Keeper of the Robes" or Stolist-priestess or priest was in charge of all the sacred adornments, which were kept carefully catalogued, often inscribed on a pillar of the temple. When it was time to dress the statue, they would bring into the sacred shrine the meryt box, a rectangular box decorated with ostrich plumes outturned at the corners. Inside this box would be the oils, unguents, and other necessities for ritually cleansing and reanointing the statue.

Wealthy worshippers would often donate jewelry and fine robes to the temple for the statue of the Goddess. A catalogue of jewelry belonging to a shrine of Isis in Spain listed many items, including gold and emerald earrings and a diadem fashioned of six pearls of two different types.

SACRED CLOTHING

What we wear against our skin has always been an announcement of who we are, or what we seek to become. Just as ritual and religion often arise out of a sense of place, a geologic or geographic imperative, so our clothing reflects the challenges of our environment, our

A nineteenth-century drawing of the statue of the Venus (Aphrodite) of Cnidos.

social statutes, and our degree of conformity with the norms of the culture in which we choose to live. It can enhance our sense of religious experience; it can hamper it. Wearing the "right" robe will be important to people whose visual or physical awareness of clothing is acute, or to those who participate with others whose are. Others may find that the mere wearing of offbeat clothing, even for a religious ritual, makes them feel awkward. (Though that may also, oddly, feel appropriate, since many of us had our first experience with uncomfortable "adult" clothing attending church services as children!) Still others may find that the wearing of any clothing at all is distracting and inhibiting. All of these feelings are valid.

However, the majority of us are accustomed to both the pleasures and the power that comes from "dressing up." We may have done so as children to imitate and invoke the adult powers which were not yet in our possession. Or, we may have experienced the sense of union in wearing a uniform marking our acceptance of and acceptance by a group we respected. We may also know, even as we accept group strictures, the dangers of too great a conformity, and subtly alter that conformity, through our clothing, in nearly undetectable ways.

Good ritual clothing can enhance the sense of specialness, of setting oneself apart from the world for the space of time spent in worship or ritual. Like anything else (other than the human mind and body) used in ritual, special clothing is a tool, a useful extra, but not essential. It can be compared to the tools of a cabinetmaker who has obtained the best possible materials, kept his or her blades bright, become accustomed to the precise feel of each tool and intimately familiar with its use. The cabinetmaker values the tools and takes pride in them, but his or her skill is independent of them; given a sharp rock and a tree branch he or she would still be capable of fashioning a useful and beautiful object.

Depending on the intent of the rite or reverence you intend to create, different types of clothing may be suitable. If your faith is fully formed you may find that most of your prayers or moments of contact occur while wearing a business suit or in bedroom slippers; valid spiritual experiences are not turned on and off with the lighting of a candle in a perfectly orchestrated rite performed only while wearing appropriate ritual garb. Formal ritual can be empowering and enlightening, but it is not the only way to experience spiritual growth.

Through the long course of the worship of Isis, many types of clothing have been chosen by different worshippers in different places. Statues of Isis-Aphrodite often depict the Goddess nude, and some Egyptian statues nearly do so, the skill of the sculptor indicating only a thin membrane of silk or cotton wrapped against Her body.

Often the exact style of clothing used to depict Isis belongs to the era just before sculpting, to lend an appearance of appropriate antiquity. This was just as important to the Greeks and Romans as it is to some present-day Pagans, and must have presented at least some of the same problems. How do you wrap that old-fashioned toga? What was

holding that priestess's frail dress on her body, other than prayer? Did the priests wear anything under those Old Kingdom kilts?

There are a few basic guidelines for temple-oriented garb. This distinction is important because at all times and places there have been worshippers of Isis who were members of the lay priesthood, simple worshippers, or priests and priestesses who did not pursue temple work but still served the Goddess. There was another class of priesthood who served more than one deity simultaneously and whose clothing might be more generic or

This modern reproduction of an Isis statue from the Tomb of Tutankhamen is typical of the barely-veiled style of Egyptian sculptors. Note the Djed (backbone of Osiris) amulet at her feet. From the collection of the author.

The Egyptian Isis: above, *the Winged Isis, with crescent and disk headdress;* below, *Isis crowned with her signature throne emblem. From the collection of the author.*

eclectic, borrowing from several traditions. Added to this already complex variety of clothing styles was the fact that different types of priests and priestesses would wear clothing which differed according to their rank in the temple.

In general, during much of the heyday of the worship of Isis, linen was the preferred fabric, especially white linen. There are a number of references by ancient writers to the "linen-clad priests of Isis." Often linen is mentioned as an item in the temple inventories. Cotton was also used widely. At some places and periods the priests and priestesses of Isis were forbidden to wear wool as part of a general prohibition against sheep products. The reason for this taboo is not clear, but it may have resulted from the distracting, scratchy quality of some wools, which may also have been very uncomfortable for temple work in warm climates.

During the Roman era, silks were transported by camel caravan over the Silk Road from China and India. The worship of Isis also spread along the Silk Road, possibly penetrating as far as Chang'an, the ancient, cosmopolitan capital of Tang-dynasty China.

Representations of Isis vary widely, particularly between the Egyptian and Greco-Roman statues and paintings. Frequently, identification of ancient images is unclear unless there are accompanying inscriptions or text to positively identify a goddess-image as Isis.

The Egyptian Isis

A common image of Isis depicts Her with the crescent and disk headdress, or capped with the throne emblem, which is unique to Her. She also often appears holding the lotus scepter, a uraeus curling over Her forehead.

Another common, but later, representation of Isis is as Isis Lactans or Galactrophousa, the Nursing Isis who cradles Horus (or the reigning pharaoh) on Her knee. This may have been the prototype for later statues of the Virgin Mary holding the Christ child.

The Winged Isis is found mainly in depictions of the Resurrection of Osiris. The action of Her wings wafting life-giving air to the nostrils of Osiris revives him.

The Greco-Roman Isis

A typical Greco-Roman Isis, holding Her sistrum in one hand and a vase in the other, is illustrated on this page.

Other Greco-Roman Isis images show Her leaning on a rudder, a sign of Her power over navigation as well as Her ability to guide Her devotees through life's storms. Images linking Her to Demeter/Ceres include a cornucopia spilling out an abundance of food, reminding us of Her power over agriculture and Her nourishing benevolence to humankind.

A Simple Robe for Men and Women

Ritual clothing can be as complicated as you care to make it. This very simple robe is easy to make and will serve you well. It is based on the *galabayah* worn presently in Egypt.

First, measure the person who will wear the robe. Place the edge of a tape measure at the top of their shoulder and have them hold it

there. Bend down until the tape measure reaches their anklebone. Note down this measurement.

Take this measurement and double it. This is how many yards of fabric you will need. Choose a natural fabric if at all possible; some cotton-polyester blends work well. This fabric must be in the 54" or 60" width. A very small person may be able to manage with the 48" width, but it is much easier for you to simply trim down the excess from

A Greco-Roman Isis with sistrum and vase.

the wider widths. (See the section entitled "The Spectrum of Isis in Ritual Garb" at the end of this chapter [pages 61–66] for additional information on fabric colors.)

Take your fabric and fold it in half. Cut a half-circle through the doubled layers of fabric to make a hole for the head. Slit this down the center about 6" on the front side of the fabric.

Measure down 12" from the top fold on each side of the robe. From your measure point, cut in about 12", then cut down at an angle, as shown. Sew a 5/8" seam along these lines. Sew along all rough edges, turning down a small hem about 1/4" in from the edge of the fabric. Turn the garment out and press.

Once complete, wear the garment a few times before you decide if you want to decorate it.

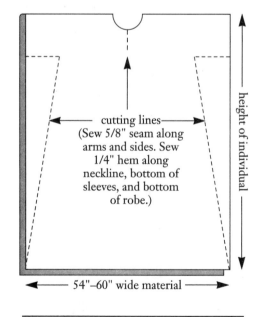

cutting lines
(Sew 5/8" seam along arms and sides. Sew 1/4" hem along neckline, bottom of sleeves, and bottom of robe.)

height of individual

◀━━ 54"–60" wide material ━━▶

Cutting diagram for simple robe.

THE KNOT OF ISIS

One detail of sacred robing for women in the Greco-Roman era was the sacred knot (also known as the Set or Thet knot, or the Knot of Isis). This is a representation of the stone Thet, or Set, amulet, created by tying together the front folds of the garment. In one common form this knot consists of an upright loop wrapped round several times at the base. Tied well, it will lie against the hollow between the breasts. If you are choosing to wear a wrapped sari-like sheath as part of your ritual costume, you can create a Thet knot in the following manner.

How to Tie a Thet Knot

1. Standing up, hold the fabric in front of you with the pattern or best side away from your body. The remaining length of the fabric should fall to your left side.

2. Grasp the upper right corner in your right hand, holding the rest of the fabric ready in your left hand.

3. Squeeze and gently pull the fabric into a rope-like length about 14" long. Place this under your left breast so the long extension is free between your breasts.

4. Wrap the fabric around your body as many times as necessary so that the end of the fabric reaches to the point between your breasts. In short, you need both ends of the fabric to tie the knot.

5. Take the long extension and fold it over into a loop with the round portion of the loop

pointing up. Turn the loop so it will lie flat against you with the opening in the loop visible from the front.

6. Take the other end of the fabric and wrap it around the base of this loop three times. Pin or tuck in the ends.

If you have plenty of fabric you may be able to wrap the base of the central loop more than three times. In this case, try pulling out one loop on each side of the base of the central loop. This will make the knot more closely resemble the stone amulet with the two side-loops trailing down.

The Thet, when used as an amulet, was made of red-colored stone or of gold. Once carved, it needed to be dipped into ankham flower water; this flower has not yet been definitely identified, but it was probably a sweet-smelling flower such as jasmine or gardenia. At the time it was dipped into water, the following words were to be recited:

The blood of Isis, and the strength of Isis, and the words of power of Isis shall be mighty to act as powers to protect this great and divine being, and to guard them from those who would do to them anything that they hold in abomination.[1]

Possession of this buckle also provided the deceased with the power to go wherever they wished in the underworld.

Normandi Ellis, in her excellent work, *Awakening Osiris*, includes a meditation on the Knot of Isis, which reads in part:

At the ends of the universe is a blood-red cord that ties life to death,

man to woman, will to destiny. Let the knot of that red sash, which cradles the hips of the goddess, bind in me the ends of life and dream … I am the knot where two worlds meet. Red magic courses through me like the blood of Isis, magic of magic, spirit of spirit. I am proof of the power of gods. I am water and dust walking.[2]

This Greco-Roman Isis displays an excellent example of a Thet knot.

JEWELRY AND AMULETS

Isis' supreme amulet was probably the Thet described previously. Many other amulets were connected with Her worship, either as funerary amulets or adapted for use by the living.

Amulets are objects into which a particular type of energy has been charged and locked. These magical tools are similar to batteries of energy which the wearer can rely upon to power a certain effect, such as protection or healing, without constantly having to reaffirm the desired effect.

Many common symbols used in jewelry were originally meant to be charged, operating amulets, but most are left powerless. A basic method to charge an amulet follows:

1. Physically cleanse the object by washing, polishing, blowing off

dust, or whatever method is appropriate, based on the material from which it is made.

2. Ritually cleanse the object using one of the methods described in Chapter Two, "Purifications for Rites of Isis."

3. Generate magical energy or healing energy as described in Chapter Eleven, "Isis the Great Physician."

4. Project the purpose of the amulet into it.

5. Maintain the flow of energy until it seems as if the amulet cannot contain any more.

6. Seal and lock the energy within the object by magically willing it to be so locked, including the instruction that the energy will maintain itself from the bountiful energy of the universe and be always available for your use as needed.

7. Coat the object with oil or pass it through incense smoke, imagining this to be like a coat of lacquer over a painted object, providing a final, hard seal.

8. Wrap the amulet in dark cloth and put it away in a place where it will not be disturbed for at least three days.

It is not necessary that this rite be performed at a specific planetary time, unless, of course, you are creating an amulet to make use of specific astrological energies. For the following amulets, and for many others, such precise timings are not necessary.

Amulets from the author's collection: above, Djed (backbone) column of Osiris; below, Thet amulet of Isis.

The Lotus Staff

Isis often is shown holding a lotus-topped staff, generally when repre-

Priests carrying staffs.

sented in Her most benevolent and beautiful aspects.

The Ueb (Set-headed) Staff

This staff, which ends in a simple representation of the head of Set, is painted red. It is carried by many of the gods, including Isis, and is used to show their dominion over the forces of evil. It directs the power of the priest or priestess.

The Vulture Amulet

This amulet, in the form of the vulture goddess Nekhebet or Mut, was considered to be a representation of Isis as the Divine Mother. This amulet was generally made of gold, and the following text was to be recited over it when it was used for funerary purposes:

Isis comes and hovers over the city, and She goes about seeking the secret habitations of Horus as he emerges from his papyrus swamps, and She raises up his injured shoulder. He is made one of the company in the divine boat, and the sovereignty of the whole world is decreed for him. He has warred mightily, and makes his deeds to be remembered; he has made the fear of him to exist and awe of him to have its being. His mother, the Mighty Lady, protects him, and She has transferred Her power into him.[3]

The Papyrus Sceptre

This can be used as an amulet or carried in ritual. In its form as a funerary amulet, it was made of mother-of-emerald or light green or blue faience. In later times, it was considered to be an amulet representing the Power of Isis-Renenet, particularly over harvests and, by extension, fertility matters as well.

The Snake's Head

This predominantly funerary amulet is associated with Isis by E. Wallis Budge in his *Egyptian Magic* because it is generally formed of a red-colored stone, and red is a color particularly sacred to Isis. As Isis

Uraeus over Isis' forehead.

possesses several snake forms, Budge believes this to be an amulet representing Her power over serpents and snakebite.

Whether or not this specific snake amulet is one "belonging" to Isis is unclear, but She certainly can be represented in snake forms. In the Greco-Roman period priestesses were shown carrying cobras in Isian processions, and snakes were frequently depicted on Her altars.

The Divine Isis also wears the rearing uraeus-snake over Her forehead. Isis and Osiris were occasionally shown as crowned snakes with their tails entwined.

The basic ankh form is shown in the center, with more complex versions to the right and left.

The Ankh

The supreme symbol of life was carried and used by virtually all of the gods in the pantheons of Egypt. Isis is frequently depicted carrying the ankh or using it to provide life-force to another being.

The origins of the symbol of the ankh are unclear. Some believe it to represent the stylized sexual organs of men and women joined together, while others believe the symbol is derived from a large-headed African fertility doll which was carried by women desiring children.

SYMBOLS, SIGNS, AND CORRESPONDENCES OF ISIS

A priestess of Isis, when asked what exactly was considered to be sacred to her goddess, replied, "Everything. Isis got all the good stuff." While this humorous answer is not strictly accurate, it seems that the goddess called "She of the Ten Thousand Names" claims easily many objects which are sacred to Her. Here are some that may be included or adapted in craft projects. For a more detailed discussion of sacred foods, please see Chapter Fourteen, "In the Kitchens and Gardens of Isis." Incenses, scents, and oils are presented in Chapter Eighteen, "Isis and Alchemy."

Animals, Insects, and Birds

Apis Bull — See "Cattle."

Beetles — See "Scarab Beetles."

Cats — Cats have long been associated with Isis, and one theory of their dispersion into Europe suggests that they were brought with the founders of the temples of Isis. Bast, whose name can be translated as "Soul of Isis," has a strong affinity with the sensual and motherly aspects of Isis.

Cattle — Isis was known in Egypt as the Great Cow, Mother of the Apis Bull, and by other titles asserting Her connection with the sacred cows of Egypt. As givers of milk and providers of nourishment, exactly as Isis provided Her milk to the pharaohs of Egypt, the association of cows with Isis is very ancient.

Crocodiles — Crocodiles were sometimes kept as pets in temples of Isis, living symbols of Isis' conquest over the negative forces of Set, who is sometimes represented as a crocodile.

Dogs — Isis is sometimes depicted riding on a dog, underlining Her association with the Dog-Star, Sirius. The guidance of the jackal, Anubis, as She searched for Her husband also links Her with canine beasts in general.

Dolphins — The constellation Delphinus was associated with special rites of Isis. The apparent power of dolphins over the waves of the sea also made them likely companions for the seafaring goddess.

Eagles — Possibly because of Isis' ties to Imperial Rome, eagles are said to be sacred to Her.

Gazelles — Sometimes called Playthings of Isis.

Griffons — Possibly because of Isis' association with hawks, griffons are said to be sacred to Her.

Hawks — Isis takes on the form of a hawk to help revive Osiris.

Lions — At the Temple of the Lions in Petra, Isis was combined with the local goddess Al-Uzza.

Peacocks — Peacocks appear occasionally in Isian iconography,

including a coin of Marcus Aurelius showing Isis accompanied by a peacock and a lion.

Pigs — Pork meat was taboo to followers of Osiris and sometimes to the priesthoods in general, due to the association with Set in his black boar form. However, Isis was, in a few examples, depicted as riding on the back of a pig and could even be referred to as The Great Sow.

Rams — Ram-headed sphinxes formed the sacred processional way to some temples where Isis was venerated. Wool was said to be forbidden to Her priests and priestesses; it is possible that this later taboo reflects an earlier tradition where the products of sheep were held to be sacred. As a Goddess of Weaving, this would be possible.

Scarab Beetles — Scarab beetles enjoy a close association with Isis. See the section, "Sacred Scarabs," in Chapter 21, "Isis and the Worship of the Hands," for additional information.

Scorpions — The Seven Scorpion Goddesses accompanied Isis after Her escape from Her imprisonment by Set. Feeling that Isis had been treated poorly

by a rich woman who refused Her shelter, they set the woman's house on fire, but Isis quelled the flames with rain, and then took shelter with a poor woman who had freely opened her doors to Her. Isis can also be represented as Isis-Selqet, a human-headed scorpion goddess with the Isian crescent and disk headdress.

Serpents — Snakes of all types are sacred to Isis and were used in Her rites, often being carried in processions. Isis and Osiris could be depicted in snake forms with their tails entwined around each other. As a symbol of wisdom, snakes are also a symbol of Isis Sophia, goddess of knowledge.

Sphinxes — Sphinxes, both animal-headed and human-headed, lined the sacred pathways to temples of Isis in Egypt.

Swallows — Isis took on the form of a swallow to fly around the pillar where Osiris' sarcophagus was contained.

Vultures — Isis-Nekhebet is the vulture form of the goddess. In Egypt, vultures were felt to be symbols of attentive motherhood.

Colors

Black — Isis in Mourning, or Isis in Search, required the worshipper or priestess to wear black. At a rite celebrated about the time of the winter solstice, a cow was draped in black and gold and driven around the temple seven times to symbolize the search of Isis for Osiris.

Gold — Gold is associated with Isis in Her sun goddess aspects.

Red — Isis wears red as Lady of Flame, and as a symbol of Her more erotic and powerful aspects.

Sea Colors — As a goddess of seafaring, the many colors of the sea can be used to depict Her.

Silver — As a lunar goddess and goddess of stars, silver represents these aspects. See the "Silver" entry under "Metals," on page 56.

White — Associated with Isis in Her lunar aspects.

Metals and Minerals

Bronze — Statuettes of Isis and other temple furnishings were often crafted of bronze, with bronze sistrums especially common. Bronze, an alloy of copper and tin, is a strong metal and was used in weaponry. The possession of bronze weapons provided a great advantage over weapons fashioned of other metals. Civilizations which possessed the secret and the materials for bronze triumphed over others, and so it is a particularly appropriate metal for Isis Victrix (the Victorious).

Copper — Copper is a warm metal with solar and cosmic associations. The Egyptians related copper to Hathor and to Isis in Her Hathor aspects. Because of its natural tendency to oxidize (or "bloom") in a rainbow of colors, copper enjoys a connection with the forces of fertility.

Modern associations include copper as a feminine, household metal, largely because of its frequent appearance in cookware. Copper's hidden presence is much more powerful. Most of us live and work surrounded by a web of copper wiring.

The Egyptians especially valued copper oxides for use in eye makeup. It was also a crucial component of bronze, an alloy of copper and tin which ushered in a new age of weaponry due to its hardness and ability to hold a sharp edge. Because of this, as well as its Sethian red color, copper also carries aggressive connotations. As a goddess of frank sexuality, Isis-Hathor also carries an aggressive aspect.

In the story of the tribulations between Isis' son, Horus, and Her brother, Set, Isis forges a harpoon of copper and uses it to skewer Set in the form of a hippopotamus.

Gold — Once used to coat the capstones of the sacred pyramids, gold was widely employed in Egypt. The yellow metal was plentiful, both in Egyptian-controlled mines and when offered as tribute from the many nations under Egypt's sway. From early times it was associated with the fire of the sun, and

embodies the warm, bright solar aspects of Isis. As the daughter of Ra, the sun god, gold is particularly appropriate for Her worship.

Gold has strong healing properties inherent in its structure. In modern times, it is still used as a remedy for many ailments, including arthritis. Because of these healing powers, gold is sacred to Isis in Her role as Divine Physician and as a nurturing Mother.

There is no metal more malleable than gold. It can be drawn into wires narrower than a human hair and can also be pounded thinner than any other metal. A single ounce of pounded gold can cover a large area, and because of this, sacred statues were frequently covered with a thin layer of gold leaf. Gold is also extremely dense, and its heaviness emphasizes its connection with the earth itself.

The Thet, or Set amulet, also known as the Knot of Isis, was occasionally made of gold instead of its more usual material of red stone or glass. Egyptians also experimented with dyeing gold, employing a red- or even purple-tinged gold for some sacred jewelry. Gold collars and diadems of delicate gold flowers were sometimes distributed by the reigning pharaoh to reward a worthy administrator or warrior.

Separate from its properties as a metal, the color gold reflects a very soothing quality of light. As such, gold-colored foil transmits a little of the solar radiance of real gold, and can be

used in its place to make sacred objects.

Silver — Although relatively common in the Roman world, silver was a rarity in ancient Egypt, and was sometimes valued more highly than gold. Only a few articles of silver have survived through the centuries. One of the finest of these objects is a pomegranate-shaped vase from the tomb of Tutankhamen. Bronze statuettes of the gods and goddesses sometimes have the eyes inlaid with silver or gold.

As a metal, silver has strong lunar associations and is frequently associated with Isis. In Roman times, a grandmother dedicated a solid silver statue to Isis in honor of a beloved grand-daughter who died young. Silver was also used in headdresses and ritual jewelry for priestesses, and to adorn statues of the Goddess. Temples would also issue festival coinage, sometimes in silver or an alloy of silver with other metals. Many cities also issued silver coins bearing images of Isis or of Isian themes.

Silver is a relatively brittle metal, which makes it more difficult to work than gold. Jewelry of silver is often made using the lost-wax casting method, which takes an imper-manent wax image and trans-forms it into a final image of silver. This is a method rich in alchemical metaphor, and can be an initiation in itself to master.

At the present writing, silver is relatively cheap (under five dollars for a nearly-pure troy ounce the size of a silver dollar).

Many coin shops offer art ingots, which are beautiful, coin-like silver pieces. If you are fortunate, you may be able to find one with a representation of one of the animals sacred to Isis, or a goddess-image such as the Statue of Liberty. These pieces usually cost a dollar or so over the "spot" or daily exchange rate for silver. An old Liberty-headed silver dollar can also serve as an altar image.

Silver wire and sheet silver are also available inexpensively. Silver wire can be bent into the shape of a protective symbol and then pounded flat with a hammer. Ankhs and Thet knots are very easy to make this way. Be sure to file off any rough edges, or coat them with a smooth substance such as epoxy.

Silver is used extensively in photographic processing to develop captured images. This is in keeping with the strong asso-ciations silver shares with the arts of divination and of pursuing occult, or hidden, knowledge.

Plants

See Chapter Fourteen, "In the Kitchens and Gardens of Isis," for these listings.

Stones and Semiprecious Gems

Amethyst — This beautiful and healing purple stone is often worn by priestesses of Isis, particularly as a round-cut, rather than faceted, stone. A temple of Isis in Rome had at least one pillar of amethyst.

Aquamarine — Isis as a Sea Goddess can be represented by this pale-blue stone.

Beryl — Crowley, in 777, associates this stone with Isis.

Carnelian — In Egypt, Thet knots were often carved of this glassy red stone.

Coral — Several varieties of coral still bear names derived from the word "Isis" (i.e., *Isisina*, *Isidella*, and *Isidae*). Again, as Isis is a Sea Goddess, coral is an appropriate stone for Her or Her worshippers.

Crystal — Egyptian artists achieved startling effects in their life-size statues by implanting eyes of painted crystal. This technique created a depth that mimicked reality and still disconcerts many visitors to Egyptian collections.

So much has been written in the last decade about clear quartz crystal that little needs to be added here. Briefly, quartz crystals are very receptive to vibrations of all kinds and can easily be charged to specific functions, such as healing, improving energy levels, or enhancing the memory. Simply hold a crystal in your hands while sending healing energy through it as you think about the function you wish the crystal to perform. (For information on how to generate healing energy, please see Chapter Eleven, "Isis the Great Physician.")

Emerald — Associated with Thoth (or Hermes), who was said to have created the Emerald Tablet with its mystical injunction, "As above, so below," emeralds have often been offered to the temples of the Goddess in ancient times and can still be used in Her worship today.

Granite — Granite was a favored material for altars in temples to Isis. Its vibrations are very compatible with Her worship, and aid in meditation.

Jacinth or Hyacinth — This reddish-orange form of zircon was among the stones adorning a silver statue of Isis offered at a shrine in Spain.

Jasper — This red stone is also suitable to represent the "Blood of Isis" for the Thet amulet.

Lapis Lazuli — One of Isis' titles was Isis of Lapis Lazuli. Mounted with gold, this rich blue stone, which often has a glittering matrix, is especially useful as a symbol of both Isis and of Her Mother, Nut of the starry sky.

Malachite — As a green stone of African origin, this stone is perfect for Isis as Goddess of Green Things and of fertility in general.

Marble — Many of the Greco-Roman temples used marble, either as building material or for statues. This smooth, polished stone is also very compatible with Her worship.

Moonstone — This association hardly needs any explanation. As Goddess of the Moon, moonstones are very appropriate in the worship of Isis.

Pearls — The moonlight-like glow of pearls made them an appropriate ancient offering to Isis, particularly as Goddess of the Sea or of Love.

Peridot — This volcanic gem, also known as olivine, is attributed to Isis by Crowley in his 777.

Ruby — Associated with Isis because of its rich, red color. The star ruby is also sacred to Isis.

Sapphire — The deep-blue sapphire is perfect for Isis as a sky and star Goddess. The star sapphire is appropriate for Her as well, and can be used as a trance or meditational tool by gazing at the star and slowly moving the stone.

Turquoise — Sacred to Hathor-Isis.

Symbols of Isis

Anchor — Initiates were thought to be safely "anchored" by their worship of Isis.

Ankh — Symbol of life, often carried by Isis in Egyptian representations, or wafted by Her wings as a breeze of life.

Bread — As a magical symbol, Aleister Crowley associates bread with Isis.

Burin — This engraving tool, used as a magical implement, is said to be a symbol of Isis. As a creatrix of writing, any inscribing or writing tool can be symbolic of Her energy.

Cornucopia — Symbol of abundance and nourishment, often carried by Isis in Greco-Roman representations.

Cup and Cross of Suffering — Aleister Crowley associates these magical symbols with Isis.

Grain Measure — The *modius*, a vessel for measuring grain, is occasionally seen in representations of Isis. This oddly-shaped vessel, wider at the top than at the bottom, is more commonly seen on statues of Serapis. Also see "Wheat."

Harpoon (or any type of aquatic spear) — Isis forged a copper harpoon for Herself to aid Horus in his battle against Set.

Horns — The horn and crescent headdress is readily identifiable with Isis, though Hathor also carries this headdress. Isis has been represented with cow horns, curved oryx-like horns, and, more rarely, pronged deer antlers. These all may in turn be symbols for the "Horns of the Moon," or the points of the crescent moon.

Horn of Plenty — See "Cornucopia."

Lamp or Lantern — These objects are associated with Isis, particularly in Her aspect of the bereft wife searching for Her husband's remains.

Lingam — See "Phallus."

Magic Circle — Crowley associates Isis with the Magic Circle in his listing of her attributes in the book 777.

Modius — See "Grain Measure."

Moon, Crescent — Crescent headdress, or cow horns resembling the crescent moon, are found in both Egyptian and Greco-Roman representations of Isis.

Moon, Full — Isis was considered identical with the moon, though this association may not have been as prevalent in Egypt. Her power over tides, particularly important to the sea-faring Greeks, also identified the moon with Her.

Pentagram — The five-pointed star was associated with Isis, and formed a component of the hieroglyphics for her name of Isis-Sothis.

There is debate among practitioners of purely Egyptian religion as to whether the woven five-pointed star was ever associated with Isis or any other deity. The woven pentagram was associated with the Virgin Mary, and in Arthurian romance was placed on a shield as her symbol of protection over the knight who bore it.

Mythologist Robert Graves, in his *Difficult Questions, Easy Answers*, includes an essay entitled "The Pentagram of Isis."

Phallus — As the one who restores the sacred Phallus of Osiris, Isis is associated with representations of the phallus. She is said to have created a new one of wood or gold for Osiris, through which She was then impregnated.

Robes of Concealment — Crowley associates Isis with both the Inner and the Outer Robes of Concealment.

Isis was forced to disguise Herself several times in the Osirian myths, once after Her escape from the prison where Set concealed Her, when She entered the service of Queen Astarte in Byblos to be near Osiris in his coffin, and again when She was raising Horus alone in the delta swamps. Once more, Isis resorted to disguising Herself as an aged woman in order to fool Set and reach the island where the gods were determining the fate of Horus and Set. These incidents associate Her with impersonation, disguise, veiling, and the ability to pass unnoticed.

Rudder — The worship of Isis was considered to be the "spiritual rudder" guiding the worshipper through the rough seas of life.

Sail — Isis is often depicted on Greco-Roman coins holding the edges of a billowing sail, and proclaiming Her power over the winds and seas.

Sceptre — As a symbol of Her divine royalty, the sceptre serves as a symbol of Her divine power over the throne, both as an occupier of it and as a dispenser of the power of the throne to the pharaoh She favors.

Ships — As Goddess of Navigation, as well as a goddess who sails in the Barque of Ra or guides the funerary boat of Osiris, ships were also Her symbols. Many ships were named "Isis," particularly those which plied the grain transport routes between Egypt and the rest of the Mediterranean.

One early commentator, Tacitus, discusses Viking ship-burial rituals and suggests that these were derived from rites of

Isis. Small ships were launched during the festival of navigation (*Isidis Navigium*) and models of ships were carried in processions.

Sistrum — A common symbol of the worship of Isis, often engraved on the stones of the tombs of priestesses, and frequently shown in other depictions of the Goddess or Her priestesses.

Situla — A small pail, usually filled with milk, carried in processions of Isis. Often these allowed the contents to drip onto the ground, blessing it.

Sponge — The all-absorbing, all-welcoming Goddess is said to have sometimes been symbolized with a sponge, though I have been unable to uncover any clear references.

Serpents — Snakes were often carried in Isian processions, and Isis and Osiris themselves could be represented as snake-bodied.

Thet or Set Knot — The Knot of Isis, perhaps a stylized symbol of the female reproductive organs, was worn as an amulet or incor-

porated into ritual clothing. See the beginning of this chapter for more information.

Throne — The three-stepped throne symbol of Isis is most commonly found on Her head or headdress.

Triangle — Triangles, either pointing up or down, can show an association with Isis. The inverted triangle with its point down is a sign of the yoni, the essential symbol of femaleness. Pythagoras, the mathematical philosopher believed also to have been an initiate of Isis, may have originated the title of Isis, "Base of the Most Perfect Triangle," which associates Her clearly with the three-sided form.

Uraeus — The small serpent emerging from the forehead or from a band around the head symbolizes Isis' divinity as Queen of Egypt.

Wand — The wand, as a symbol of magical power and because of its phallic associations, is also seen as a symbol of Isis. The magical staffs that She carries in Egyptian iconography, such as the lotus staff and the Set staff, are forms of magical wands.

Wheat — Blades of wheat were often held by Isis, particularly in areas where She was identified with either the goddess Demeter or as patroness of the grain fleets of Egypt.

Wings — The Winged Isis was most commonly found in funerary statuary, or as a healing entity. Greco-Roman statues of Isis did not show Her with wings, though Isis identified with Nike (Victory) could bear wings. Priestesses might have a crossed-wing design on their sacred robes.

Yoni — Any vulvar symbols, such as cleft-yoni representations, can apply to Isis as the Gateway of Life and as the Great Mother and Divine Midwife.

Woods

Cedar — The cedar trade with the area that is now Lebanon was important to the Egyptians, who used the fragrant wood extensively. The worship of Isis was often introduced into the foreign ports where the wood was loaded on ships for transport to Egypt. Due to the love of ancient civilizations for cedar wood, this species is nearly extinct in Lebanon today.

Citrus Wood — Citrus wood was sometimes used in creating ritual objects for the worship of Isis.

Pine and Fir Woods — These woods were used for creating the ships launched at the Festival of Navigation, the *Isidis Navigium*. The high masts of these ships were sometimes made of single fir trees, which were then extensively decorated, perhaps a forerunner of modern Christmas trees.

One festival of Osiris included the ritual carving-out of a figure of Osiris from a pine tree. The figure was then returned to the heart of the tree and left there for a year, at the end of which the figure was burned and a new one made.

Pine cones were often offered to Osiris.

THE SPECTRUM OF ISIS IN RITUAL GARB

As Lady of Light, Isis claims dominion over all colors of the spectrum, and Her many-colored robes were designed to dazzle the eyes of Her worshippers. Although white was often the preferred, or at least the most common, color for the priesthood to wear in ordinary circumstances, there were many exceptions. The Melanophores, or Wearers of Black, chose to wear black robes to symbolize the mourning Isis searching for Osiris.

Ancient clothing styles were conservative, changing slowly over a long period of time. Most Western garb today is confining; the term "buttoned down" is slang for a restricted personality with little mental or physical freedom. Egyptian, Greek, and Roman clothing relied heavily on the artful draping of fabric. Some portions were sewn, or fastened with brooches or pins, but most styles demanded a careful positioning of the cloth itself. In a sense, the ancients veiled their bodies, rather than clothed them.

While it is not necessary to have special clothing to successfully pray or do ritual, you may find the use of a special garment an enhancement to your rites. Fabrics gradually gather to them vibrations compatible with the atmospheres to which they are exposed.

Color, weight, and type of material all play a role in changing your personal environment. Some of these changes are obvious: certain fabrics keep you warmer, others keep you cooler. Your state of body definitely influences your state of

mind. If you embark on creating a special robe, use a fabric that you like to touch.

Remember that robes tend to retain body heat; in combination with candles, incense, groups of people, and small working areas, you may understand why some prefer to work nearly naked. Some priests depicted in Isian paintings wore only their kilts, while others were shown in a full toga. A ready-to-wear ritual robe for both women and men can be found in the form of the modern *galabayah*, a straight, loose robe with sleeves often found in Middle Eastern stores or in shops carrying African clothing.

Priestesses' Robes

Isis and Her priestesses have been depicted in so many colors, fashions, and styles, that there is virtually no limitation to what a priestess can wear and still be "in style" with ancient costume. Isis was often depicted in temple and tomb paintings as wearing a slim Egyptian sheath dress covered with vivid woven or embroidered patterns. One style consisted of the crossed wings of the sacred vulture wrapped about Her hips.

The writer and initiate Plutarch, in his book *On Isis and Osiris*, describes the robes of Isis as "variegated in color (for Her essential power concerns the material which becomes everything and receives everything), light and darkness, day and night, fire and water, life and death, beginning and end."

Plutarch contrasts these multi-colored garments with the robe of Osiris, which he says has nothing dark or variegated about it. Instead, the robe of Osiris is "one simple color, the color of light; for the origin of things is unadulterated and the primal element which is spiritually intelligible is unmixed. For this reason they put on this dress only once, and then take it off, preserving it unseen and untouched, whereas they use the Isiac robes many times."

Dion Fortune's priestess of the Isis of Nature, Vivien Le Fay Morgan, describes her preferences for color, clothing, and adornments in Fortune's classic magical novel, *Moon Magic*. Her heroine avoids

A priestess of Isis.

primary colors, but chooses instead the subtle, blended tones and opalescent shades contrasted with vivid lipstick and long lacquered fingernails, though for ritual work her hands might go unadorned. She favored furs, and full-length robes of rich fabrics. Rings and gems of many kinds were worn by her, carefully chosen for their effect by day or night. Emeralds were reserved for the nighttime, along with pearls and opals; day found her wearing amber or coral, malachite, lapis, or jade.

Priests' Robes

Apuleius describes the robes he donned after his successful completion of the initiation into the Mysteries of Isis. Ever careful of his vows of secrecy, he mentions that he feels free to speak of his robes only because they were viewed by many people at his presentation to the congregation after the ritual, and so his listing of them in such detail is not to be regarded as a betrayal of the initiation he received.

Apuleius was wearing twelve stoles, a vestment of fine linen richly embroidered with flowers, and an Olympian stole covered with Indian dragons, Hyperborean griffins, and other beasts from "the other part of the world," apparently Asia and the Indian subcontinent. He carried a lighted torch in his right hand, and wore a garland of flowers which held white palm fronds spreading out in a kind of halo headdress, evoking the rays of the sun.

While Apuleius' initiate robes were elaborate, the everyday garb of a priest usually consisted of a simple garment, white in color. Sometimes a priest of Isis would wear only a kilt, leaving the chest bare or partially draped with a stole. Very high-ranking priests might wear a leopard skin in addition to their kilt.

In later times, Greco-Roman priests would wear a draped garment, and would be distinguished primarily by their shaven heads, often shaving the eyebrows, eyelashes, and all other body hair as well. Priestesses in the Greco-Roman period often had curled hair, or kept their hair "long and abundant" (as Apuleius described the Hair of Isis Herself in his encounter

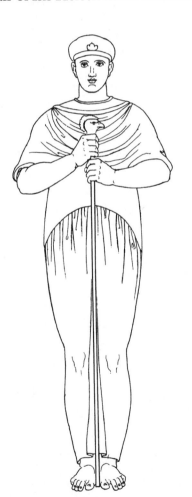

A Priest of Isis in the Greco-Roman style.

with Her by the seashore). In Egypt, women also often shaved their heads, but wore wigs in the ceremonies.

The Effect of Light

Candlelight, in essence a flickering source of warmed sunlight, is very beneficial to the human brain. Incandescent lighting can vary from warm to cold; generally speaking, soft lighting is not only more flattering to the human form but also healthier. Both candlelight and incandescent lighting add yellow to the colors you are wearing.

Fluorescent lighting, hailed as cheaper and more efficient energy usage, has a very negative effect on the human mind. The flicker rate and the harshly-reduced spectrum make thinking and maintaining alertness extremely difficult. It would be interesting to research whether or not the sharp drop in scholastic achievement in the United States mirrors the educational community's move toward windowless, artificially-lit classrooms filled with fluorescent bulbs.

Full-spectrum fluorescents reduce some of these negative effects, as do filtering panels placed over the lights. Wearing a hat or visor can also reduce some of the deleterious effects of fluorescent lighting.

Oddly enough, though similar to fluorescent lighting in construction, neon lights can offer a very pure source of colored light in vivid shades that are almost impossible to find elsewhere. Though some health problems may exist with neon lights, for the purpose of providing pure colored light they are excellent.

The Influence of Color

The right design of clothing is, to force a pun, immaterial to how effective your work with Isis will be. However, good design of ritual clothing *can* enhance your experiences. Another potential enhancement is that of color. The colors you wear affect the amount of various spectrums of light reflecting into your eyes.

Orthodox medicine and science are beginning to realize, and to publish, the dramatic effects of different types of light on the human brain. The colors that "look best" on you may have little to do with the colors your brain craves. Holding fabrics up to your eyes— even covering your head with them- can show you what colors feel best to your mind. You will find some colors stimulating, others relaxing. For ritual clothing you will generally want to choose colors which induce a meditative state of mind.

You may be surprised at which colors evoke the desired response in you. These may also change with different emotional states, your overall health, and the time of year.

Where you live may also influence your need for colored light. Someone who lives in the desert is not likely to be craving yellow light; another person who lives by the sea will probably always have their fill of the blue spectrum. Persons living in smoggy areas and working under fluorescent lighting may be suffering from colored light deficiency in practically the entire spectrum, and may want to compensate with vividly colored clothing for both ritual and everyday use.

Some fabrics reflect more light than others. Silks, though expensive, have a sheen and purity of color that is hard to match in other fabrics. Rayon, although synthetic material, is very human-friendly and has some of the reflective qualities of silk at a much lower price. It also flows well when made into ritual wear. Cottons are also good when dyed with vivid colors. However, they will usually fade over time, and this will affect how you perceive the color.

Combining colors can also be very effective in inducing or clearing states of mind. The colors you wear will also be modified by the amount and source of light in the areas you wear them, and by colors worn alongside them, both fabrics and metals.

Choosing a Color

Deciding what color will enhance your own spirituality is extremely personal and can only be determined by experiment. Here are some common associations which may help you explore the spectrum.

Pastel shades are kinder, gentler versions of their more vivid cousins, and have a less pronounced effect. Colors all have their own inherent brightness, which also affects their usefulness. Yellow is extremely bright, so even a pastel yellow will pack a strong punch of yellow energy.

At the opposite end of the brightness scale, the dark blues may tend to absorb rather than reflect light, as will matte black fabrics. However, a dark color in a fabric that reflects back light will send out its own color as well as bits of the rest of the spectrum.

Glossy-dark or black fur will throw back tiny splinters of light of all colors—check this out the next

time you encounter a friendly Labrador retriever lying in the sunlight. However, this reflection of the rest of the spectrum is usually too subtle to effectively use in correcting deficiencies or setting moods. Wearing only black will enhance the effect of the colors in your surroundings on your state of mind, and will also cause the shade of light reflected back from your skin and hair to be of greater importance. The oils in the skin make humans of all shades reflect back white light.

Blue — Calms and soothes. Lack of the blue spectrum can cause irritability and nervousness. Too much blue can be depressing, as the expression "feeling blue" indicates. Lapis or royal blues, however, are not usually depressing.

Green — Increases creativity. Lack of green can contribute to mental lethargy and clichéd thinking. Green is the most prevalent color in the spectrum, and difficult to overdose with. Even flesh colors have a surprising amount of green in them, which is why it is easy for television broadcasts to tint humans slightly green if the equipment is not set up properly.

Magenta and Fuchsia — These are red-heavy purples which are more stimulating than the blue-heavy varieties.

Orange — Stimulating. It is similar to yellow light and is a healing color.

Purple, Violet, and Lavender — Since all of these shades contain varying amounts of both red and blue, these colors can be very

balancing while exerting a mildly stimulating effect.

Many people are so strongly attracted to these colors that they avoid wearing other colors, which is not generally advisable. Wearing only purple can lead to deficiencies in the yellow and green ranges, as well as deficiencies in whatever portions of the pure red and blue spectrums are not included in the particular shade of purple worn.

Red — Increases energy; mentally and sexually stimulating. Lack of the red spectrum can be depressing. Too much red can lead to restlessness, irritability, and anger.

Turquoise — Calming, but without the sedative effect of some pure blues. Turquoise can provide a euphoric influence, and is a good color for spiritual work.

Yellow — Generally stimulating. Lack of yellow light is depressing. Some yellow-light deficiencies can be counteracted by using a heat lamp.

☽· ☿ ·☾

Colored lights can also be incorporated into personal rituals. Glass oil lamps with colored oils and candles in colored glass containers can also provide needed frequencies of light.

When experimenting with enhancing your rites and ritual frame of mind with color, you will probably discover that you are much more aware of color in general. Your perception of subtle differences between colors of similar shade will surprise you.

☽· ☿ ·☾

Chapter Six
The Sixth Hour of Daylight

EXALTING ISIS

PRAISESONGS AND INVOCATIONS

THROUGHOUT HISTORY, THE WORSHIPPERS of Isis have spoken and sung to Her. Praisesongs, lavishly listing the fruits of Her benevolence and reciting Her history, have been found at many temples. Modern authors have provided us with invocations that create a resonance in the invoker, calling down a portion of the divine Power so that the priestess and goddess share the same essence.[1]

Possibly the most evocative—and invocative—chants created in this century are those found within Dion Fortune's magical novels. They are best appreciated within the context of the novels, but here is one of them.

Isis Invocation

I am the star that rises from the sea, the
*   twilight sea.*
I bring men dreams that rule their destiny.
I bring the moon-tides to the souls of men,
The tides that flow and ebb and flow again;
That flow and ebb and flow alternately,
These are my secret, these belong to me.

Isis-Aphrodite (Venus).

I am the Eternal Woman, I am She—
The tides of all men's souls belong to me.
The tides that flow and ebb and flow
again;
The secret, silent tides that govern men;
These are my secret, these belong to me.
Out of my hands he takes his destiny;
Touch of my hands bestows serenity—
These are the moon-tides, these belong
to me.
Isis in Heaven, on earth, Persephone,
Diana of the moon and Hecate,
Veiled Isis, Aphrodite from the sea,
All these am I and they are seen in me.
The high full-moon in the mid-heaven
shines clear,
I hear the invoking words, hear and
appear ...
Shaddai el Chai and Rhea, Binah, Ge,
I come unto the priest that calleth me.[2]

Apuleius' Adoration of Isis

From J. Gwyn Griffith's translation of Apuleius' novel, *Metamorphoses:*

At about the first watch of night I was awakened by a sudden fright and I saw the full orb of the moon gleaming radiantly with splendid sheen and coming out just then from the waves of the sea; and aware of the mute mysteries of the dark night, I knew that now the eminent goddess was prevailing with especial power and that all human affairs were governed by her providence, while not only cattle and wild beasts, but lifeless beings too were invigorated by the divine favour of her light and majesty; further that the very bodies in earth, sea, and sky were at one time blessed with growth by her favour, and at another time afflicted through her with decline. Now that fate, it seemed, had taken its fill of my many great misfortunes and was offering, though late, a hope of deliverance, I decided to address in prayer the sacred image of the goddess now present in person. So shaking off at once my torpid slumber, I gladly and eagerly arose and, anxious to purify myself, I went to bathe in the sea. Seven times I plunged my head under the waves, since the divine Pythagoras pronounced that number to be very specially suitable in sacred rites. Then with a tear-stained face I prayed to the all-powerful goddess thus:

"O Queen of Heaven— whether thou art Ceres, the primal and bountiful mother of crops, who, glad in the return of her daughter, removed the brutish acorn provender of old, and showed to men gentle nourishment, after which thou now honourest the soil of Eleusis; or whether thou art heavenly Venus, who didst unite the difference of the sexes in the first beginnings of nature by creating Love, and after bringing forth mankind with its unceasing offspring, art worshipped in the island shrine of Paphos; or the sister of Phoebus, who didst relieve the delivery of young ones by soothing remedies, thus rearing such teeming masses, and art now adored in the celebrated temples of Ephesus; or whether as Proserpine, dreaded in cries that pierce the night, repelling attacks of ghosts with thy threefold countenance, and keeping barred the bolts of the earth, wandering the while in groves here and there, thou art propitiated with differing rites—whoever thou art, illumining all city walls with that womanly light, nourishing with bright fires the joyous seeds, and bestowing uncertain illumination only during digressions from thy path, by whatever name or ceremony or visage it is right to address thee, help me now in the depth of my trouble, strengthen my crushed fortune, grant respite and peace after the endurance of dire ills; regard this as enough of toil, enough of danger. Remove the cruel four-footed form, restore me to the sight of my loved ones, restore me to my own self as Lucius. And if some deity is angered so as to pursue me with implacable cruelty, at least allow me to die, if I am not allowed really to live."

When I had thus poured out my prayers, adding pitiable wailings, sleep again spread over my wilting spirit and overpowered me on that same sandy bed. I had scarcely settled down when lo! from the middle of the sea face divine arose, showing above the waves a countenance which even gods must admire; and then gradually the radiant image of the whole body, when the brine had been shaken off, seemed to stand before me. I will try to communicate to you her wonderful appearance if the poverty of human speech affords me the means of description or if the deity herself lends me her rich store of rhetorical eloquence.

First, her abundant, long hair, gently curled over her divine neck or loosely spread, streamed down softly. A crown of many designs with many kinds of flowers had girt her lofty head; in its centre a flat disk above the forehead shone with a clear light in the manner of a mirror or indeed like the moon, while on its right and left it was embraced by coils of uprising snakes; from above it was adorned also with outstretched ears of corn. Her tunic too was of many colours,

Isis-Ceres (Demeter).

woven entirely of fine linen, now bright with a white gleam, now yellow with saffron hue, now fiery with roseate ruddiness. But what most of all overwhelmed my sight further was the cloak of deepest black, resplendent with dark sheen; it went round about, returning under the right side to the left shoulder, a part of the garment being dropped in the manner of a knot; and hanging down with many folds, the whole robe undulated gracefully with tasselled fringes to its lowest edges.

Along the embroidered border and in the very body of the material there gleamed stars here and there, and in their midst a half-moon breathed a flame of fire. But wherever the sweep of that magnificent mantle moved, a wreath garlanded of all manner of flowers and fruits was indivisibly joined to it. The things she carried were of quite varied kind. For in her right hand

Isis-Diana.

she bore a bronze rattle in which a few rods in the middle, thrust across a thin sheet of metal that was curved like a belt, emitted a tinkling sound when the arm made three quivering jolts. From the left hand then there hung a golden vessel on whose handle, where it was conspicuous, there rose a serpent which reared its head high and puffed its neck thickly. Her ambrosian feet were covered by sandals woven with leaves of victorious palm. Such was the great goddess who, breathing the blessed fragrance of Arabia, deigned to address me with divine voice.

"Lo, I am with you, Lucius, moved by your prayers, I who am the mother of the universe, the mistress of all the elements, the first offspring of time, the highest of deities, the queen of the dead, foremost of heavenly beings, the single form that fuses all gods and goddesses; I who order by my will the starry heights of heaven, the health-giving breezes of the sea, and the awful silences of those in the underworld: my single godhead is adored by the whole world in varied forms, in differing rites and with many diverse names.

"Thus the Phrygians, earliest of races, call me Pessinuntia, Mother of the Gods; thus the Athenians, sprung from their own soil, call me Cecropeian Minerva; and the sea-tossed Cyprians call me Paphian Venus, the archer Cretans Diana Dictynna, and the trilingual Sicilians Ortygian Proserpine; to the Eleusians I am Ceres, the ancient goddess, to others Juno, to others Belona and Hecate and Rhamnusia. But the Ethiopians, who are illumined by the first rays of the sun god as he is born every day together with the Africans and the Egyptians who excel through having the original doctrine, honor me with my distinctive rites and give me my true name of Queen Isis.

"I am here taking pity on your ills; I am here to give aid and solace. Cease then from tears and wailings, set aside your sadness; there is now dawning for you, through my providence, the day of salvation ..."[3]

A Hymn of Isidorus

Here is one of the praisesongs written by Isidorus, who worshipped Isis at Madinet Madi in the Fayoum Oasis district of Egypt, sometime during the first century B.C.E.

The original of this hymn was inscribed on blocks at the temple, and provided a model for the worship of those who came to Her sacred space.

Hymn Three

O Ruler of the highest Gods,
Hermouthis, Lady,
Isis, pure, most sacred, mighty, of
mighty Name, Deo,
O most hallowed Bestower of good
things,
To all men who are righteous,
You grant great blessings: to possess
wealth,
A life that is pleasant, and most serene
happiness:
Material gain, good fortune, and
happy soundness of understanding.
All who live lives of greatest bliss, the
best of men:
Sceptre-bearing kings and those who
are rulers,
If they depend on You, rule until old
age,
Leaving shining and splendid wealth
in abundance
To their sons, and sons' sons, and men
who come after.
But the one whom the heavenly Queen
has held the most dear of princes,
Rules both Asia and Europe,

Keeping the peace; the harvests grow
heavy for him
With all kinds of good things, bearing
fruit ...
And where indeed there are wars and
slaughter
Of countless throngs,
Your strength, and godly power
Annihilates the multitude against
him;
But to the few with him it gives
courage.
Hear me Agathetyche,
When I pray to You, Lady,
Whether You have journeyed into
Libya or to the south wind,
Or whether You are dwelling in the
outermost regions of the north wind
ever sweetly blowing,
Or whether You dwell in the blasts of
the east wind where are the risings
of the sun,
Or whether You have gone to Olympus
where the Olympian gods dwell,
Or whether You are in heaven above,
a judge with the immortal gods,
Or whether having mounted the
chariot of the swift-driving sun,
You are directing the world of men,
Looking down on the manifold deeds of
the wicked
And gazing down on those of the just.
If You are present here too, You
witness individual virtue,
Delighting in the sacrifices, libations
and offerings,
Of the men who dwell in the Nome of
Suchos, the Arsinoites,
Men of mixed races who all, yearly,
are present
On the twentieth of the month of
Pachon and Thoth, bringing a
tenth for You
And for Anchoes, and Sokonopis, most
sacred gods, at Your feast.

Isis and Osiris.

O hearer of prayers, black-robed Isis,
the Merciful,
And You Great Gods who share the
temple with Her,
Send Paean to me, O healer of all ills.[4]

An Ancient Hymn from Cyme

I am Isis, the mistress of Every Land,
and I was taught by Hermes, and
with Hermes I devised Letters, both
the Sacred and the Demotic, so that
all things might be written with
the same [letters].

I gave and ordained Laws for men,
which no one is able to change.

I am eldest daughter of Kronos. I am
wife and sister of King Osiris. I am
She who finds fruit for men. I am
mother of King Horos.

I am She that rises in the dogstar. She
called Goddess by women. For me
was the city of Boubastis built.

I divided the earth from the heavens. I
showed the Path of the Stars. I
ordered the Course of Sun and
Moon. I devised business in the Sea.

I made strong the Man. I brought
together Woman and Man. I
appointed to Women to bring their
Infants to birth in the tenth month.
I ordained that Parents should be
loved by Children. I laid punish-
ments on those disposed without
natural affection towards their
Parents.

I made with my brother Osiris an end
to the Eating of Men. I revealed
Mysteries to Men. I taught [men] to
honor Images of the Gods. I conse-
crated the Precincts of the Gods.

I broke down the Governments of
Tyrants. I made an end to
Murders. I compelled Women to
take the love of Men. I made the
Right stronger than Gold and
Silver. I ordained that the True
should be thought Good. I devised
Marriage-contracts.

I assigned to Greeks and Barbarians
their languages. I made the Beau-
tiful and the Shameful to be distin-
guished by Nature. I ordained that
nothing should be more feared than
an Oath. I have delivered the
Plotter of Evil against other men
into the hands of the one he plotted
against. I established Penalties for
those who practice Injustice. I
decreed Mercy to Supplicants. I
protect [or honor] righteous guards.
With me the Right prevails.

I am the Queen of Rivers and Winds
and Sea. No one is held in honor
without my knowing it. I am the
Queen of War. I am the Queen of
the Thunderbolt. I stir up the Sea
and I calm it. I am in the Rays of
the Sun.

Whatever I please, this too shall come
to an end. With me everything is

reasonable. I set free those in bonds.
I am the Queen of Seamanship. I
make the navigable unnavigable
when it pleases me.
I created Walls of Cities. I am called
the Lawgiver.[5] I brought up Islands
out of the Depths into the Light. I
am Lord of Rainstorms.[6] I over-
come Fate. Fate hearkens to me.
Hail, Egypt that nourished me.[7]

Creating New Chants

Chants are songs which can be
either sung or spoken. They generally rhyme, which helps induce a
receptive state of mind in the
listeners and chanters and aid the
memory. Chants are usually charac-
terized by strong rhythms, but slow,
hypnotic meandering can also be
found in powerful chants. The
simplest chant, and a very ancient
one, is a recital of names or titles of
the Goddess.

A very simple chant model
consists of three names of the
Goddess starting with the same
word, then an invocation statement
such as "Isis be with us!" or "Come
to us, Goddess!" This is a wonderful
type of chant to do spontaneously,
since you really can't go wrong as
long as you can think of three
names of the Goddess (or can
quickly improvise a few new ones!)
and add a short sentence inviting
Her to make Her presence known.
After a few verses, this chant form
gathers a great deal of power. It can
also be done as a round started by a
priestess or priest, letting each
participating individual do a verse or
a single line of a verse. Here is a
short sample.

Lady of Light (name line)
Lady of Life (name line)
Lady of Green Plants (name line)
Come to us now! (invocation line)
Goddess of Magic
Goddess of Healing
Goddess of Brightness
  Bless us Your children!
Mistress of power
Mistress of Righteousness
Mistress of the Evening Star
  Teach us Your wisdom!
Isis of Philae
Isis of Memphis
Isis of Alexandria
  Show us Your places!

… and so on. As Isis Myrionymous,
Isis of the Myriad of Names, the
possibilities are unlimited. See
"Goddess of Ten Thousand Names"
on the following page for additional
attested names of Isis.

The Naming of the Places

Another simple but moving hymn
model is the Naming of the Places.
A similar type of hymn to Isis
consisted of Isis declaring Her
attributes in different places and
Her powers for and over humanity.
Copies of some of these hymns have
been found at several temple sites,
and in some cases the names of the
authors (such as Isidorus, one of
whose hymns is given previously)
and some details of their lives have
survived the centuries.

At its simplest, these ancient
hymns were listings of all the places
where the worship of Isis was
known by the author. This format
can be easily adapted to your own
area and your own experiences.
Where have you been when you
meditated on or prayed to Isis?

Choose a pleasing way of listing the town, place, or even streetname. Listen to the combination of words aloud. Try to alternate accented syllables with unaccented ones, as in that quintessential poem of American childhood, "Mary Had a Little Lamb." This meter creates a surging rhythm that is easy to remember and lends power to your recitation. Use rhyme if you like. The number of lines and syllables, perfect adherence to meter, and rhyme scheme do not really matter. What does matter is that the resulting poem/hymn/chant works for you.

Because chants which you create yourself are uniquely yours, you will probably find them much easier to remember than material which you merely read. Feel free to change your chants with each recitation to reflect new events or to recall a time or place particularly significant to you now. Feel equally free to become attached to a few verses which you always repeat intact.

Here is one of my "Naming of the Places":

At dusk by the Pacific Ocean
On the sand of the beach at Laguna
In the woods of the mountains of
*   Julian*
By the dark mines of tourmaline at
*   Pala*
In the light of the Moon rising over
*   Coronado*
In the busy shadowed streets of San
*   Diego*
Wet in the waves of the sea cave in La
*   Jolla*
By the tiered fountain above Del Mar
Looking over the hills where coyotes
*   still roam in Costa Mesa*

In a flattened field outside Novato
In the desert oasis of Palm Canyon
In the bright air of Alpine
Between the tall towers of Los Angeles
On roadways clotted with commuters
I have sought and found You, Holy Isis.

Simplicity is powerful. Simply saying one or more of the many Names of Isis aloud or silently is a prayer-chant. Done in a group with different participants starting at different times or each reciting a different Name of Isis creates an incredible vortex of energy which can be offered to Isis and directed toward a purpose pleasing to Her, such as healing or peace.

GODDESS OF TEN THOUSAND NAMES

Study all her names and you will learn
the relations of Earth with Heaven.
—The Sage (speaking of Isis) in Isha
Schwaller de Lubicz's
Her-Bak, Egyptian Initiate

The mere speaking of Her names was a sacred litany. Though many titles of Isis are long lost, and many more remain to be discovered, here are a few of the many names She has been called by—and answered to— through Her long history.

Africa
Agape
Albula
Alexandria
All-bounteous
All-hearing
All-receiving
All-seeing
Amenti — The Hidden One
Ankhet — Producer and Giver of
    Life

Anqet — Embracer of the Land, producer of fertility in the waters

Aphrodite

Arbiter in matters of sexual love

Aset — one pronunciation of Her Egyptian name

Ast — another pronunciation

Athena

Au Set — variant pronunciation of Aset, the Egyptian name of Isis

Aut — a title of Isis at Denderah

Base of the Most Beautiful Triangle

Benefactress of the Tuat (the Underworld)

Bride of God

Child of Nut

Cornucopia of All Our Goods

Creation

Creatrix of the Nile Flood

Crown of Ra-Heru

Daughter of Geb

Daughter of Neb-er-Tcher

Daughter of Nut

Daughter of Ra

Daughter of Seb

Daughter of Thoth

Dea ex Machina — The Goddess in the Machine, the divine

Diadem of Life

Dikaiosyne — an aspect associated with justice

Dispeller of Attack

Divine Mother

Divine One

Dweller in Netru

Dynamis

Dynastis

Earth

Embracer of the Land

Epekoos — The All-hearing

Euploia — Giver of Good Sailing

Eye of Ra

Female Horus

Female Principle in Nature

Female Ra

First Offspring of Time

First of the Muses in Hermopolis

Freedom

Fresh Tuft

Friendship

Fructifier

Galactotrouphousa — Suckling Isis, who bestows the miracle of the milk of life

Gentle

Giver of Life

Goddess Fifteen

Goddess of All Goddesses

Goddess of Moisture

Goddess of the Crossroads

God-Mother

Greatest of the Gods

Great Goddess

Nut giving birth to the Sun, which shines on her daughter, Hathor-Isis.

Great Goddess of the Underworld
Great Lady
Great Lady of the Underworld
Great Sorceress Who Heals
Great Virgin
Great White Sow of Heliopolis
Green Goddess
Guardian
Guide
Hallowed
Hent — Queen
Heqet — Isis as great magician
Hera — Isis as identical to Hera
Hestia — Isis as identical to Hestia
Hidden One
Immortal
Ineffable Mistress (in the sense of
    "Lady")

Isis-Hestia.

Inventrix — inventor of all things
Isis-Aphrodite
Isis-Aphrodite-Astarte
Isis-Aphrodite-Pelagia
Isis-Astarte
Isis-Fortuna — Goddess of Fate and
    Fortune
Isis-Hathor
Isis-Inanna
Isis-Nike — Isis combined with the
    victory Goddess
Isis-Tyche
Jewel of the Wind
Joy
Justitia — Isis of Justice
Khut — The Light Giver
Kourotrophos
Lady Isis
Lady of Abundance
Lady of Beauty
Lady of Beer
Lady of Bees
Lady of Bread
Lady of Every Country
Lady of Flame
Lady of Green Crops
Lady of Increase and Decay
Lady of Joy and Gladness
Lady of Life
Lady of Light
Lady of Love
Lady of Peace
Lady of the Great House
Lady of the House of Fire
Lady of the Land
Lady of the Mouths of Seas and
    Rivers
Lady of the New Year
Lady of the North Wind
Lady of the Sea
Lady of the Shuttle

Lady of the Solid Earth
Lady of the Two Lands
Lady of Thunder
Lady of War and Rule
Lady of Warmth and Fire
Lady of Words of Power
Lady Rich in Names
Lady Who is a Chariot in the Form of Fire
Leader of the Muses
Light-giver of Heaven
Linen-garbed Queen of Egypt
Linopeplos — Linen-garbed Isis
Living One
Lochia
Lofty Pharos of Light — Isis praised as the Lighthouse of Alexandria
Lotus-bearing
Lydia Educatrix — Isis as the Educatress of Lydia
Maia
Maker of Kings
Maker of Monarchs
Many-formed
Many-named
Matter
Mediatrix between the Celestial and the Terrestrial
Medicina Mundi — The Power that Heals the World
Menouthis — this aspect of Isis was worshipped at both Menouthis and Alexandria, and was revered as an especially potent healing goddess
Meri — Isis as sea-goddess
Mistress of All the Elements
Mistress of All Things Forever
Mistress of Enchantments
Mistress of Eternity
Mistress of the Earth

Mistress of the Land of Women
Mistress of the Pyramid
Mistress of the Word in the Beginning
Mistress of the World
Moon
Most Great
Most Mighty One
Mother of God
Mother of the Gods
Mother of the Horus of Gold
Motivating or Intervening Power
Myrionymos — Isis of the Myriad of Names, Isis of the Ten Thousand Names
Name of the Sun
Nanaia — Isis as identical to the goddess Nanaia

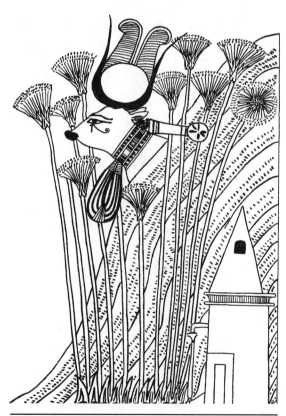

Isis-Hathor as Cow-Goddess looking forth from the funeral mountain at Thebes.

Nature
Nepherses — The Beautiful
Noreia — Isis as identical to the
    goddess Noreia
Nurse
Of Beautiful Form
One

*The Goddess Mut (Great Mother), an
aspect of Isis-Sothis.*

Only One
Panthea — The All-Goddess
Pantocrateira — The All-ruling
Pelagia — Isis of the sea and as a
    protectoress of ships
Persephone
Pharia — Isis of the Pharos Light-
    house at Alexandria
Phronesis — personification of
    Wisdom
Placidae Reginae — The Queen of
    Peace
Ploutodotai — Isis, Giver of Riches
Pluonumos — Isis of the Many
    Names
Polyonymos — The Many-named
Power Shooting Forth the Nile
Power That Heals the World
Pterophoros — The Winged Isis
Queen of Heaven
Queen of Peace
Queen of the Earth
Queen of the South and North
Ray of the Sun
Renenet — Goddess of the Harvest
Resurrection and Life
Ruler of the World
Saeculi Felicitas — our age's
    happiness
Salvatrix of Sailors
Savior
Savior of Mankind
Selene — The Moon
Sesheta — Goddess of Literature
    and the Library
She of Green Wings and Crescent
    Moon
She of the Moon
She Whose Praises are Innumerable
Skilled in Calculation
Skilled in Writing
Sochit — The Field-Goddess

Sophia — Isis as Divine Wisdom

Sothis — Isis as the Goddess of the star Sothis (Sirius) and of the New Year

The All-Goddess

The Beautiful Goddess

Throne — Isis as Giver of the Throne

Throne-Woman — See "Throne" above

Uadjet — Isis as the Cobra Goddess

Understanding

Urthekau — She Who is Rich in Magic Spells

Usert — Isis as Earth-Goddess, giver of life

Venerandum — She Who Must Be Adored

Warlike

Wife of Ra

Wife of the Lord (Osiris)

Wife of the Lord of the Abyss (Osiris)

Wife of the Lord of the Inundation (Osiris)

PERSONAL NAMES OF PRIESTESSES, PRIESTS, AND DEVOTEES

A few names of priestesses, priests, and devotees of Isis have come down to us, through writings of the time and from temple and tomb inscriptions. Here is a sampling:

Alexandra (f)

Anthia (f)

Antonius (m)

Anuph (m)

Apollodorous (m)

Arsinoe (f)

Augusta (f)

Augustus (m)

Calasiris (m)

Cantria (f)

Cleopatra (f)

Cultilia (f)

Cynthia (f)

Demetria (f)

Diodora (f)

Dionysia (f)

Dorion (m)

Dynamis (f)

Elpis (f)

Fabia (f)

Flavia (f)

Harpocras, Harpocrates, Harpocration (m)

Isadora — Gift of Isis (f)

Isias (f)

Isidorus — Gift of Isis (m)

Isidotus — Gift of Isis, Given by Isis (m)

Isigenea (f)

Ision (m)

Isocrates (m)

Iuliana, Juliana (f)

Jason (m)

Klea (f)

Lucius (m)

Mithras (m)

Nicippe (f)

Paedusis — Lady Professor (f)

Paesis (f)

Parthena (f)

Paulina (f)

Petosiris — Gift of Osiris (m)

Selene — The Moon

Serapion (m)

Tesenisis — Daughter of Isis (f)

Tetratia (f)

Theopompis — Lady of the Sacred Procession (f)

Tryphaena (f)

SELF-NAMING RITE

At some point in your worship of Isis, you may feel that your given name no longer applies to yourself as priestess or priest. While it is definitely not essential to take a special new name, you may find another name more appropriate for this period of your development. Over your spiritual lifetime you may change this name more than once, so it is best to use it only within your sacred rites, rather than with the world at large.

Think carefully on your new name. You may want to combine a name with a description, such as "Pharia-Lighthouse-Priestess" or "Serapion, Servant of Serapis."

Make or acquire a new ritual robe. Stand before your altar. Light candles or oil lamps, and offer incense and flowers.

Holy Isis,
You of the Myriad of Names,
Today I stand before You to declare my new name.
You have filled me with such joy and richness
That my old name is outworn.
I declare to You that I, who came to You as (old name) am now (new name),
Your servant.
Teach me, (new name), in Your ways.
Let me gain knowledge of all Your holy names.
Many-formed,
Many-named,
Great Isis!

Chapter Seven
The Seventh Hour of Daylight

THE NOONTIME RITE

T HE SPHERE OF THE sun has ascended to the apex of the sky and hangs above us, shedding its brightest light onto the Earth. The energy in its rays is at its most powerful, driving down into the earth. This is a new manifestation of light, direct and even harsh. To this new Power, and to Isis as the Sun, another rite is offered.

At noon, the Awakening Rite which greets the deity at dawn is augmented by a midday rite which celebrates the highest passage of the sun. Generally, in each

temple, the deity worshipped was identified with the sun for the purposes of this rite. Additional offerings were made and other minor rites performed. In temples of Isis, myrrh incense was burned at midday.

In our culture, the lunchtime break coincides approximately with the sun peaking overhead. As with the Morning Rite, whatever daytime hour means midday to you can be used for this observation if you choose to follow it. This rite was not as extensive nor considered as crucial as the Morning Rite, when the temple's or individual's contact with the Goddess was restored after the mythological challenges of the night had been met and vanquished. The Noontime Rite was less solemn. Individual prayers and requests could be presented to the Goddess.

As with your morning breakfast, feel free to sanctify your noontime meal as an offering. Although you may be physically away from your temple area, take this opportunity to visualize your temple, either what you use at home or a temple image that you may remember or have created.

This rite, although primarily a celebration of divinity, can also offer health benefits to those who perform it. Many people, including myself, are negatively affected by the absence of the spectrum of light contained in sunlight. This lack can

cause depression and apathy, and has even been suggested as a cause of the unusually high suicide rates in northern countries. Sunlight is also beneficial to some types of vision problems.

Seek out a place in your everyday work environment which feels special to you and can be used as your physical temple-away-from-home for this rite. Wise contemporary architects are beginning to include spaces which enhance the sense of the sacred even in the most mundane environments. A hotel complex in San Diego incorporates towers built with a six-sided crystal structure and an area which is flooded with sunlight when it has an equinox alignment, precisely in the manner of the ancient temples. Some office complexes offer reflecting pools, which can be excellent meditation spots.

The noontime rite holds an important opportunity to recognize Isis as a sun goddess, an aspect which is often lost in admiration of her strong lunar powers. Recognizing this aspect is an important step to expanding your own awareness and capabilities, especially in dealing with the brightly-lit, intensely material world of commerce.

While you may find that you prefer Isis' lunar or oceanic attributes, and work mainly with those, it is important to welcome her many other aspects. Our greatest avenues for personal growth often lie in the directions with which we are by nature most unfamiliar or uncomfortable. The solar aspect is a highly concentrated form of the energy of starlight, brought up close, unfiltered by the veiling energies of deep

Thoth, scribe of the gods and greatest of magicians.

Seb (Father Earth-God) and Nut (Mother Sky-Goddess) with the solar boats.

space. This stellar aspect provides a departure point for exploring more of Isis' role as an all-encompassing cosmic goddess whose influence stretches far beyond the "small town" of our solar system.

ISIS AND THE SUN GOD RA

Although Isis is not related to the sun god Ra in early writings, a later spell joins them as father and daughter. This relationship may have been established to aid the priests of the sun god to explain Isis' persistent power even in times and areas where the Osirian cult was restricted to a religion of the under-world and the dead, while the sun gods ruled supreme in daylight and on Earth. Isis travelled freely between both worlds, functioning in some contexts as a divine mediatrix between the earthly and cosmic gods and goddesses.

Ra was considered to grow weak as the day wore on, travelling across the afternoon sky in the "Becoming Weak" boat of Semket after having spent the morning sailing in the boat called Matet, or "Becoming Strong."

Isis was particularly determined to gain power over the sun because of another incident in Her mythology. After the birth of Horus, Isis lived alone in the papyrus swamps, going daily to beg food for Herself and Her infant son.

One day She returned in the heat of the day to find Horus, son of his slain father, lying seemingly dead on the ground with foam on his lips, stung to death by Set in the form of a scorpion. Isis threw Herself on the mercy of Ra, begging him to stop the sun in its course across the heavens to give Her time to save the boy by magic.

Ra finally relented and the sun froze in the sky, while Thoth, here a form of Ra, came down from the sky and taught Isis a powerful spell to restore Her son to life. Once Horus

The god Horus as a child.

was healed, the sun moved forward on its path.

A curious story is found preserved in the Turin Papyrus, which tells of the relationship between Isis and Ra, in this story Her father. In this tale, dating from the New Kingdom (1539–1075 B.C.E.), Ra has grown old and incompetent. He drools from the mouth; his actions are misguided; the cosmos and humankind are threatened with ruin.

Isis decides that She cannot allow the destruction of the universe to occur, and becomes determined to obtain the Secret Name of Ra, the supreme word of power which will allow Her to heal him and also to be able to rule in his place if necessary. This tale may also relate to acts of ritual suicide—or murder—of pharaohs who were growing too incompetent to rule.

Out of the mud formed by the spittle of Ra She creates the figure of an asp and sets it in the path of Ra, for only something created out of his own nature could have the capacity to harm him.

As Ra wanders about the earth, he passes near the snake. The viper

strikes him and pierces the skin of Ra, forcing into his flesh its powerful venom.

Feverstruck and bewildered, Ra suffers as Isis offers to heal him if he will only give Her the power to do so. He refuses to divulge his secret name, but eventually relents as the poison burns through him.

Isis heals him with his name and restores him to health—but now the power is shared. Isis has succeeded in stealing fire from heaven in the form of the name of the sun god Ra, simultaneously confirming and expanding Her own divine power.

This myth is a difficult one at first glance, and is subject to many interpretations, including that of alchemical allegory, which is discussed in Chapter Eighteen, "Isis and Alchemy." Here Isis, who is a consistently beneficent goddess in Egyptian myth, sparing Her adulterous sister Her wrath, saving the life of the murderous Set at the last moment, presiding over births and healings, seems to stoop to black-mail in order to acquire power.[1]

Ra, contrary to the normal concept of a supreme deity, is temporarily or permanently decrepit and unable to fulfill his divine duties. The myth might have made sense had the worship of Isis super-seded that of Ra, but instead, the two worships existed simultaneously, with that of Isis actually preceding that of Ra.

Arthur Versluis, in his eloquent book *The Egyptian Mysteries*, presents an intriguing explanation of this myth and provides insight into the nature of Isis. He suggests that the decrepitude of Ra is actually a metaphor for the decline of worship among an increasingly ignorant

Ra with some of his attributes.

populace and priesthood. No longer capable of direct interaction with the Supreme, humanity empowers Isis to act as a divine mediatrix, stepping down the power of the supreme and intangible deity, whose actions are so obscure that they appear to be those of a senile god.[2]

This role as mediatrix and salvatrix is one which Isis indubitably fulfilled in later times, and it was in these roles that She received the most heartfelt devotion from the masses. It was She who could modify fate and travel between both the worlds of the dead and the worlds of the living.

NOONTIME GREETING

This rite should be performed outside or in view of the sun. Welcome this opportunity to absorb the natural light of the sun into your body. If you cannot come in reach of the sun, relax, breathe deeply, and take a moment to vividly recall a bright moment you have spent in the sunlight, and imagine yourself saying the rite from that location.

If you can't remember these words, or don't find them meaningful to you, create your own greeting, or simply greet the Goddess as the divine friend She is. A glance at the sun and a spoken or unspoken "Hi, Isis!" is a valid expression of this rite.

The essence that is Isis is neither diminished nor enhanced by your performance of this rite or any other. What is enhanced is your own perception of the divine and your own ability to fully experience the spiritual dimensions of existence, and to transmit that ability and experience to the world you exist within.

The action of sunlight has such a strong effect on the third eye during this rite that it is easy to forget the other energy centers of the body. Take a moment to plant your feet firmly on the earth (or the floor) and breathe deeply, feeling the energy contained in the oxygen

you breathe penetrating every cell of your body. Note the flood of energy in your heart region.

The Egyptians knew the seventh or noontime hour of the day as "The Hour of the Expansion of the Heart," which rises for Horus. Let the heat and light pouring over your body awaken the feeling of Divine Love.

Hail Isis
Lady veiled with the cloak of the sun
Whose warmth coaxes forth the green
  grass
Whose light illuminates the Earth
Let us live in luminance
Lady of fire and light!

Alternate Greeting

From the land of morning I hail You
  Isis
I thank You for Your guidance
  through the hours between night
  and noon
Welcome to the softer sky of afternoon
Look ahead to the respite of dusk and
  evening.

SOLAR ECLIPSE GREETING

Eclipses can be times of great clarity, as the influences which we are accustomed to are abruptly removed or transformed and everyday objects and situations can be seen in a genuinely "new," if temporary, light.

Nepthys, as a goddess of dusk and Isis' twin, is also associated with eclipse energies, both solar and lunar. These moments of "unnatural" twilight are under her influence.

At rare intervals, you may have the opportunity to view a partial or even a complete solar eclipse. If so, you may want to use the following special greeting during the eclipse. If you prefer to work with only the Isis energies, substitute Her name for that of Nepthys.

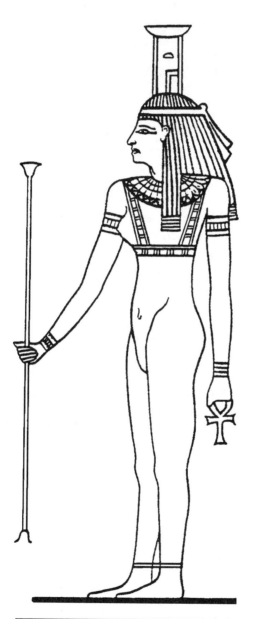

Nepthys, Isis' twin, Goddess of Dusk, is also associated with eclipse energies.

Hail Nepthys
The Moon and the Sun are One.
Lady of the bright crescent and the
*   dark circle*
Mistress of the Night concealed by the
*   Light*
Multiply my eyes that I may see You
*   in all Your forms.*

THE MEDITATION OF THE SUN: ASCENDING IN THE BARQUE OF RA

Isis is a sun goddess, a transmitter of solar power or a reflector of the light of the sun. She is "Light," "Shining," the one who alleviates the darkness between death and living states. She is warmth and light combined with moisture, the perfect conditions for life and growth.

Here the veil of moon and water conceals a fiery solar heart, which in turn conceals the dark blanket of space which finally parts to reveal the Sun-behind-the-Sun, the star Sirius.

Sirius itself physically conceals and by its perturbations reveals its dark twin star, a black sun. So the veils of the goddess part and swirl, part and swirl. Isis dances before us, and each veil of initiation may close to conceal or open to reveal, each flash of change another illumination in the cycle of initiation, another turn in the maze.

The solar initiation of Isis can be one of the most satisfying, because it is closely connected with the rational aspects of the mind, the everyday faculties with which we are familiar and thus take for granted. When this initiation occurs there is a clarity and absence of doubt. It does not slip away in the bright light of morning; it *is* the bright light of morning.

The solar initiation confers the capacity to be dynamic on both the inner and outer planes, in alternating phases of power. Often, after this initiation occurs, there is a positive material benefit, since the individual may finally be integrating the lunar, intuitive aspects of the personality with the solar, rational ones.

The solar initiations will also often involve a member of the opposite sex. This may or may not be a romantic union, but may be the union of teacher and student or friend and friend.

In seeking a solar knowledge of Isis, it is useful to perform the Noon Rite regularly, and to meditate on the sun in its various phases throughout the daily rites. Note the point at which the sun rises and sets. Place a sundial in your garden. Make sun tea. Charge crystals with solar energy. Consider the mixed blessing of nuclear power. Understand that the sun fuels itself by fusion, endless forced combining of the elements. Experiment with children's solar photography kits that allow you to develop an image using the power of the sun. Play with a prism and light a dark area using mirrors and reflected sunlight.

A nineteenth-century engraving of Cleopatra during the battle of Actium.

Chapter Eight
The Eighth Hour of Daylight

── ISIS AS A GODDESS ── OF WAR

ISIS, WORSHIPPED FIRST IN Egypt and then throughout the Greco-Roman world, is well-known as a goddess of love, motherhood, and magic. Her role as a maker of kings and as a goddess of war is often forgotten among the crowd of titles which generated for Her yet another title, that of Goddess of Ten Thousand Names.[1] In fact, Isis was not only a creator and patron goddess of kings but was also a maker of

queens, several of whose stories have survived to the present day.

Many queens and royal princesses must have found the story of the tribulations of Isis and Osiris familiar, particularly the family squabbles and forced marriages to assure politically acceptable unions. Isis Victrix, the Isis of Victory, was a natural choice to become the personal salvatrix of several powerful queens.

CLEOPATRA THE SEVENTH

Cleopatra the Seventh is the best known of the warrior queens who worshipped Isis and the most openly devoted to the faith. Cleopatra styled herself "The New Isis" and often appeared dressed as the goddess. Forcibly married to her younger brother Ptolemy, in an echo of the brother-sister marriage myth, her brother's advisors plotted to rid themselves of the intelligent,

Above, *Cleopatra the Seventh's hieroglyph;*
below, *Cleopatra the Seventh.*

strong-willed queen in favor of her more pliable sister, Arsinoe.

Apparently Isis, The One Above Fate, had other plans for Her priestess Cleopatra. Although Rome was more likely to support her brother's claim than hers, a mighty advocate came forward in the form of Julius Caesar. While his aid to Cleopatra is generally attributed to her great beauty and powers of persuasion, it may have been her role as High Priestess of Isis which predisposed Julius Caesar to support her claim.

Rome at the time was violently opposed to the foreign worship then making converts at all levels of Roman society. Julius Caesar, however, exhibited a curious tolerance toward the alien faith. Though he acted to suppress independent guilds, believing that they were a covert threat to the stability of government, he left the Isian fraternities in peace.

Caesar apparently met with an individual termed "The High Pontiff of Isis" in Egypt, although the identity of this leader is unclear, and may have been assured of the cooperation of the international and influential Isian priesthood if he supported their claimant to the throne of Egypt. Cleopatra may or may not have gained access to Julius by being hidden in and then unrolled from a rug, as popular legend suggests.

However their first meeting occurred, their first encounter may have been orchestrated by the Isian clergy, who recognized in the devout Cleopatra and the powerful general a chance for a royal union on the scale of the divine Isis and Osiris. On a more pragmatic level, their union would end the tearing-down of temples and shrines to Isis by the Roman authorities.

Despite the setbacks of later events, this is the scenario that unfolded. Although Julius was murdered by the treachery of those he trusted, in a curious parallel with the death of Osiris, the faith of Isis continued unchecked.

When Cleopatra recreated her divine union with Julius Caesar by allying herself with his friend and "heir" Marcus Antonius, she was again transferring the power of the throne of Egypt to another Roman known to have sympathy for the religion of Isis, who could be counted on not to interfere with the growth of that worship.

Although Cleopatra was ultimately defeated after bringing to her embrace two of Rome's finest warriors, the faith she espoused expanded and flourished for centuries after her death.

CLEOPATRA SELENE — REFLECTING HER MOTHER'S GLORY

One of the greatest evangelists for the faith of Isis came in the person of the little-known Cleopatra Selene, one of a set of twins Cleopatra the Seventh bore to Marcus Antonius. Raised in Rome after her mother's death, Cleopatra Selene was married to King Juba of Mauritania, who apparently needed the marriage to legitimize his claim to that throne.

Very calmly, Cleopatra's daughter proceeded to follow in her mother's footsteps, establishing a major temple to Isis in her capital of Caesarea. Shortly after the founding of this temple in the heart of a

Roman city, Rome itself permitted a Temple to Isis to be erected within its walls.

Cleopatra Selene ruled alone when her husband was detained in another part of the Empire, and she issued coinage as a Ptolemaic Queen, sharing her coins with depictions of Isis and other Egyptian symbols. She continued her mother's habit of dressing as Isis for occasions of great significance. Remembering the brilliant city of her childhood, Cleopatra Selene attempted to recreate the glory of the city of Isis, Alexandria, on the shores of her new homeland at Caesarea.

Cleopatra Selene was also an astute politician, and might well have led armies to battle, but her skills as a diplomat and negotiator made this unnecessary. For years she met with troublesome chieftains and artfully prevented open rebellion against the Roman Empire she

Julius Caesar.

Antonius and Cleopatra as Osiris and Isis—a nineteenth-century illustration.

ironically represented. Within a year after her death, the delicate balance she had maintained was shattered and Mauritania was torn by strife between different factions.

ZENOBIA, QUEEN OF THE NABATAEANS, CONQUERATRIX OF EGYPT

Both Cleopatra and Cleopatra Selene might have seen echoes of themselves several centuries later in the form of Zenobia, Queen of the Nabataeans, who claimed both physical and spiritual descent from Cleopatra the Seventh.

The Nabataeans were a mysterious, semi-nomadic people who nonetheless carved cities out of mountains and deep desert canyons. Petra, the hidden city which for many centuries was the Nabataean capital, held a rose-red temple to Isis carved from the walls of the canyon city.

It was the need for temple incense which first drew the Nabataeans and the worship of Isis together in about the first century B.C.E. Zenobia's possible ancestress, Cleopatra, once waged war on the Nabataeans to preserve access to frankincense, the trade of which the Nabataeans almost completely monopolized.

As Roman power grew, the wealthy and independent

Nabataeans became a source of irritation to the Emperors, and repeated attacks on their stronghold at Petra led the Nabataeans to relocate their capital to the mountain city of Palmyra. However, the Emperor Severus conquered Palmyra as well, killing the chief of the city, Odenathus, when he was suspected of plotting a rebellion.

Rome erred in believing that the death of Odenathus would be sufficient to break the spirit of the desert-hardened Palmyrenes. His younger son, also called Odenathus, went back into the desert and gathered the support of the Bedouin and other tribesmen, training them to fight against Roman forces.

Odenathus found his future queen in the daughter of his chief military advisor, a tribesman named Zabba. Supposedly descended from Cleopatra through her Greek mother, Bath-Zabbai (or Zenobia) was beautiful and brilliant, as well as a superb military strategist. She personally supervised the training of the calvary of Palmyra, whom she taught to triumph over traditional Roman-style tactics by using a harassing, insect-sting style of guerrilla warfare.

Emulating Cleopatra, Zenobia mastered the Egyptian language, perhaps studying with one of the native Egyptian priests at the Temple of Isis-Aphrodite in Palmyra. She and Odenathus lulled Rome into believing that they were content vassals fighting only to further the interests of Rome against the unconquered nations of Mesopotamia. This unlikely argument, supported by a careful list of enemies of Rome whom they had subjugated, so persuaded the Roman

Senate that they named Odenathus the Emperor of the East.

But in 267 tragedy struck. Odenathus was murdered by a nephew and Zenobia was made regent of the East, holding the throne for their eldest son. As a widow, Zenobia found herself in power over an empire reaching from the Caucasus mountains to the Libyan deserts. She led her troops in battle to defend her possessions, wearing a helmet and armor and a robe secured by a buckle made of diamonds.

Zenobia continued to expand Palmyrene power and finally attacked and conquered a large portion of Egypt. Rome realized that perhaps her interests and ambitions were not the same as that of the Empire and the Emperor Gallienus went against Palmyrene might. He was defeated and killed.

But a different emperor, Aurelian, rose up to challenge the Empress of the East. Aurelian had another challenge to meet as well. The Roman senate, safe in Rome, was questioning why their emperors seemed to be having such trouble subduing an adversary who, after all, was a mere woman. Aurelian detailed his difficulties in a letter to the Senate which answered any questions about the strength and ability of Zenobia as a ruler and as a warrior. He wrote:

My accusers would not know how to praise me enough, if they knew this woman—if they knew her prudence in council, her firmness of purpose, the dignity with which she directs her army, her munificence when need requires it, her severity when it is just to be severe.

If any Roman suspected that her so-called victories were actually due to her husband or her father, Aurelian quenched these thoughts by adding,

I must remark that the victory of Odenathus over the Persians, the flight of Sapor, the march to Ctesiphon, were her work. I can assert that such was the dread of this woman among Orientals and Egyptians that she held in check Arabians, Saracens, and Armenians …[2]

Ultimately, Aurelian defeated Zenobia. Unlike her predecessor Cleopatra, Zenobia did not avoid walking in the triumphal parade of her conqueror. Yet Zenobia's history, which along with Aurelian's becomes surprisingly obscure for two such dynamic personages, was not yet finished.

Zenobia may have been beheaded by him after the triumphal procession at Antioch, as one account gives, or, following Cleopatra to the last, she may have committed suicide. But it is also rumored that Aurelian had a daughter by Zenobia, or that he married a daughter of hers.

It is likely that Zenobia survived walking in his triumphs at Antioch and Rome and lived out her years in a villa on the Tiber near to the Villa of Hadrian with its extensive Isian statuary and shrines, but on what terms is not known.

QUEEN SERPOT AND PRINCE PEDIKHONS: BATTLE OF DEATH AND LOVE

Late Egyptian literature of the post-Imperial era gives another example of a warrior queen relying on Isis to bring her victory. A portion of the Petubastis cycle of stories is called *Egyptians and Amazons* and deals with a warrior queen ruling over a nation of women.

In the story fragments translated in Miriam Lichtheim's *Ancient Egyptian Literature: The Late Period*, Queen Serpot, ruler of the land of Khor, is in her fortress which is about to be attacked by Prince Pedikhons, who has been wreaking havoc in the area. Knowing that she is severely outnumbered, Queen Serpot prays: "Give me help, O Isis!" The queen, who is designated in the text by the feminine version of the word "Pharaoh," calls on her younger sister, Ashteshyt, for help.

Ashteshyt, whose name may be derived from the Egyptian name of Isis, Aset, agrees to disguise herself as a man and go to reconnoiter the enemy camp. Based on Ashteshyt's information, the pharaohess decides to attack. She again invokes Isis to help her and orders her people to make preparations for the attack.

The battle goes in Serpot's favor. She is described as fighting like a hawk falling on prey, like the serpent Apophis attacking Ra. Prince Pedikhons retreats and decides that his only chance at victory lies in defeating Serpot in single combat the following morning. Serpot accepts the challenge despite her sister's offer to fight in her stead.

By Isis, the Great Goddess, the Mistress of the Land of the Women, it is I who shall don armor and go to the battlefield against the evil serpent of an Egyptian today![3]

Ancient Egyptian weapons.

She and Prince Pedikhons meet alone at the battleground. Savagely they engage in combat. The text says that "They took death to themselves as neighbor," fighting with all the bravery, guile, and skill they had gained in years of battle. Neither submits to the other. Finally, after fighting from dawn until dusk, they agree to a truce for the night to commence anew in the morning.

For the first time they see each other outside the heat of battle. Although the end of the text has many missing portions, Queen Serpot is now laughing and Prince Pedikhons is calling her "my sister," the traditional Egyptian endearment between lovers.

As with the rest of these warrior queens, mere military victory is not sufficient. Invariably the good of the entire nation is their goal, and war is pursued as a means to an end rather than an endeavor complete in and of itself. The Isian concept of true victory entails a dynamic, harmonious uniting of opposites for the benefit of both attacker and attacked, not an unlikely philosophy for a goddess who proclaimed: "I am She who made men and women to love one another."

ISIS VICTRIX RITE FOR PROTECTION AND DEFENSE

This rite can be used whenever you feel unjustly opposed or threatened.

Grasp an object of power in your right hand. This could be a wand, sistrum, crystal, or blade. Pointing the object, breathe deeply and feel the air flowing into your lungs, into your body, along your limbs, and in and through the object you hold. Firmly draw a circle around you, visualizing electric blue or flaming red light radiating down from the object. Once you feel the circle is well drawn, imagine it widening and stretching to cover your room, your house, your block or even your nation. If danger or distress is associated with a specific direction, face that direction and say the following:

> I call on the Light of Isis and the
>   Power of Isis to protect me and
>   mine;
> From all things of darkness,
> From all manner of unjust attack.
> Those that mean me harm,
> You shall not pass this barrier!
> Those that cause me pain,
> You cannot pass this barrier!
> The Light of Isis stops you!
> The Power of Isis stops you!

> I glow with the Light of Isis!
> I speak with the Power of Isis!
> No evil shall pass, no evil shall enter!
> Isis stands by me, She raises the copper
>   harpoon!
> She is my protector! She battles for
>   me!
> Isis the Ever-victorious, She battles for
>   me!
> Horus stands by me, he raises the
>   copper harpoon!
> He is my protector! He battles for me!
> Horus the Great Warrior, he battles
>   for me!
> You shall halt, you shall cease your
>   attacks,
> You shall lose this unjust battle against
>   me!
> Your weapons shall fail you, your
>   weapons shall turn against you!
> Isis is my protector, She battles for me!
> Horus is my protector, he battles for
>   me!
> She of the Ten Thousand Names
> Protects me in Ten Thousand Ways!
> Isis is my protector and She shall over-
>   come you!
> Horus is my protector and he shall
>   overcome you!
> Be gone! Be away!

Clap your hands in the direction of the adversary to end this rite. If this rite is done correctly, you will feel strong and powerful. In the event that you feel too angry after performing this rite, you may wish to follow it with a purification shower. Take advantage of this time to visualize the "washing away" of whatever force opposes you.

Chapter Nine
The Ninth Hour of Daylight

— Isis as Sea Goddess —

I am she who ere the earth was formed
Was Ea, Binah, Ge
I am that soundless, boundless, bitter sea
Out of whose deeps life wells eternally …

Isis Rite from Dion Fortune's
The Sea Priestess[1]

Isis Pelagia — Isis of the Sea. Isis Euploia — Isis of Good Sailing. Sailing with the crew of Ra on the nighttime journey through the Underworld. Poling a boat of papyrus through the shallow delta bayous, searching for the sundered parts of Osiris. As the special goddess of the city of Alexandria, whose massive lighthouse sent out a beam so strong that ships far at sea could make their ways to the Port of Egypt. Invoked at the shore by Lucius, Isis manifested in sea mist and moonlight.

Like Yemaja, the Yoruba goddess who still enjoys processions to the beach in African and South American countries, Isis was worshipped at the shore and on the sea. Special patron of the grain ships bringing the bounty of Egypt to Rome's ports, the worship of Isis took root in the busy commercial ports. Seafarers often left Her offerings before embarking on treacherous journeys across the sea.

In the glitter of moonlight on the waves, Isis sometimes makes Herself

Isis Pharia holding a billowing sail with the Lighthouse of Alexandria in the background.

known, taking shape in mist and foam. Some say that Her worship first arose in the temples of long-lost Atlantis, and that the waves of the cataclysm swept priests and priestesses of Isis to the shores of the Atlantic, where they established new temples in Her honor.

Waves and tides are secrets of Isis, and in the sweep of waves against the sand and rocks Her heartbeat can be heard, pulsing, churning, bringing life and death with each turbulent wave.

INVOCATION TO ISIS

From Dion Fortune's *Sea Priestess:*

*I am she who ere the earth was formed
    Was Ea, Binah, Ge
I am that soundless, boundless, bitter sea
Out of whose deeps life wells eternally.*

*Astarte, Aphrodite, Ashtoreth
Giver of life and bringer in of death;
Hera in Heaven, on earth, Persephone;
Levanah of the tides and Hecate—
All these am I, and they are seen in me.*

*The hour of the high full moon draws
    near;
I hear the invoking words, hear and
    appear—
Isis Unveiled and Ea, Binah, Ge,
I come unto the priest that calleth me.[2]*

THE PLOIAPHESIA FESTIVAL

The Greco-Roman Festival of the Ploiaphesia, or *Isidis Navigium*, was when a boat dedicated to Isis as Goddess of the Sea was launched to open the season of navigation.

Originally Isis' role as a sea goddess was considered to be a later addition of Greco-Roman times, but early Pyramid Texts associated Osiris with "The Great Green" (the Mediterranean) and with the Syrian sea. Isis Herself was always present in the Boat of the Gods, which sailed through the Underworld at night. In the Osirian legend, She is also thought to have travelled by sea to Byblos to recover Her husband's body from internment in a palace pillar, so Isis' own associations with sea and sea-travel are relatively early.

As Egyptian trade with the Mediterranean increased, many boats were named "Isis," a practice which persists in a small way even today, with several Nile tourist barges taking the Goddess' name on their prows. Eyes of Horus were also painted on ships to defend against storms, and are still occasionally seen on modern ships in the Mediterranean and Aegean seas.

In Egypt, Isis could be symbolized by the mooring-pole used to fasten ships, and in later times rudders and anchors were used as symbols of Isis' power to guide souls through life and death, and to be a source of stability in rough weather and times.

A Modern Ploiaphesia

On a day when the sailing weather is excellent, go to the shore with jubilation, music, and dancing. Decorate the ship to be launched with banners, flowers, lights, and any other decorations that attract you. Deck the decks with gilded palms or winnowing fans.

If possible, have someone willing to don scuba gear swim under the ship with a raw egg, mentally visualizing the extraction of any impurities into the egg. If you like, everyone can take eggs and go over the ship with them. Then the eggs should be taken some distance away from the ship and smashed where they will wash into the water.

Take a torch or candle around the ship to purify it, all the time calling on Isis to guide it and protect its occupants. Fumigate the ship thoroughly with frankincense incense, avoiding any areas where open flame or sparks might be hazardous.

Once the purification is complete, launch the ship with a libation of wine or milk to the Goddess Isis, and set forth. Feast in Her name, and invoke Her protection for all who sail the seven seas.

Other ships can accompany the Ship of Isis, and may participate in the purification rites as well.

History of the Festival

The Ploiaphesia, or *Isidis Navigium*, was the hallmark festival of the worship of Isis in Greco-Roman times. Celebrated widely, it asserts Her benevolent power over the tides and the sea at the beginning of the season of navigation after the harsh weather of winter. The Launching of the Ship of Isis was the prototype for many similar festivals associated with Christian festivals.

Two dates were celebrated as the Ploiaphesia. The more commonly observed date, March 5, was the original observance and actually corresponded with better seafaring weather. Later, in an effort to positively associate Isis with the Roman Emperors, an additional Launching of the Ship of Isis was included in the emperor-worship holiday on January 5–6.

Apuleius, in *The Golden Ass*, describes the festival of the Ploiaphesia as it was celebrated at the seaport of Cenchreae on the north coast of Africa. At this point in the novel, Lucius, a hapless victim of evil magic who has been transformed from human shape into the form of an ass, has had his desperate prayers answered with an appearance of the Goddess Isis. She instructs him to attend Her festival and eat of the roses Her priest will be carrying, as Lucius will then be returned to human form.

ISIS AS GODDESS OF TRAVELLERS

Isis has always wandered, first in search of Osiris and later as Her worship spread from place to place. Her travel to Byblos in search of Osiris was commemorated as an annual event. After the dismemberment of Osiris, Isis was said to find each portion of his body and bury it in a temple in a different locale of Egypt, accounting for the many

An Eye of Horus—often painted on ships as a protective device.

temples dedicated to Osiris throughout Egypt. Isis travelled from temple to temple throughout the year, visiting other deities. And of course, She rides in the Boat of Ra through the heavenly journeys each night.

Travellers quickly adopted Isis as their particular patron. She had at least one temple near the base of the Pharos lighthouse, and a huge rose granite statue stood nearby, welcoming tired travellers. She was believed to provide good winds from Her wings, and a small sail was an ancient symbol of Her breath of life, which was wafted to the nostrils of the deceased.

Offerings were made by travellers at Her temples before beginning journeys, and after they were successfully completed. Worshippers of Isis enjoyed a fellowship in foreign places; the temples and rites were familiar, and travellers in the faith were always assured of a warm welcome. Some worshippers went on pilgrimages which lasted for months and covered great distances.

MEDITATION OF THE WATERS

Isis is the flow of the tides, the life-giving chaos of liquid hydrogen and oxygen bound together. She is the great Wave moving in the seas of Time and Space, the flowing without beginning, and without end. She is the water that brings the sands of the shore, and She is the water that takes away each grain again. Moisture is Hers, in rain, in springs, in ice and in its melting. Even the Name we know Her by whispers of ice and the hiss of water running over rocks, or seafoam from the crashing-up of waves on jutting rocks.

Isis is also the flood of rivers. From the flood comes the mud, which draws into the Earth and Water initiation.

Think of birth from a closed vessel of fluid within the mother's body, which in turn is warmed by the race of blood in veins and arteries.

In seeking this initiation, walk along the shore. Swim in a pool or in the open sea. Lie in water in the bathtub or jacuzzi. Observe the flow of your own fluids, sexual secretions, saliva, sweat. Shower frequently, with different temperatures of water. Set floating candles in vessels of water. Boil water and watch the bubbles. Observe the swirl of fluids pouring into a cup, or the mixture of cream into coffee. Go boating or take a ferry ride. Visit a marine park. Consciously go half a day without fluids. Drink extra water. Look at still waters when they have pooled from the rain. Walk in rain. Look at pictures of other planets and consider how uniquely beautiful our blue and green jewel is among them.

☽· ⟨⊕⟩ ·☾

Chapter Ten
The Tenth Hour of Daylight

— FESTIVALS OF ISIS —

THE NURTURING LAND OF the faith of Isis, Egypt, was bright with festivals and holy days. As Her worship spread into the Greco-Roman world, with its complex panoply of public rites, festivals, and high holy days, even more days and dates became associated with Isis. One Greco-Roman festival calendar from the temple complex at Socnaipou Nesos lists over 150 days of special observances, with one festival in honor of Isis' birthday lasting sixteen days.

Many rites of Isis were nocturnal, and colored lights (possibly candles in glass containers, or lamps of colored translucent stone filled with salt and oil) decorated temples and private homes the length of Egypt much as Christmas lights decorate some parts of the world today. The Egyptologist and novelist Georg

Ebers describes a festival of lights such as the ones celebrated for Isis:

> The feast ... was celebrated by a universal illumination which begins at the rising of the moon. The shores of the Nile looked like two long lines of fire. Every temple, house, and hut was ornamented with lamps, according to the means of its possessors ... The palm-trees and sycamores were silvered by the moon light and threw strange fantastic reflections onto the red waters of the Nile—red for the fiery glow of the houses on their shores ... Now and then a brightly lighted boat would come swiftly across the river and seemed as it neared the shore to be cutting its way through a glowing stream of molten iron. Lotus blossoms, white as snow, lay on the surface of the river, rising and falling with the waves and looking like eyes in the water.[1]

THE BEAUTIFUL WANDERING STARRY YEAR: SEVERAL CALENDARS OF EGYPT

Establishing the exact day of traditional festivals is very difficult when those festivals are not attached to a particular event, such as the rising of a star or the advent of the solstice. Egypt alone employed three to four different calendars simultaneously, some drifting so far from the reality of the season that fall festivals were celebrated in spring.

Mythologist Robert Graves describes an esoteric Osirian calendar that is possibly the earliest used in Egypt, though it may have been restricted to purely ritual use. This "Osirian year" consisted of five seasons of seventy-two days. Each section of the year was associated with one of the Osirian deities: Osiris, Isis, Horus, Set, and Nepthys. Graves suggests that these periods correspond with birth, initiation, consummation, fruitfulness, and a period of decline which would ultimately usher in the next period of birth.

Other Egyptian calendars generally assumed a three-season year. One temple calendar in use was the ritual Sothic calendar which began the year on *peret Sopdet* (the first day the star Sirius [or Sothis] rises just before dawn, often termed the "heliacal rising" from the Greek name for the sun, *Helios*). This event coincided with the flood of the Nile. This annual reckoning was known as the *renpit nofert*, the beautiful or perfect year.

There was also a civic calendar in use that was based on a 360-day year and which rapidly became out of alignment with the real changes of the seasons. Occasionally, the accumulated error was corrected by an astute pharaoh, further confusing the calendar situation until everyone was informed of the changes. This 360-day year was popularly termed the Wandering Year or the *renpit geb* (Lame Year), as it limped from season to season, rarely matching the events of nature.

Since the basic Egyptian year commonly in use was based on a 360-day cycle, five days were added each year to bring it into accord with the observed 365-day cycle.

Although exact dating for the festivals is an area open to much dispute and reinterpretation, I generally follow the calendrical system detailed in Dr. Robert Brier's *Ancient Egyptian Magic*. Dr. Brier uses an updated form of the Sothic calendar, placing the modern heliacal rising of Sirius (on about August 1) as the beginning of the Egyptian year with the first day of the month of Tahuti.

Since even the ancients found the profusion of calendars confusing, as is evident in the writings of many ancient (and bewildered) chroniclers, allow yourself flexibility in interpreting these dates. Generally, if an event is based on a significant cosmic event, such as the solstice, full moon, or new moon, try to adhere to the actual dates and times of those events. The energy these occurrences manifest is not imaginary and is strongest at the exact time of the celestial event.

THE EGYPTIAN YEAR

Akhet

 The season of Akhet, the Inundation of the Nile.

Tahuti — Aug. 1–30
Paopi — Aug. 31–Sept. 29
Hethara (also written as Athyr) — Sept. 30–Oct. 29
Koiak — Oct. 30–Nov. 28

Proyet

 The season of Proyet, the emergence of the land and of green things.

Tybi — Nov. 29–Dec. 28
Mechir — Dec. 29–Jan. 27
Panemot — Jan. 28–Feb. 26
Parmuti — Feb. 27–Mar. 28

Shomu

 The season of Shomu, of summer and of harvest.

Pachons — Mar. 29–Apr. 27
Payni — Apr. 28–May 26
Epipi — May 27–June 26
Mesore — June 27–July 26

BIRTHDAYS OF THE GODS AND GODDESSES

1st Epagomenal Day

July 27
Birthday of Osiris

2nd Epagomenal Day

July 28
Birthday of Horus

3rd Epagomenal Day

July 29
Birthday of Set

4th Epagomenal Day

July 30
Birthday of Isis

5th Epagomenal Day

July 31
Birthday of Nepthys

6th Epagomenal Day

Leap Year day

The five days inserted into the calendar to bring the twelve-month cycle of thirty days each to equal the actual 365 days of the observed year, were given to the gods as birthdays. The tale behind this event is that Nut had been forbidden by her husband, Geb, to bring forth children on any day of the year. Tahuti (Thoth), hearing of this and loving Nut, undertook to gamble with the moon-god for a fraction of his light. Tahuti, god of wisdom, won, and of this extra light he fashioned five additional days and gave them to Nut so that she could bear her children on these days "not of the year."

In later times, a sixth epagom-enal day was added to help adjust the calendar, exactly as our "leap year" does for us in modern times. This additional day can be assigned to a different deity, such as Anubis, and celebrated accordingly.

Birthday festivals of the gods should include a rite or hymn in honor of the particular deity, and whatever entertainments may please the gods. Dancing is very suitable for Isis and Osiris; Horus and Set might find war-dancing or martial exhibits suitable; Nepthys is espe-cially well-suited to divinatory rites, and she enjoys dance-offerings as well. Feasting is an important part of all of these celebrations.

Osiris, husband of Isis. The first day of the new moon is sacred to him.

A New Year's Spell For Luck

On the first of the five (or six) epagomenal days, draw the figure or hieroglyph of Osiris on a piece of linen. Repeat this process each day with each deity. Use a sweet unguent as your "ink" and draw with a toothpick or small brush.

A simple unguent or ointment can be made by taking a plain cosmetic cold cream and mixing it with a few drops of essential oil. The mixture can be thinned with a little water. To darken your "ink," try adding a little dark-colored powdered herb, such as sage. As you draw the image of each deity, medi-tate on his or her attributes and ask for their benevolent influence in your life.

When the linen strip is completed, you may display it as an altar piece or roll it up and tie it with a piece of string sealed with a dollop of wax. This can be carried with you to bring the luck of the gods to all of your endeavors throughout the year.

MONTHLY OBSERVANCES AND DAILY ASSOCIATIONS

In addition to the special holidays, each month had several lunar festi-vals. The first day of the new moon is considered sacred to Osiris, and a rite called the "Unfinished Blessing" was performed in Egypt. Osiris is also worshipped during the full moon feast on the fifteenth of each lunar month as well.

A Feast to the Lunar Isis

On the fifteenth day of each lunar month, when the moon is at its fullest, the "Fifteenth-Day Feast" to

Isis and Osiris was held. This may be the origin of Isis' epithet, The Goddess Fifteen. Dion Fortune describes a more modern lunar feast in her book *The Sea Priestess:*

There was almond curd such as the Chinese make; and scallops in their shells and little crescent honey-cakes like marzipan for dessert—all white things. And this curious pallid dinner-table was relieved by a great pile of pomegranates ....[2]

To perform this rite-feast, a variety of lunar foods should be selected and prepared. See Chapter Fourteen, "In the Kitchens and Gardens of Isis," for a menu and recipes. The menu is a suggestion, but feel free to improvise or substitute, especially if this allows you to make use of special items grown in the area where you live.

The foods should be primarily white or light-colored, though accents of red (which will look black in moonlight) are perfectly acceptable. Where possible, the foods should be round or crescent-shaped. All of the foods should be the finest and freshest available. Choose unblemished fruits, organically grown if possible, and if you use meat, choose from those companies who raise humanely. (For the calorie-conscious, range-grazed meats are lower in calories than pen-fed animals.) Use silver or white serving plates.

Feast Blessing

This can be done in front of the group, by the group as a whole, or silently by the presiding priestess or priest.

In praise of Isis and Osiris
In thanks for the foods that are provided
In worship of the great Beings
Hail to all the Holy Ones
Hail to the God and Goddess
Hail to the Goddess and God!
Let us be merry in the moonlight
Sacred Ones, feast with us
Sacred Ones, dance with us
Sacred Ones, play with us!

Repeat until you feel that the invitation has been answered. Eat and enjoy the company of your friends, both humans and deities.

Special Days

Isis was specially honored in rites on the first and fourth day of the waxing moon cycle, after the new moon. She is associated with all of the junctures of day and night: dawn, noon, sunset, and midnight. Rites for these times are in Chapters One, Seven, Thirteen, and Nineteen.

The Hours of the Day and Night

We owe our twenty-four-hour day to the Egyptian system of dividing day and night into twelve hours each. Isis plays a particularly crucial and powerful role as Goddess of the Hour during the twelfth hour of the night (5–6 A.M.); at the seventh hour of the night, midnight, when She joins the boat of Ra and causes it to proceed; the eighth hour of the night, 1–2 A.M.; the ninth hour of the night, 2–3 A.M., for which She was the particular Goddess in charge; the ninth hour of the day (2–3 P.M.); the second hour of the night (7–8 P.M.), known as the

"Hour of She Who Knows How to Protect her Consort"; and also at the fifth and sixth hours of the night (10–12 P.M.).

Due to the multiplicity of calendars, and the needs of individual temples in different areas, virtually "every day's a holiday!" when it comes to Isian rites, especially in Egypt.

Listed below are a few celebrations you may wish to include in your own special observances.

Although the Egyptians were fully aware of the astronomical events marking the change of seasons, these times did not hold the same significance to the farmers as they did for much of the rest of the world. The true seasons for the Egyptian peasant were dictated by the flood of the Nile, not the position of the sun.

Since many of us are used to marking the turning of the seasons by celebrating the solstices and equinoxes, these rites can be combined with rites of Isis. The New Year's celebration coincides approximately with Lammas; the rites of Koiak begin on Samhain (Halloween); the birth of Horus to Isis occurs neatly on the Winter Solstice; and the March 5 Ploiaphesia will survive a delay until the spring equinox.

THE NEW YEAR'S CELEBRATION

Tahuti 1 / August 1 — *"Shay met em ronpu!"* (May you live a hundred years!) This phrase was used widely as a greeting during the New Year's celebrations, when gifts were often exchanged and entertainment beckoned from every corner. The Nile flowed, raised by the tears of Isis;

the Nile had risen, flooded by the ejaculation of Osiris; the Nile had filled to overflowing with the rain from the distant mountains of Nubia.

The art of drama began in the temples. While we remember today many ancient Greek and Roman dramatists, we may forget that the earliest playwrights drew their inspiration from the mystery plays performed in the temples to honor their gods. And in turn, these temples borrowed the ancient mystery dramas from the land of Khem—Egypt—particularly from the many extensive dramas enacted to illustrate the life, death, and resurrection of Osiris.

Here is a simple ritual drama which can be enacted by a group on the celebration of the New Year. While parts are indicated for priestesses and priests, any interested person can take these roles for the enactment of the drama. If memorizing lines is difficult, consider taping the drama beforehand, and letting the actors mime their parts. This has a precedent in Egyptian practice, where the lector-priest, or "Man of the Papyrus Scroll," would read the ritual aloud while other priests and priestesses performed the sacred action.

A brief rehearsal and walkthrough will ensure a smoother performance of this drama. Photocopying the text, cutting it out, and gluing it onto index cards is recommended. Cards are easier to handle during the drama and less distracting for the observers.

As designed, the rite can be performed by as few as five people (with a little imagination and doubling-up, even fewer) or as many

as nine. If you are blessed with a small village of people willing to participate, the priestesses and priests who stand in the quarters or bring news from the directions can be doubled.

There is no limit to the possible number of sistrum-shakers, drummers, bell ringers, and others who form the procession; this is a good opportunity to let everyone, including interested children, participate.

If children do take part, assign each a special task, as this helps keep their interest alive and makes them feel a part of the show. Suggestions for tasks include holding various objects at hand for the priestesses or priests, bearing flowers, shaking sistrums (though this can be overdone), or serving a very useful function, keeping people's too-long robes from dragging on the ground by following them as train-bearers. Of course, there can also be a crowd of onlookers.

Someone who is not the main priest/ess leading the ritual should take the head of the procession and lead it so that it surrounds the area of the action. The priests and priestesses taking the quarter positions simply step out of the procession into their quarters, letting the procession uncoil around them. The priests and/or priestesses who will bring the news from the directions are not in the procession, but instead wait in the area from which they will come at their points in the ceremony.

A badly-led procession can easily lead to a traffic jam in the Sacred Space, and this is to be avoided if possible. The leader of the procession may want to carry a staff or papyrus frond, which can be gently used to keep processioners from going astray. Cries such as "Hey—you're in the wrong place—get over there!" are to be avoided.

I may be taking some time to focus on leading the procession because of an experience early in my magical life where, as the most junior member present, I was given the task—and honor—of leading the procession for an ordination rite. About midway through, I realized that no one had told me where to stop, and I did not know where on the grounds the rite would begin. I went on, earnestly sweeping the ground with a papyrus staff, until I finally realized the rest of the group had all stopped about ten yards behind me and the rite was ready to begin. Shamefaced, I rejoined the group. At least I had led no one astray but myself.

This drama is best performed outside, but it can be performed inside as well. As it is a ritual drama, and not strictly a ritual, special magical preparation of the Sacred Area is optional.

Drama of the New Year

Participants proceed into the Sacred Area in a solemn procession, slowly shaking sistrums in unison. The mood is somber.

On an altar in the center of the sacred area, a bowl of water sits. An incense burner provides fragrance, and an oil lamp or candle provides light. A small bowl of salt or natron is also on the altar.

Priest/ess: *The calculations of the astronomer priests have been made, the time has come. Today shall be* *the beginning of the New Year. Yet the waters are not flowing, the rising of the star has not been seen, the birthcries of the Goddess Isis have not been heard, Hapi has not emerged from his cave.*

From this temple in the hours of darkness priests and priestesses have gone to seek signs of these sacred things. And now, in these quiet hours,

We wait to learn if the forces of chaos have triumphed;

We wait to learn if the powers of light will prevail;

We wait to learn if all shall be as it has been.

(Silence for a moment.)

Priest/ess (to the East): *Do we have word yet of the rising of Sothis? Beautiful star, does it glow in the East, heralding dawn, sharing the sky with Ra?*

East Quarter: *The priest/ess has gone to the roof of the temple; s/he has not yet returned.*

Priest/ess: *Shall the star return and coax the Nile to rise? I cannot see, the water is dark and unfathomable.*

Sothis, star of Isis, great glow of the East, second Sun of the sky, sparkling one of great beauty, mistress of the sky of dawn, companion of Ra, seeker of Osiris striding across the sky, fail not to rise! Shed your light upon us, on this, the beginning of the New Year.

Priest/ess (to the South): *Do we have word yet of the stirring of Hapi in his cave? Great God of the*

Nile, will he release the waters that wait to flood?

South Quarter: *The priest/ess has gone beneath the ground and to the cave of Hapi; s/he has not yet returned.*

Priest/ess: *Shall Hapi release the waters, shall the flood rise to the mark of abundance on the sacred measure of the Nile?*

I cannot see, the water is still and unmoving.

Hapi, lord of the Nile, great God of the inundation, he who waits in his cave, sacred one of Philae, source of all waters, burst forth from your sacred cave! Spill out the waters of life! Let the fields be moist and wet and abundant for the coming year! Come forth with the waters, joyous God! Do not let us perish, great unseen one!

Priest/ess (to the West): *Do we have word yet of the birth of Isis? Beautiful Goddess, has She emerged yet from the womb of Nut?*

West Quarter: *The priest/ess has gone within the birth house; s/he has not yet returned.*

Priest/ess: *Shall the Goddess return to us, with all Her light and joy? I cannot see, the water is turbulent and unyielding.*

Isis, Divine One, Lady whose weeping causes the Nile to flood, Great Sothis, star of the morning, maker of the sunrise, wife of the lord of inundation, divine creatrix of the Nile flood, return to us, on this day-between-the-days, on the birth of the New Year.

Goddess of Green, Goddess of Gardens, Goddess of Plants, Lady of Abundant Harvests, Daughter

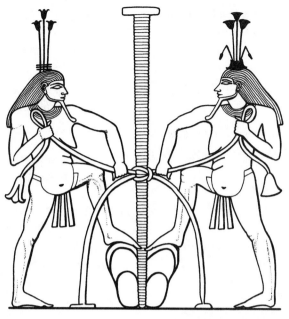

Hapi, shown both as God of the Nile of the South and God of the Nile of the North. Although male, he was depicted with breasts by the ancient Egyptians to indicate his powers of fertility and nourishment.

of Nut, come forth from Your mother's womb!

Priest/ess (to the North): *Do we have word yet of the sacred rise of the Nile, do the waters grow fast and full?*

North Quarter: *The priest/ess has gone down to the banks of the sacred river; s/he has not yet returned.*

(Silence for a moment.)

Priest/ess: *Shall the fields be rich in this New Year? I cannot see, the water is stagnant and cloudy.*

> *Sacred waters of the Nile, tears that Isis has shed, great water, eternal river, rope that binds the north and south, bringer of moisture to the fields of Kemet, return to us as you have returned so many times. Great Nile, flood over the fields!*

> *I hear a sound; let them enter.*

(Herald-priest/ess approaches from East, or goes to stand in the East Quarter.)

Priest/ess: *Have you word of the appearance of Sothis?*

Priest/ess: *I have word: Sothis glows in the sky, more brightly than ever before!*

> *Rejoice, rejoice!*
> *Sothis glows again!*

(Herald priest/ess approaches from the South, or goes to stand in the South Quarter.)

Priest/ess: *Have you word of the freeing of the waters?*

Priest/ess: *I have word: Hapi has come forth from his cave,*

> *The waters are released!*
> *Rejoice, rejoice!*
> *Hapi has come forth!*

(Herald priest/ess approaches from the West, or goes to stand in the West Quarter.)

Priest/ess: *Have you word of the birth of Isis?*

Priest/ess: *I have word: the Goddess is reborn, beautiful of limb, great of heart!*
Rejoice, rejoice!
The Goddess is reborn!

(Herald priest/ess approaches from the North, or goes to stand in the North Quarter.)

Priest/ess: *Have you word of the rising of the Nile?*

Priest/ess: *I have word: the river rises, it rises to the mark of abundance and beyond!*
Rejoice, rejoice!
The river rises!

Priest/ess: *Look now upon the waters: the omens are clear!*
All in abundance; the fields shall be fertile, the harvest great; the gods and goddesses pleased;
The hearts of men and women light;
Peace and prosperity will prevail;
Many new things shall be created within this New Year.
A year among years, this year shall be!
Our rites have succeeded; this holy day is one of celebration!
Hail to the four sons of Horus,
Who have blessed our rite with their presence!

Let the temple stand open to the multitude
Let us now go to honor the great river, the great star,
The great Goddess and the great God with feasting, music, and dancing!

(Procession out of space with great joy, sistrum-shaking, etc.)

All chant: *There is new cool water in the world this morning.*
There is a new beginning, there is a New Year.
There is a new Goddess in the world this morning.
Isis, born of Nut, has blessed us here.
Feel the newness of the Goddess
Feel the swelling of the waters
Feel the brightness of the heavens
Sothis rising, the Nile in flood.

Finish the day's festivities with a feast, music, dancing, whatever brings you and your companions joy.

THE GOING-FORTH OF ISIS

Hethara 8 / October 7 — At various times in the sacred year, the god or goddess of a temple would follow a sacred pathway to another temple to "visit" the deity dwelling there. This date was one of the going-forths of Isis. A procession would take an image of Isis, usually the most splendid one the temple possessed, and follow a carefully designed route to another temple, with many pauses at special sites along the way.

At each of these stops, a brief rite would be performed in the presence of the public. Often, divinations would be offered by the priests or priestessess. Finally, the procession would arrive at the second temple and the image of Isis would be placed in an honored location. Depending on the shared mythology, different rites would be performed and a festival held at the second temple.

A modern going-forth rite offers a wonderful opportunity for Pagan priests and priestesses of different faiths to join together. Select a day for the sacred procession, such as Hethara 8, or any other appropriate day. Arrange with one or more priestesses and/or priests to accept a visit from Isis on that day. Purify yourself and whatever vehicle will carry the image of the Goddess. Cars can be purified with a standard car wash, followed by a dousing with a bucket of water to which a cup of hyssop tea has been added. Seal this with an anointing of fragrant oil, placing a drop on each door, each bumper, in the center of the roof and under the car. Add a few drops to the interior, or place a few drops on a cotton ball placed in the car.

The visiting procession should bring food and other offerings. The temples being visited can also provide food offerings for the ceremonies.

Going-Forth Rite

Working with the officiants of the other temples, create a brief arrival and greeting rite appropriate to Isis and the other deity involved. This should occur at the entrance to the "temple precinct" (often the front gate, or on the lawn or stoop). A member of the procession approaches and can make known the arrival of the Goddess thus:

We bring you greetings from the Goddess Isis, who waits to enter.

The priest/ess of the temple may answer:

The House or temple, coven, grove, circle, etc. of (Deity) welcomes the Goddess Isis. Enter this holy space.

The image of the Goddess is brought inside, and placed beside or opposite an image of the deity of that temple. This is the time to perform another brief rite, short ritual drama, or other ceremony, whatever the officiants prefer. Food offerings are made and shared among the participants, and music or dancing may be performed. If other visits are scheduled, after a time the procession leaves, bringing along any from the visited temple who wish to come along.

THE SACRED RITES OF KOIAK — THE OSIRIAN MYSTERY

Your nature, Osiris, is more secret than other gods,
You are the moon in heaven.
You rejuvenate yourself at your own desire,
You become young according to your own wish.
You appear in order to dispel darkness, anointed and clothed,
for the gods and magic came into existence to illuminate your majesty and bring your enemies to shambles.
Truly, you are the Nile,
great upon the banks at the time of the beginning of the season;

Men and gods all live by the moisture which comes from you.

Rameses IV's inscription to
Osiris at Abydos

The full Osirian mystery cycle is generally considered to belong to the month of Koiak, though differences between various calendars also affected this holiday. Varying opinions place the Koiak festivals on various dates from our present-day September to January. In addition, major or nearby temples would sometimes adjust the actual celebration dates to allow the populace to attend more than one version of the festival. Smaller temples generally used shorter versions of the rites, while at larger temple complexes the rites could go on for a week or more.

Although much of the festival material was sorrowful, the attitude of the citizenry was joyous. Here, for a few days, foodsellers and souvenir vendors would set up at the temples, entertainers would perform, and the populace at large would watch the dramatized presentations put on by the temple staff. Some of the citizenry would participate, battling on the side of Horus

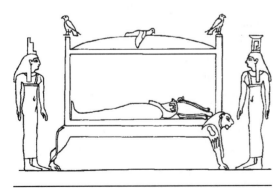

Osiris on his funeral bed, attended by Isis (at his feet) and Nephthys (at his head).

or Set, or joining as "extras" in the dramatic outdoor scenes.

The gravity of the events leading up to Osiris' death and dismemberment was alleviated by the joyous finding of Osiris by Isis, and in some versions, by the final triumph of Horus over Set.

To observe this holiday, read aloud the "Rite of Restoration" given in Chapter Eleven, "Isis the Great Physician," while standing in front of your altar or shrine. Imagine that Osiris is the one being restored, and that you speak to him. Make a small figure of clay and lay it on the altar in front of you. When you finish the rite, stand or lean the image in an upright position, signifying the restoration of Osiris.

PLOIAPHESIA — THE FESTIVAL OF NAVIGATION

Parmuti 7 / March 5 — See Chapter Nine, "Isis as a Sea Goddess," for details of this celebration. This rite can also be shifted to coincide with the spring equinox.

NIGHT OF THE TEAR DROP OF ISIS

Epipi 18 / June 14 — This is the night that Isis is believed to weep over Osiris, which begins the Flooding of the Nile. This festival is still celebrated by Muslims under the name *Lelat Al Nuktah*, or Night of the Drop. Women put lumps of dough outside their doors, representing family members. In the morning, they see if there are cracks in the dough. If so, it is a sign of long life for the person represented by the dough. If not, it is thought to be a bad omen. *Gerekh en Haty* is the Egyptian name for this night. On this night at Philae, the clergy would throw gold coins and other objects of gold into the Nile.

EVE OF THE EPAGOMENAL DAYS

Mesore 30 / July 26 — The five days for the birthdays of the gods and goddesses are about to begin, and a feast is held. Any rite done on this day is thought to have power throughout the coming year. Singing is especially encouraged.

ISIS IN MODERN FESTIVALS

Modern-day carnival celebrations throughout the world have many resemblances to the great Egyptian, and specifically Isian, festivals which were celebrated in Egypt and wherever the Egyptian cults gained acceptance. The ship-models of the *Isidis Navigium* are still carried in fiestas and other celebrations, often with no explanation provided for their presence, except that they have always been included.

In modern Mardi Gras celebrations in New Orleans, the many floats are manned (and womanned) by "Krewes," members of guilds whose primary purpose is to create a float for the celebration. These groups share some similarities with the guilds of laypeople who were associated with the mysteries of Isis; many of these Krewes have coalesced under Egyptian names, including one well-established group parading under the name of "Isis." Other Egyptian names of Krewes include Nefertiti, Cleopatra, and several others. The aluminum tokens thrown from the floats carry on the tradition of temple-minted festival coinage; the dancing,

drinking, and carousing can't be much different from the ancient festivals, such as that of Hathor at Denderah, where more beer was said to be consumed in one day than in the whole of the rest of the year!

The transformative role of masks and costumes can also be seen as a secular equivalent to the much more controlled and complex ceremonies within the context of the ancient mysteries, specifically the mysteries of Isis.

Masks were in common use among the priests, particularly those dedicated to Anubis, who often appeared in processions wearing the imposing jackal mask. One controversial theory of Egyptian artistic representations proposed by Professor Arelene Wolinski maintains that most of the depictions of animal-headed gods were actually their masked priests and priestesses; the theological distinctions could be crucial to an understanding of the ancient Egyptian faiths.

Drama, which was, as we have noted, born of the plays presented by the mystery temples and slowly assimilated into the mundane world, originally relied on masks to convey emotions.

The very fixedness of a mask's expression seems to help induce a meditative or trance state in the bearer; the constantly changing human expression is for once frozen and allowed to be examined. Energy can accumulate between the flesh face and the false one, and the inanimate shell can absorb *mana*, lifeforce, and be perceived as unnervingly real by those approaching it. The chakras in the head and neck are particularly active, as the restricted range of

movement forces concentration in those areas. Many persons who believe themselves incapable of convincing acting can nevertheless create and maintain a suitable voice to match their temporary face.

So next Mardi Gras, bring the Goddess or Her priests and priestesses into the wild throng crowding the streets.

))·⊖·((

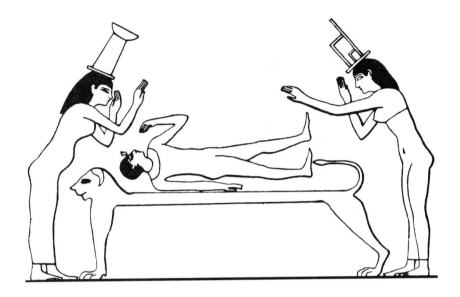

Chapter Eleven
The Eleventh Hour of Daylight

ISIS THE GREAT PHYSICIAN

I am here taking pity on your ills;
I am here to give aid and solace.

Isis, speaking in *Metamorphoses*, by Apuleius

To BE HEALED IS sacred. It is a blessing on the body from the workings of the soul. Imbalances, sometimes from causes beyond our understanding, are corrected and health is restored. In the age of modern, interventive medicine, to be brought back to wellness, especially if it includes spiritual wellness, is as much a miracle as it was in the healing temples of old. Some of the invocations in mysterious languages have been altered, but the essentials are identical.

Isis' power for rites of healing was well established from early times. Galen,

115

Top, *Osiris, left, and Serapis, right, both identified with the worship of Isis;* bottom, *Asclepius, a physician-god whom the Greeks associated with Isis.*

an early medical writer, tells us that a powerful, multi-use medicine was called "Isis" in recognition of the healing powers of the compound.[1] Another classical writer reminds us that "All the world is eager to bestow honors on Isis because she clearly reveals herself in the cures of disease."

The reputation of Isis as an extraordinary healing goddess grew through her patronage of the royal city of Alexandria and its Museum and Library, over which she symbolically ruled with her consort Osar-Apis, or Serapis. The School of Medicine was renowned as the capital of medical learning, and Alexandrian physicians were considered to be the finest in the ancient world. Part of their skill resulted from the royal permission to allow the dissection of human bodies, using the corpses of executed criminals. Since the priests of Anubis had long explored the human body during the process of mummification, this permission is not surprising. But to Greek and Roman doctors, who rarely could explore the inner workings of the human form, this permission was a great step forward. Their intimate knowledge of physiology permitted Alexandrian doctors to make more accurate diagnoses and better understand the functions of the human body. Medical manuals from Alexandria were eagerly sought and scrutinized by physicians in other cites and countries. The great lighthouse, the Pharos at Alexandria, must have been a welcome beacon of promised healing to travellers approaching from the sea. A monumental statue of Isis stood near the

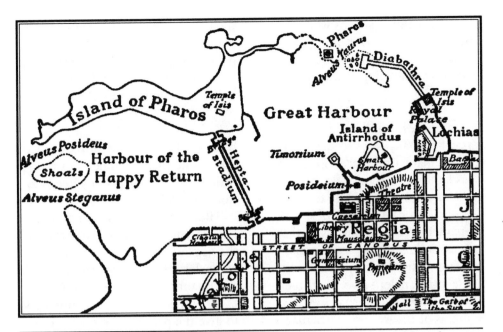

Detail of a map showing Alexandria at the time of Cleopatra's reign. Note the Temples of Isis.

Chapter
Eleven

*Isis the
Great
Physician*

117

lighthouse, drawing the ships into the arms of Her protective harbor.[2]

In the minds of the Greeks, Isis was associated from early times with the physician-god Asclepius, and a chapel to Isis was built within his temple compound at Athens.

DREAM INCUBATION

Both temples of Isis and temples of Asclepius practiced the healing therapy of dream incubation.[3] A person suffering from a malady, often one which had resisted standard cures, would come and stay at the temple and follow a carefully prescribed daily regimen. Under close guidance from the priests, the patient slept within the temple in expectation of receiving a dream from the Goddess which would reveal the method of cure to the sufferer. That these cures were often successful is attested by the many commemorative stelai and votive

objects retrieved from the temples. In addition, trained members of the priesthood would administer less esoteric cures which would also provide relief.

In the public processions, priests and priestesses called *pastophors* would carry small models of the shrines of Isis, but in everyday life at the temple their roles were often much more crucial. They were the first-line physicians attached to the temple. While the spiritual responsibilities were lighter for them than for some of their associates, they were required to be expert in all major branches of medical knowledge, through memorization of the six Books of Thoth.

Once mastered, the *pastophors* possessed a thorough knowledge of general anatomy, common and rare diseases, the compounding of medicines, treatment of the eyes and preservation of vision, gynecology, and surgical techniques. At a time when women physicians were rare, and prevented from training even in Alexandria, there were female *pastophors* practicing at the Temples of Isis.

Around the healing temple sites communities would spring up, similar in many ways to spa resorts. In fact, many of the present-day spas famous for their waters remain on sites once occupied by temples to Isis and other healing deities. Remains of ancient hostels, eating places, and rival temples of other healing deities reveal just how closely the ancient spas resembled their modern counterparts. Many temples of Isis were of particular renown as healing temples, and these sites often remained in use until a late period.

DISEASE AND HEALING

Isis, embracing both orthodox medicine along with what the modern world terms psychic healing, disregards any limitations in the methods by which one may heal or be healed. Her blessing can be invoked through any channel, whether it is contemporary medicine, psychic healing, Asian medicine, or non-traditional techniques. Ideally, the best and most appropriate portions of all healing therapies can be brought together under the name of Isis to provide a conduit for healing energy to reach the sufferer.

Disease results from an imbalance of energy in the body, causing systems to break down or malfunction. This may be the result of exhaustion, making one susceptible to germs and viruses, poor diet, faulty genetics, and even past-life traumas. Complicating the issue of health is

the fact that we live on a tough little planet much too close to the sun; the daily radiation bath we receive slowly mutates our cells beyond what the basic repair and maintenance systems we possess can fix.

Healing takes place when the balance of energy is restored, and there is neither too much nor too little of anything the body needs to function and survive.

Because disease is a function of energy, energy must be restored to the organism—ourselves or those we seek to heal—in the right quality and quantity to restore balance. Usually this must be done gradually, to give the person being healed time enough to receive, absorb, and use the healing energy. Depending on the urgency of the disease, both psychic healing and modern medicine have crucial roles to play. In general, chronic illnesses resistant to everyday therapies may respond well to psychic healing, as do some other ailments which have built up gradually and are not immediately life-threatening. Modern medicine needs to be invoked, however, for most modern emergencies.

Please do not substitute psychic healing alone for standard medical care. I have witnessed the slow withering of a close relative who chose to treat a minor cancer with faith healing, until the disease had progressed beyond any chance of cure and killed him. I have seen others try psychic healing simply because they believed it would be cheaper or because they didn't like their regular doctor and didn't want to bother finding a new one.

Dion Fortune, one of the foremost occultists of this century, stated in *Aspects of Occultism* that she doubted that spiritual healing had much effect against most cancers, tuberculosis, or syphilis, since she had seen so many cases where spiritual healing had been utterly useless against these ailments. She felt "far better results are obtained by physical methods if they are applied in the early stages."[4]

Healing is a dynamic partnership between the stricken individual, the healer(s), and whatever powers this association of individuals can resonate with. One key factor in psychic healing, often overlooked, is whether or not the individual really wants to get well, or, more often, wholeheartedly believes that he or she deserves to.

Illness is still taken by many to be a type of divine punishment; whether or not this is realized at the conscious level, many people die because they believe in their hearts that they have been cursed or abandoned by the deity they worship through some act or failing of their own. In some cases, this may be close to the truth: an individual may have sinned in their own mind against the powers they worship, and out of guilt may suppress their own healing powers, making them more susceptible to the disease which they then allow to punish them. The all-powerful deities we worship are much more forgiving than are our own souls and hearts.

Healing psychological and spiritual barriers is essential to successful results. This is an area where modern orthodox medicine abdicates its role of authority, routinely ignoring these very real needs. It is an area where a trained, experienced psychic practitioner can help clear away spiritual debris and make an individual ready for healing, orthodox or otherwise.

MANIFESTING HEALING ENERGY

The cautions above, urging the use of modern medicine for modern diseases, are especially important in light of the fact that healing energy itself is very simple to generate. It is a natural skill that everyone possesses, including animals, though only a few species choose to reliably project healing energy for humans. Among humans, some individuals project this power more easily, and these are frequently the people who are excellent with plants or sick children. But everyone alive has the capacity to provide healing energy, and the quantity and quality of that healing capacity can be refined with practice and study.

Initially, because it comes so easily to so many people, you may be tempted, as I was, to discount it entirely as a result of static electricity or friction, and the apparent benefits which follow merely the result of suggestion. While psychological factors definitely play a part in any kind of healing, the energy projected is real, and not merely a result of the everyday imagination.

Centering

Whenever you perform healing work, it is essential that you take the time to center and connect yourself with the healing energies of the universe. Your personal reservoir of healing energy is limited, and if you fail to connect with the universal supply, your energy balancing work for yourself or others may leave you exhausted or accidentally taking on the symptoms of those you attempt

to heal. Routine energy-balancing work, properly done, should leave you feeling slightly invigorated; during balancing you may find that your own minor ailments are also cleared.

To center and connect, breathe deeply and imagine your aura penetrating into the earth and rising to the stars. Ask the help of Isis or another healing deity to provide you with the necessary connection to the universal energy sources.

Before beginning, always be sure you have permission to heal. As odd as it may seem, there are many who value their illnesses or are using them as tools for growth or to repay karma. Whether or not this is a reasonable decision is the burden of the individual. Their choices are not something to be lightly tampered with "for their own good." When in doubt, offer the energy you generate to the spirit of the ill person, to be used for whatever positive purpose their soul chooses.

Healing energy can also be used on your pets and plants. The relief it provides can be particularly welcome to injured animals, since they are generally not given painkillers while recovering from surgery or injury. Again, seek the finest medical diagnoses and treatments available to use along with your energy balancing and healing work, and ask permission of the plant or animal. If you feel resistance, or if an animal is too panicked to allow your mental connection, direct your energy to calm them and clear confusion. If there is still resistance, reach out to the deity with whom you heal. Determine if you are meant to continue with healing efforts.

How to Generate Healing Energy

If you haven't worked with healing energy before, try the following exercise. It will begin to familiarize you with some of the sensations you may feel as healing energy moves within your body.

Begin by inhaling deeply, and then rub your hands together rapidly for a count of five. Pause and hold your palms toward each other about two inches apart. Move your dominant hand slightly away from the other hand. You will probably feel the energy field in your still hand respond as your moving hand changes position. Breathe deeply again. You will feel the sense of energy increase and subside.

You may also be aware of the ebb and flow of healing force in other areas of your body, particularly in the energy centers called the *chakras* or *plexuses* strung throughout the body. As you do this exercise, if there is anything giving you pain, such as a cut or a bruise, trying placing your hands on either side of the injury without touching the skin, and move your dominant hand back and forth around the wound. If you have made a good "connection," you will feel a pleasant tingle or mild tightness in the skin around the wound. After a short time, you will probably notice the energy begin to subside. This is normally the cue that no more energy can be absorbed, and that it's time to finish the session. When you stop, the discomfort or pain will generally have lessened or vanished. Often, the ailment will continue to improve for a short time after the energy transfer has stopped.

When you finish transferring energy, clap your hands away from you or shake them vigorously. This acts as a purification and clears you of any problem-related energy you may have encountered during the energy transfer. If you still feel exceptionally drained or clogged, use some of the purification techniques described in Chapter Two.

Using this energy treatment can be excellent first aid while awaiting medical treatment. I recently practiced this on myself while waiting for X-rays after my feet decided to skip the bottom ten steps of a flight of stairs. My muscles were stiffening so badly I doubted I would be able to walk the next day. Modern medicine provided me with anti-inflammatories, I provided the energy healing, and the result was that I was on my feet, with no apparent damage other than a bad bruise, by the next day. Which did the most good? I believe that both interacted to be stronger than either used alone.

My first experience with healing work involved an animal whom I knew would not receive any treatment. A dog belonging to some acquaintances had not eaten for several days and was growing steadily weaker and more listless. The owners had no intention of taking her to a veterinarian and I had no car to do so myself. I grew worried about the dog, a friendly but not-too-bright German shepherd; already her owners were talking of "putting her down," since she was not capable of performing her duties as a watchdog. My concern was considered to be foolish, city-girl sentimentality.

At that time, early in my exploration of religious alternatives, I had great naive confidence in my ability and right to heal. When no one was watching I decided to see what I could do, and walked around the dog where she was lying, head on her paws and a sad look in her deep brown eyes. As I walked, I generated healing energy at her from my hands, and from the rest of my body as well. I walked around her in a circle because it seemed a "magical" thing to do, and whispered a prayer of healing, something along the lines of "it's healing that you're feeling, be fleet, go and eat." This obviously was not high bardic poetry or a spell handed down from antiquity, but fortunately healing prayers and chants don't need to be.

Before I had completed my third circuit around the ailing beast, the dog happily got to her feet, walked around the circle with me, and headed for her food bowl a dozen yards away, eating and drinking as if nothing had ever been wrong. This was a dog who had not bonded to me in any way and never would; she simply started eating during my little ritual. The dog lived on for a number of years.

ANCIENT HEALING PRAYERS

Isis, known as Great of Magic, was also hailed as The Great Physician, Inventrix of Medicines, Isis Medica, and The Great Sorceress Who Heals. It is not surprising that the most primitive magical spell-prayers for healing were associated with Isis along with efficient healing temples and scientifically compounded medicines.

One ancient prayer is given by Guido Majno in his fascinating book, *The Healing Hand.* Originally

intended to be said while bandages are being removed (an often painful process), it could also apply to any situation where "binding" is a problem. The negative reference to the color red probably refers to inflammation and, by association, to Set, the "red god." I have modernized the language slightly from the "thee and thou" form of translation found in Majno's book.

Rite for Fevers and Inflammations

Loosened is he
Who is loosened by Isis.
Loosened was Horus by Isis
Of the evil he felt
When his brother Seth
Killed his father Osiris.
O Isis, great in sorcery,
May You loosen me,
May You deliver me,
From everything evil
And vicious
And RED.
From the spell of a god,
From the spell of a goddess,
Of a dead man,
Of a dead woman,
Of a fiendish man,
Of a fiendish woman
Who will be fiendish within me,
The like of Your loosening
The like of Your delivering
Your son Horus.
For I stepped into fire,
I stepped out of water;
I shall not be caught
In this day's trap.
Behold You have saved me
From all things evil
And vicious
And RED.[5]

Another healing spell is given by Dr. Walter Jayne in his book, *The Healing Gods of Ancient Civilizations.* Found in the Ebers Papyrus, one of the major surviving compendiums of mostly magical healing spells, this is a generalized protection against disease and sickness. The language has been slightly modernized.

Healing Spell From the Ebers Papyrus

May Isis heal me
As She healed her son Horus
Of all the pains
Which his brother Seth
Brought on him
When he slew his father Osiris.
O Isis!
Great Enchantress heal me,
Save me from all evil things of
*   darkness,*
From the epidemic and deadly disease
And infections of all sorts that spring
*   upon me,*
As You saved and freed your son Horus.
For I have passed through fire
And am come out of the water;
May I never light upon that day
When I shall say,
"I am of no account and pitiable."
O Ra,
Who has spoken for Your body,
O Osiris,
Who prays for Your manifestation.
Ra speaks for the body,
Osiris prays for the manifestation.
Free me from all possible evil,
All hurtful things of darkness,
From epidemic and deadly fevers of all
*   kinds.*[6]

ISIAN WORLD HEALING RITE

This simple rite can be done at anytime, anywhere. It can be added to the four daily rites or done separately. The energy raised in this rite increases with time and practice, and will work toward healing you as you work toward healing the world.

Sitting or standing, lift your shoulders slightly and exhale. Invoke the Goddess Isis by saying Her name, mentally or aloud. Breathe in deeply again, and awake healing energy in your hands. At first you may need to generate this energy as indicated previously. Later, merely thinking of it will usually be sufficient to start the flow. Picture energy flowing into you from above and out from you in all directions, emanating in a thin layer over the entire surface of the earth. Imagine individuals in far away places feeling this light veil of healing energy fall on them, available for whatever positive purpose they need.

After a few moments, you will feel the energy flow from you start to slacken. At this point, mentally release the remainder of the energy you have received, and consciously cut off the flow of energy from your body. Move around, clap your hands, or stop the flow in whatever way feels effective to you. Some individuals may prefer to perform this rite shortly before a meal, since the act of eating will tend to shut down the energy flow automatically.

During this rite, you may repeat a simple prayer or invocation of the Goddess, if this does not distract you from generating the essential healing energy. Some things are ineffable—unable to be spoken—and you may find that adding conscious words to this rite detracts from your full participation.

Healing Prayer

Isis, glorious Goddess,
You of the healing wings,
World Mother, Wound-Mender,
Breaker of the chains of pain,
You who hold the world in the palm of
*   Your hand*
Heal from me, heal through me,
Heal by me, heal for me,
All Glory to You, Holy Isis!

What I say is usually not so wordy. I inhale, exhale with the word "Isis," and think, "Heal the World," as the flow begins to go out from my hands. Where you are is not important; I've done this rite while alone, with others, or even while driving.

ISIS AND MODERN DISEASE

There are few things on earth more horrible than the rending apart of a human being through the cruel ravages of AIDS or any slow, wasting disease. These Sethian plagues are probably the major spiritual and medical challenge faced by this planet in the latter part of the twentieth century, destroying talented and creative people, and making us afraid to embrace one another. It can be extremely hard to keep faith in our gods and watch over the slow decline of those we love.

The Osirian mythos offers painful models; perhaps, temporarily, the power of evil is in ascendancy now, just as the myth tells us that Set did for a time triumph over Osiris and Isis. There will be resurrection, but the physical forms of

Chapter
Eleven

Isis the
Great
Physician

123

many persons may well be destroyed before AIDS is defeated. However, this is no cause to abandon the individual battles. With the rapid advancements in life-saving and life-extending drugs, holding back the tide of this now-deadly disease may result in the first generation of individuals who survive it. Healing spells, even the protective battle spell given in Chapter Eight, "Isis as a Goddess of War," in the section entitled "Isis Victrix Rite for Protection and Defense," can help ease symptoms. Psychic healing can also be effective; physical massage can sometimes bring relief, especially to those who have been starved of touch. Aromatherapy can bring pleasure even after other senses have failed. If we give up, we give in to the forces of blind chaos and senseless destruction, and we are not of their nature.

It may be useful to perform a version of the Lamentations after the passing of one whose body has been so painfully ravaged. Spiritually, I believe that this rite can help the recently deceased become comfortable in his or her new form and accept that the body has rejuvenated. Some persons, so used to the impediments of the flesh, still handicap themselves with less-than-perfect bodies in the beyond. Others, whose illnesses have marred their outer spirits as well, find themselves the subjects of healing in the Otherworld, and this rite may assist their spiritual healing.

This piece is based loosely on the form of the Lamentations, the ancient songs performed by Isis and Nephthys for Osiris and all those who followed him into the Beyond.

As with virtually everything in this book, modify it for your personal circumstances if you need to. Participant(s) in this rite ideally should purify themselves first, using any of the methods detailed in Chapter Two, "Purifications for Rites of Isis," but this is not essential. The rite can be done by one or by many, and does not require any special preparations. It can be done in a temple area or other sacred space, or anywhere. A circle does not need to be cast and no tools are needed.

This rite serves a dual purpose: healing for the deceased, and healing of grief for the participant(s).

If appropriate, this rite can be preceded by a designated period of lamentation before the chant begins. In Egypt, professional mourning-women were hired to shed tears, cry out with eerie ululations, and generally carry on with wildly dramatic expressions of sorrow. This was ostensibly to provide a respectable burial procession for the dead, but relatives and friends were probably able to express their inner grief more freely, if less noticeably, when a dozen or more trained and highly noisy mourners were drawing the attention of any curious onlookers. Here, a period when crying and screaming are encouraged can be very cathartic and help in the healing of those left behind. Have plenty of tissues and water on hand. Drums, sistrums, flutes, and other noisemakers can help people express their grief through sound even if they are uncomfortable or unable to shed tears.

Mourning for the dead.

Chapter
Eleven

*Isis the
Great
Physician*

125

Rite of Restoration

Come to your house,
Come to your house.
Beautiful being,
    return to your house.
Your body awaits, renewed and ready.
Come occupy your form
    for your travels Beyond.
Swift and sharp is your mind,
    your beautiful mind.
Wit without limit,
    your beautiful mind.
Strong and mighty are your limbs,
    your beautiful limbs.
Moving without limit,
    your beautiful limbs.
Clear and bright are your eyes,
    your beautiful eyes.
Seeing without limit,
    your beautiful eyes.
Full and pink are your lips,
    your beautiful lips.

Speaking without limit,
    your beautiful lips.
Red and moist is your tongue,
    your beautiful tongue.
Tasting without limit,
    your beautiful tongue.
Clear and soft is your skin,
    your beautiful skin.
Protecting without limit,
    your beautiful skin.
Strong and steady is your heart,
    your beautiful heart.
Beating without limit,
    your beautiful heart.
Deep and full is your breath,
    your beautiful breath.
Breathing without limit,
    your beautiful breath.
(Additional descriptive verses or lines can
    be added here if needed.)
All things are perfect within you,
    all functions are restored within you.

Wholly perfect, wholly restored.
Awaken into this body of light,
justified spirit, your trials are passed.
The measure is made, the weight is balanced.
As a new Being you go forth in the daytime,
you go forth in the Light.
As a new Being you go forth in the nighttime,
you go forth in the Night.
Go forth, beloved one,
Isis is before you,
Nepthys is behind you,
Anubis guides you,
Osiris welcomes you.
Until rebirth you shall remain
An honored guest at his table.
At the Table of Osiris
You take your seat.
Whole and perfect,
Among the Blessed,
You take your seat.

After this rite, drink water and eat together. Neither joy nor sorrow should be expected from the participants; let it be as it is. Grieving takes its own path and its own time for all of us. "Celebration" of an individual's life shortly after a death can be more painful than healing, since some sorrowing individuals may also feel guilty that they are unable to feel the joy necessary for a true celebration. Acceptance of sorrow and loss must come first; even in the recreation of the death of Osiris, many days of mourning preceded the briefer Hilaria, or festival of finding him again.

Chapter Twelve
The Twelfth Hour of Daylight

——— ISIS AND OTHER ———
DEITIES

DESCRIBING EVEN A FEW of the relationships of Isis with other gods and goddesses, both within Egypt and without, is a challenging task. For example, if Isis is mated with Osiris, and Osiris was killed by Set, why is She paired with Sobek, sometimes considered a form of Set, at the major temple complex of Socnaipou Nesos? For every concrete fact, there is frequently an opposing and apparently contradictory bit of information.

Also perplexing at first is the ease with which Isis meets and melds with other deities. She finds herself perfectly at home with deities which some "purists" would regard as too far outside Her pantheon to accept this mesmerizing goddess. National, linguistic, and psychological boundaries mean little to Isis: She both wanders and finds companionship where She pleases. She is truly a Universal Goddess who knows no barriers … and can break through the puny ones we humans may erect through small-ness of mind.

In exploring Isis and Her inter-actions with other deities, I have attempted to limit myself to those interactions I or my colleagues have experienced personally, or which have a historical or mythological

Above, *Isis in the form of a hawk hovers over the body of Osiris as Anubis stands at his feet;* below, *Osiris, holding a crook and flail, is enfolded in Isis' wings.*

basis. You will probably experience many others as you join with Isis in Her travels.

ISIS AND EGYPTIAN DEITIES

Isis and Osiris

Historical: The relationships of Isis and Osiris and of Isis and Horus-Osiris formed a keystone for the Pharaohs, who generally perceived themselves as Horus in life and Osiris after death, always guarded and protected by the Wings of Isis. Antony and Cleopatra politically mined the imagery of "New Isis" and "New Dionysus," following the popular identification of Osiris with Dionysus at that time.

Isis was initially worshipped separately as a goddess of the throne, not as the consort of Osiris, though this union was created at an early date.

Mythological: Born brother and sister from the womb of the Goddess Nut, in life they love each other, and guide Egypt. From the tomb Isis enlivens Osiris, restores him, brings him to fullness, and gives him the choice to remain in the Underworld. From doubled death Isis restores Osiris to whole-ness; from death-in-life he restores Her, by answering at last Her cry to "Come to Me!" Osiris rescued Isis from eternal mourning and empty sadness.

Physical Portrayals: Isis is often portrayed standing behind the Throne of Osiris, usually with one hand on the back of the chair. She may also stand behind Osiris with Her wings folded down on each side of him, forming a sacred protective space around him. Osiris is frequently depicted as having green or black skin, and often holds the crook and flail, symbols of kingship. When portrayed as dead, Osiris is often seen as "ithyphallic" (with an erect penis), while Isis hovers over his body in the form of a hawk. Often, Isis and Nepthys are portrayed standing at each end of the funeral couch, with Osiris lying between them.

Spiritual: It was by the actions of Isis in restoring Osiris that She was able to restore Herself; Her sterility during Osiris' lifetime, left unexplained in myth even as the two bring great fertility and prosperity to the land, is balanced by Her fertility after his death.

For Isis to be fertile it was necessary that She experience Her own Passion, in the medieval religious sense, and suffer and search for Osiris. As a living goddess, perfectly equilibrated by the living Osiris, there was no opportunity or necessity for new life to form. The formation of the triads of Isis-Osiris-Horus and Isis-Osiris-Set brought the potential of motion and life back into play. No longer together on the same plane of existence, Isis and Osiris could now create a new alternating polarity between the realms of life and death, dynamic and fruitful.

Osiris, active now on the inner planes which are often considered more "female" in nature, was beyond the reach of the mundane concerns tying up the energies of the gods. He ascended to become a more distant divinity, more cosmically oriented, similar to the role played in the Osiris myths by his

mother Nut, who could not be bothered to attend the bickering tribunals overseen by Ra, but could only be contacted through letters from the other gods. (Possibly Nut was only too aware of the result; her recommendation to give the throne to Horus was completely ignored, and the yammering continued.)

Isis and Horus

Mythological: Any discussion of Horus must first acknowledge that there were two distinct gods by this name in Egypt, and even the Egyptians were not quite sure where one ended and the other began. The one we are concerned with is Horus the Younger, the son of Isis and Osiris,

Chapter
Twelve

*Isis and
Other
Deities*

129

Horus, son of Isis and Osiris.

said to have been conceived in the womb of Isis even as She was still waiting to be born from the womb of Nut.

Horus was said to have been born weak in his lower limbs, and nearly died of scorpion or snake-

bite while Isis was away begging food. Isis trained him to grow up to avenge his father, but their own relationship seems rocky. Some versions of the myths state that Horus at one point rapes Isis; in another, he slices off Her head in anger when She releases Set. (Thoth, nearby, is said to have replaced Her head with a cow's head, which explains Her conflation with Hathor.) The god Merul, worshipped in Nubia and at Philae, is also said to be the son of Isis and Horus.

Physical Portrayals: In Egyptian iconography, Horus is usually portrayed as a well-built, hawk-headed man. When represented as a child, however, he is not hawk-headed. In Greco-Roman times, Horus was called Harpocrates or Aion. The most common represen-tation of Harpocrates is a small boy holding a finger to his lips in what has been described as a gesture of youth—or of silence, gently cautioning initiates not to reveal the sacred secrets.

Spiritual: Isis and Horus represent both a fierce and a mutually nurturing mother-son attachment. The relationship is not considered to be a negative or weakening one for Horus. Isis is extremely active in assuring Horus' strength and inde-pendence, though this independence leads to friction between them.

Isis and Anubis

Historical: The worship of Anubis was prevalent in Egypt due to his close association with the Osirian deities. Some of his rites may have been derived from another jackal-headed deity, Wepawet.

Harpocrates, readily identified by his finger-to-lips gesture.

Anubis weighing the souls of the dead.

Chapter
Twelve

*Isis and
Other
Deities*

131

Many Greco-Roman temples to Isis and Serapis also acknowledged Anubis, sometimes as a healing deity. When Greco-Roman authors disparaged Egypt's "animal-headed gods," they were usually speaking of Anubis, who attracted a large cult following and was almost always included prominently in Isian processions.

A class of worshippers called *Anubophores* reverently carried his statue in processions, while priests of Anubis wore his mask. His worship in the Roman Empire was so common in some areas that one future emperor of Rome, Domitian, escaped death by donning the garb of a priest of Anubis to pass undisturbed through the irate populace.

Plutarch, in discussing the division of the day and night between Isis and Nepthys, suggested that Anubis was considered to be the horizon line running between day and night, touching both and partaking of their natures. Robert Temple's theory of a Sirian origin for the Egyptian gods suggests that this "horizon" was really an orbit path relating to the Sirian star system.[1]

Mythological: The most common tale presents Anubis as the son of Osiris and Nepthys, who bore him after her furtive mating with Osiris. However, out of fear of Set, Nepthys abandoned the misshapen baby in the wilderness, where Isis found and raised him. At least one ancient source calls Anubis the Son of Isis.

Anubis, known as *Anupu* in Egyptian, helped Isis in her wanderings to find the body of Osiris, and with her is said to have created the art of embalming. He takes charge of the recently dead in the underworld, and is frequently shown

Left to right: *Nephtys, Osiris, and Isis.*

leading the dead to the Hall of Judgement where Osiris presides. He is also essential to the ceremony of the "Opening of the Mouth," and originally provided the magical iron needed for the ritual adze.

Physical Portrayals: Anubis is most frequently shown as a jackal-headed human or in an entirely jackal or dog-like form. He can also be represented wearing the costume of a Roman centurion. One obscure representation shows him as an archer, which may be a pun connecting him to Sirius, the Dog Star, also known as the Arrow Star. Anubis is shown as an entirely human figure in one relief at Abydos, one of the two most important spiritual centers of the Osirian religion.

Spiritual: The form of Anubis is a powerful and protective energy, and can be contacted as a guide in astral explorations and as a guide to new knowledge. A lesser form of Anubis can be requested to act as a guard around a temple or home. His presence is quiet but deeply powerful.

Isis and Nepthys

Mythological/Spiritual: The connection between Isis and Nepthys is an ancient one, dating back to early representations of twin goddesses, sometimes unnamed, mourning the death of Osiris. There are many emotional complexities between these two goddesses. First of all, they are said to be sister goddesses, both born of the womb of Nut. They are mated to brothers, Set and Osiris. While the union of Isis and Osiris is stated to be one of freely given love that seized them both while they were still in the womb of Nut, there is no information on the union of Set and Nepthys, which seems to have been forced upon them.

Despite Osiris' love for Isis, Nepthys is still able to seduce him, though she takes on the disguise of Isis to do so. As they are twin goddesses, this would not be difficult. Set, for his part, desires Isis, at least as the conveyor of the throne, a function which Nepthys does not apparently share with her sister. He knows, as an inscription at Denderah states, that "Without Her, one does not stand upon the throne."

Later sources give Anubis, the jackal-headed god, as the offspring of the union between Nepthys and Osiris. Abandoned in the desert by Set's order, Isis finds him and takes him to raise. After the death of Osiris, Isis and Nepthys join in mourning and sometimes Nepthys is also included in tales of the search for Osiris. Here, as in other areas of the myth, Isis' strong family feeling overrides less noble emotions such as revenge or jealousy. As she later spares Set even after he has nearly killed her son Horus, here she accepts Nepthys as her companion.

Some of these connections become clearer when the family structure is abandoned and the chief players are looked at as split gods and goddesses. In this view, Isis is both herself and her dark, nebulous sister Nepthys; she functions both as the noble wife and the surreptitious mistress. Osiris, too, is seen as both Set and Osiris; the pacific Osiris is balanced by the violent Set; the Green God of Vegetation is complemented by the fiery red nature of his desert-dwelling brother.

Nepthys, whose name in Egyptian is *Nebthet*, is considered primarily a goddess of death by some authors, and an aspect of the Black Isis by others. Nepthys was also sometimes called "Lady of Books," and was credited with the writing of the Lamentations and other hymns. In this guise, she was closely associated with Seshet, the sacred lady of writing for the royal house of the Pharaohs and determiner of the length of their reigns.

Nepthys' particular times of day were dawn and dusk. She was believed to have been born at Het-Sekhem, which remained a center of her worship. Plutarch defined Nepthys as "the mistress of all that is unmanifest and so immaterial, while Isis rules over all that is manifest and material."

Despite her underworld connections, Nepthys enjoyed the title of "The Creative Goddess Who Lives Within An." She was also considered a goddess of sexuality and was thought of as a female counterpart to the perpetually erect god Min. At Mendes in the Delta region, she was renowned as a goddess of healing.

Physical Portrayals: Nepthys is a twin to her sister Isis and generally can only be distinguished by her headdress, which to my eye has always resembled a birdbath. The stem of the "birdbath" encloses the symbol of the Throne of Isis.

The Goddess Seshet, "Lady of the House of Books," associated with Nepthys.

Isis and Set

Historical: The worship of Set was always tolerated by the Egyptians. Some pharaohs were particularly indebted to Set, and used the term "Set" in their names, though this could also be derived from the Isian Set knot. Some foreign conquerors of Egypt also revered Set as the opposer of the traditional order, hoping to justify their conquest of Egypt in that light.

Mythological: In constant opposition, Isis and Set battle and simultaneously reflect each other. They continually interact. In a sense, the nebulous qualities of Set's wife Nepthys seem to be more of an appropriate match for the enforced passivity of Osiris, and the forceful qualities of Isis well matched by the dangerous dynamism of Set.

Set's crimes against Isis are well documented in the myths: he desires Her, kills Osiris, imprisons Isis, attempts to kill Her son Horus, battles both physically and legally against Horus for the throne of Egypt, attempts to rape Horus ... the list continues.

Defenders of Set—and they always existed in Egypt, tolerated alongside the popular faiths—claimed that he was the elder son of Nut and Geb, born before Osiris, and so had a better claim on the throne and thus on Isis. In this view, Isis and Osiris are the transgressors, Osiris claiming a throne he was not entitled to through the inappropriate love of his sister, Isis.

Physical Portrayals: The "Set Animal" used to represent the god has been variously identified as a wild ass, a dog, an anteater, or an okapi (a zebra-like animal), among others. No one knows for certain; some believe that the animal itself is long extinct. He is sometimes shown wearing the crowns of Upper and Lower Egypt, generally in images produced during the reign of pro-Set pharaohs.

Spiritual: The powerful energies of Set are sometimes represented as a chained crocodile or hippopotamus, with the end of the chain held by Isis, indicating his submission to Her. Under this configuration, the powers of Set are said to be under

Set as a chained hippopotamus, subjugated by Horus.

Tahuti (Thoth) and his ape.

Chapter
Twelve

*Isis and
Other
Deities*

135

the dominion of Isis and can be directed for benevolent purposes, but this is an uneasy truce at best. As a godform, the energies of Set are contentious and strife-ridden, and his devotees, even under the chained guise, rarely lead peaceful lives.

Isis and Tahuti (Thoth)

Mythological: In the mythologies, Thoth is the deity who gambles with the moon to obtain enough light to form five days when Nut may give birth, opening the way for the Osirian group of deities to come forth. He also helps Isis to escape from the prison where Set places Her after the death of Osiris, and is also the intermediary between Isis and Ra when Isis calls upon the sun to stop its motion until Her son Horus can be cured of a fatal scorpion sting. Both Thoth and Isis are credited with the creation of writing, and one of Thoth's titles is "Lord of Divine Words." It is Thoth who gives the breath of life

to the newly-born god, Osiris, as he is born from the body of Nut.

Spiritual: Thoth is clarity and honesty personified. He is the wise supervisor of the scribes, knowing the pathways of writing well enough to disentangle his charges' work when necessary. He is the holder of the keys to the repository of wisdom, and his temples are said to "possess secret chambers where knowledge not even known to the Pharaoh is kept." He is a literalist who can find hidden flexibilities in spoken and written language. As a divine intercessor between the gods and other gods or humans, he is perhaps more inclined to righteousness than most of the deities he serves.

Some tales state that Thoth is the father of Isis. In later times, he was associated with alchemy and was considered to be the author of many alchemical treatises. The aphorism "As above, so below" comes from the Smaragadene Tablet (Emerald Tablet) attributed to Thoth.

Thoth is generally depicted as an ibis-headed god with a writing tablet. He can also be indicated with the "ape of Thoth," the cyno-cephalus (or "dog-headed") ape.

Isis and the Scorpion Goddesses

When Isis fled from the prison where Set placed Her after he had murdered Osiris, She was accompanied by the Seven Scorpion Goddesses. The Metternich Stele, dated to about 370 B.C.E., provides Isis' listing of Her companions: "The two scorpions Tefen and Befen were behind me; Mestet and Mestetef were one on each side of me; Petet, Thetet and Matet went in front to prepare a way for me."

These guardian goddesses later punish a woman who refuses shelter to Isis by lighting her dwelling on fire. Isis, troubled by the woman's distress, calls down rain to quench the flames. The woman then recognizes Her as a goddess and is willing to offer Her help. Isis Herself was sometimes called the "Scorpion of Behdet," particularly in association with Horus of Edfu.

Selkit (or Selqet, or Serket) was another scorpion goddess with close associations with Isis. One representation of Selkit shows her as a sphinx-like woman with the body of a scorpion, arched tail raising over her body, and her head crowned with the horn and disk headdress of Isis. This Isis-Selkit is an extremely protective aspect of the Goddess, and not to be used lightly. Her fiery nature in this form should be used with caution.

Above, *scorpion-bodied statuette of Isis-Selkit, from the collection of the author*; below, *the Goddess Selkit.*

The god Khepra in a solar boat.

Chapter
Twelve

*Isis and
Other
Deities*

137

Isis and Khepra

Khepra was possibly the original sun god of ancient Egypt, before the worship of Ra or other sun-gods became ascendent. Khepra was regarded as self-created and the sole parent of Tefnut and Shu, who in turn were the parents of Geb and Nut, who then produced Isis, Osiris, Set, Nepthys, and Horus. Khepra was regarded as having created Tefnut and Shu by copulating with his own shadow and forming from his semen Shu, god of the air (and of daylight itself), and Tefnut, goddess of moisture. All these gods together formed one version of the nine-member Ennead, or "Company of the Gods."

The beetle was believed by the Egyptians to create itself from inert matter, probably because of the way beetles emerged from the mud of the Nile. One variety of beetle rolls balls of dung and mud in front of itself, either for food or as shelters for its eggs. Sometimes two beetles work together to move a dung ball, and the mother beetle often stays in the vicinity of the ball until the young crawl from it.

The image of the scarab became a very popular amulet for both the dead and the living in Egypt, and is still popular and commonly available. See the sections entitled "Egyptian Runestones" and "Divination with Scarabs" in Chapter Twenty-Two, "The Oracles of Isis," for a method of divination using scarabs.

Isis and Bast

The cat goddess Bast was frequently associated with Isis, and cats were common in temples of Isis. One theory of the distribution of domestic cats throughout Europe and the Middle East suggests that they followed the spread of temples of Isis.

Physical Portrayals: Bast is presented as a cat on her haunches or as a cat-headed woman. She often carries a sistrum. Some representations of the standing cat-headed Bast include kittens playing at her feet. In her purely cat form, her statues often bear a gold earring and other jewelry.

Spiritual: The Egyptian *Bast* can be broken down into Ba-Ast, which can be translated as the "Soul of Isis." The combination of fierceness and calm found in many cats is a good metaphor for the nature of the goddess Isis Herself. One title of Bast is "Daughter of Isis," though the mythology of this relationship is vague. It may have been believed that Bast was the daughter of Isis by

Above, *an Egyptian cat talisman;* below, *the Goddess Bast.*

Ra (Isis is called "Wife of Ra" in some materials).

Bastet was especially worshipped in her city, Boubastis, which was known for its festival where it was said more beer was drunk on that day than during the rest of the year in all of Egypt. Bastet was thus associated with divine intoxication, dancing, and music, as well as sexuality. In these aspects she was very similar to Hathor, who was also frequently considered an aspect of Isis (although from the Hathorian viewpoint, of course, Isis was considered an aspect of Hathor).

Isis and Hathor

Historical: Isis and Hathor were portrayed almost interchangeably in some roles, most notably as the Divine Nurse to the Pharaoh. It is possible that a portrayal of Isis as the "House of Horus" may have given rise to the birth of a separate goddess who performed this function. The Greeks identified Hathor as Aphrodite (as they also did Isis).

Mythological: Although the remaining mythology is slight on the relationship of Isis and Hathor, they were considered similar deities in many ways from relatively early times. In the account of the trials of Set and Horus, Hathor cheers the surly Ra by dancing and exposing herself to him, ensuring his return to the legal proceedings. The name "Hat-Hor" means "House of Horus," which associates her with both the ancient Elder Horus and the younger Horus Son of Isis.

Physical Portrayals: The iconography (symbols and attributes) used for Hathor and Isis is very similar;

both are crowned with horns and crescent. In some cases the goddesses can only be distinguished if the hieroglyphs of their names are indicated.

Hathor often wears a band around her head, tied in the back. Isis generally does not wear this ribbon.

Spiritual: Both Hathor and Isis are primarily positive goddesses who desire the happiness of their followers. Isis and Hathor almost always were present in each other's temples. In some senses, Hathor possesses all of the joyous aspects of Isis while avoiding Her funerary and underworld aspects. She is a maiden, a lover, to some extent a mother, but not a widow as Isis becomes. She is perplexed by no great trials or tragedies, though in some accounts, it is Hathor instead of Sekhmet who, as the Eye of Ra, destroys humankind (and is only placated by beer tinted red to substitute for blood). One priestess suggested that Hathor is "Isis Before She Got Married," and this humorous analysis holds at least some truth.

ISIS AND ASIAN DEITIES

Isis and Kali

Historical: No historical material that I have found links the worship of these two deities, but they are both claimed as forebears to the Black Madonna, the dark Virgin worshipped throughout Europe. Gypsies, who have been associated, rightly or wrongly, with Isis and Her worship, spring from the land of Kali.

Mythological: No myths link these two deities.

Chapter
Twelve

*Isis and
Other
Deities*

139

Above, *Hathor*; below, *a bust of Bast from the collection of the author.*

Spiritual: Isis, in Her Black or Dark Aspect, is known as the "Breaker in Pieces," a title shared by Kali. See "Earth Meditation" in the section entitled "Into the Coils of the Labyrinth," in Chapter Sixteen, "Isis as Love Goddess," for more information on the darker aspects of Isis.

Isis and Ganga

Ganga was a Hindu goddess of the River Ganges. In the Oxyrhynchus Papyrus, a listing of Isis' names and attributes in other lands suggests that She presides over the Ganges. This may simply be an extension of Isis' influence over the Nile to implied influence over any major river.

Isis and Harita

Historical/Mythological: William MacQuitty, author of *Island of Isis*, believes that Isis was combined by some with the plague goddess Harita or Hariti. This deity was said to be the mother of five hundred demons, but was converted to Buddhism by Buddha himself. Other authors trace her presence in the development of the Kuan Yin iconography.

Kuan Yin.

Isis and Tara

Historical: The multiformed Tara is perhaps the truest Great Mother goddess of the East, both beloved and feared by her followers.

Physical Portrayals: Tara may carry a lotus, or be depicted with a crescent diadem. The moon and lotus are also frequently mentioned in songs of praise to Tara. She usually wears a knotted belt similar to the Thet knot of Isis.

Spiritual: Tara and Isis share many attributes, and a number of titles as well. Like Isis, Tara is a saviouress, a mother goddess, a healer, and a protector. She is considered to be a Bodhisattva as well as a perfect Buddha; she has attained all yet still turns back to stretch a hand to aid her followers.

Isis and Kuan Yin

Historical/Mythological: Kuan Yin became a popular goddess relatively late, so it is very possible that Isis was incorporated into some aspects of her myth. Originally supposed to be a male deity, the exact evolution of Avalokitesvara into Kuan Yin is not clear, and may well have been influenced by Greco-Indian knowledge of Isis.

Physical Portrayals: When Alexander the Great invaded parts of India, he left Greek kings in charge of the conquered territories. These kings naturally brought in Greek architecture, arts, artisans, and religious observances. In the province-state of Gandhara, Greco-Indian art flourished, and it was here that many of the conventions still found in modern Indian depictions of their gods and goddesses were created. Isis had many opportunities to influence depictions of other goddesses, and this may be why Kuan Yin was later portrayed with the Knot of Isis and the Lotus as two of her special attributes. She is also often portrayed holding one or more children.

Spiritual: Isis and Kuan Yin share many bright aspects, particularly as protectresses of small children and granters of favors to women. The essential energy of the Bright Isis and Kuan Yin are nearly the same, and can be invoked with success.

Isis and Nu Kua

The lesser-known Asian all-goddess, Nu Kua, shares many aspects with Isis. She and her consort are most often portrayed as snake-bodied, a representation used for Isis and Osiris as well as Isis and Serapis, their tails spiraling together in a sacred knot. Forming a primal, sacred couple like Isis and Osiris, Nu Kua and her brother Fu Xi brought similar aspects of culture to their people, including agriculture, metal working, navigation, healing, and other skills and arts.

ISIS AND GRECO-ROMAN DEITIES

Isis was associated and combined with many Greek goddesses, including Hera, Aphrodite, Demeter, Persephone, and others.

Isis and Serapis

Historical: Until recently, many scholars believed that the worship of Serapis had been engineered by the Ptolemies to provide a point of synthesis between their own Greek gods and the deities of conquered Egypt, and, later, throughout the Mediterranean. However, the worship of Serapis, Osar-Apis, or Ausar-Apis appears to have arisen more or less spontaneously. This is supported by recent analyses which seem to show that in areas where the Ptolemies would have been expected to attempt religious colonization of this type, temples to Isis and Serapis are only sporadically found. In other areas, where the Ptolemaic kings and queens had nothing to gain by asserting their presence and power, temples and other evidence of worship are often frequent.

Plutarch gives a description of Serapis which concentrates on his underworld aspects.[2] Serapis was also revered as a god of action, and was especially favored by men serving in the Roman Legions, with many votive tablets attesting to his popularity. In some places, weapons were dedicated to Serapis.

Asar-Hapi (Serapis).

Mythological: There is little mythological or literary material linking together Isis and Serapis. Despite this lack, we have the evidence of dozens of temple sites which they shared compatibly for many centuries.

Physical Portrayals: Serapis is usually depicted as a non-Egyptian, muscular man in early middle age, with curling beard and hair. In association with Serapis, Isis is sometimes depicted as a Roman woman of the upper class, wearing a fringed shawl and tiny curls. She may also carry some attributes of Demeter, such as a blade of grain.

Isis and Serapis are also portrayed as snake-bodied divinities with their tails entwined together.

Spiritual: Serapis is a more lively aspect of Osiris, particularly renowned as a god of healing. Isis and Serapis, when invoked as a pair, present a somewhat staid but otherwise model married relationship. Their roles as providers of grain, symbolized by the *modius* (or grain-measure) often depicted on Serapis' head, was particularly crucial to the Roman empire, which depended on Egypt as the "granary of Rome."

Isis and Zeus

Historical/Mythological: Isis was connected to Zeus through two main pathways, that of her identification with Io, and through the identification of Serapis with Zeus. Statues of Zeus-Serapis were common, and the deities in some places were considered identical. The cry of "One Zeus Serapis!" even hinted at a type of monotheism based on this composite deity.

Spiritual: The relationship of Isis with Zeus was similar to that of Isis with Ra, an uneasy alliance at best. Isis has never accepted subordinate roles to gods very well, and mythologists could not easily marry Her to Zeus. On occasion, Isis was identified with Hera, but, here again, the identification was limited.

Isis and Artemis/Diana

Historical/Mythological: Artemis and Isis were considered aspects of

Above, *Serapis and Isis;* below, *Serapis.*

the same divinity at many places in the Greek and Roman world. Xenophon's novel, *Ephesiaca*, follows the adventures of a priestess equally dedicated to both, and to whom they are essentially different names of the same divinity. Artemis, as a virgin huntress, seems to be a far cry from the mothering, erotic aspects of Isis. Yet many shrines and temples held both goddesses, and individual sites might be dedicated to either Isis-Artemis or Artemis-Isis. The identification of Diana with Artemis was so extensive that these two goddesses were often considered identical. As lunar deities, this also provided another meeting point with the worship of Isis.

Physical Portrayals: A crescent on the forehead frequently identifies either Diana or Artemis, and of course ties both deities to Isis as well.

Spiritual: As independent goddesses, both Isis and Artemis/Diana urge self-reliance and self-sufficiency. Isis required chastity of some of Her followers at certain times, and Artemis was also a divinity called upon by women in childbirth.

Isis and Io

Historical/Mythological: Io was said to be a priestess of Hera who was desired by Hera's husband, Zeus. This was not particularly unusual— Zeus generally desired everyone. Janet and Stewart Farrar, in their excellent *The Witches' Goddess*, state that Io was actually an early Moon-Cow goddess, who gave her name to the Ionians. Io is also sometimes associated with Europa, who gave

Above, *a nineteenth-century engraving of Diana, showing the characteristic lunar crescent upon her head;* below, *the many-breasted Artemis (Diana) of Ephesus.*

her name to the continent of Europe.

When Hera learned of Zeus' indiscretions with Io, he turned Io into a heifer in an effort to protect her from the wrath of his wife. But Hera turned herself into a gadfly and chased the poor cow-goddess to Egypt, where, supposedly, she became Isis.

This story is a late confabulation of Greek origin, and cannot be taken as a valid tale of Isis appearing in Egypt. The flow of divinity and information is much more likely to have been from Egypt to Greece than the other way around.

Physical Portrayals: Io is usually portrayed as a young woman in Greek clothing with a crescent on her brow or small cow horns visible in her coiffure. Mosaics and frescoes

of Io often show Egyptianizing elements, such as crocodiles, Nile scenes, sphinxes, and so on.

Isis and Demeter/Persephone

Historical/Mythological: It was said even by the Greeks that the mysteries of Demeter originated in Egypt, and it appears that early nighttime mystery rites of Isis were adapted by the Greeks in the story of Demeter. As the Mother in Search, elements of Isis' search for Her husband Osiris are echoed by Demeter. As the Bride of the Dead, Persephone finds herself mated to the Underworld Lord, who here can be seen as a version of Osiris.

Physical Portrayals: Demeter and the Hellenized Isis are often almost indistinguishable from each other if no inscription is present. Demeter may have an Egyptianized head-dress, or the Hellenized Isis may hold wheat in Her hand rather than a sistrum.

Kore, another name for Persephone, has occasionally been combined with Isis, and a few statuettes of the goddess Kore-Isis exist.

Spiritual: As a mother goddess who loses a loved one, the story of Demeter is not far removed from that of Isis. Demeter, like Isis, goes in search of the lost one, and only with great difficulty achieves a partial success in reclaiming the lost one to life.

Isis and Dionysus

Historical/Mythological: The fun-loving aspects of Osiris, as musician, lover, and dancer, were identified with Dionysus. As Isis and Osiris were believed to have invented wine and beer, this association was plau-

Demeter.

sible. Osiris' ecstatic, shamanic aspects were well represented by Dionysus. Isis was considered in some areas to couple with Dionysus.

Spiritual: As an evoker of joy and divine intoxication, Dionysus represents aspects of Osiris not revealed in the surviving literature, which is primarily funerary. Dionysus can be considered the aspect of Osiris Isis so loved: active, erotic, divinely intoxicated, and intoxicating.

Isis and Aphrodite/Venus

Historical/Mythological: Isis and Aphrodite were worshipped as one in many places. Isis' love and passion for Osiris was a major point of identification.

Physical Portrayals: Egyptianized statuettes of Aphrodite are known. These Isis-Aphrodite images are usually nude or wearing only jewelry.

Spiritual: Isis and Aphrodite look kindly on the foibles of human emotion, and both are believed to favorably answer prayers for love. They also share aspects as sea goddesses, and both accepted prostitutes among their worshippers. Sacred prostitution, while more uncommon with Isis, was not unknown, and one story states that Isis prostituted Herself during the years She was hiding from Set.

ISIS AND CELTIC-SCANDINAVIAN DEITIES

Isis and Herne

Historical: The march of the Roman Empire took Isis into the heart of the country of Herne, and

at least one Celtic plaque appears to depict Cernunnos, who can be considered another aspect of Herne, with the foreign Egyptian deities.

Mythological: No myths linking these two deities.

Spiritual: The energies of Isis, who has been portrayed with deer antlers instead of the more common cow horns, blend surprisingly well with Herne, and they form a mated pair easily in the mind.

The masculine force of the stag god is similar to that of the Apis Bull of Egypt. Working with Isis and Herne energies increases the sense of connectedness with the earth and all living things. Herne as leader of the Wild Hunt finds his mate in Isis, Lady of Thunder and Wind.

Isis and Freya

Historical: Tacitus, an ancient Roman writer, in his *Germanicus,*

Priest of Dionysus.

notes that the Rus, a Scandinavian tribe, worshipped Isis, though the evidence he offers is ambiguous. It was his belief that the Viking custom of ship-burial was related to Egyptian practices.

Another Scandinavian goddess, Nehallenia, was depicted with wheat, a horn of plenty, and a ship, all symbols of Isis.

Above, *Freya in her chariot drawn by cats;* below, *Freya on the battlefield.*

Mythological: No myths specifically linking the two goddesses.

Spiritual: As Chooser of the Slain, the commander of the Valkyries Freya goes to Earth and selects the most valiant among the dead so that they may enter Valhalla, the afterlife presided over by Odin, whose subjects fight and fall all day only to be resurrected to feast and drink all night. Freya's gathering of the dead from the fields of battle resonates with Isis' gathering of Osiris so that he may receive the life of the underworld. Janet and Stewart Farrar, in *The Witches' Goddess,* point out that Freya/Frigg was the wife and sister of Odin, and owned a falcon-plumed robe which granted her the power to fly, paralleling Isis' ability to change herself into a falcon. Freya's chariot drawn by cats recalls the chariot of Isis, as well as Isis' association with the feline world.

Isis and Odin

Historical: See "Isis and Freya."

Mythological: No myths link the two deities. The spurious *British Edda* attempts to correlate Thor, the son of Odin, and Horus/Osiris, the husband-son of Isis.

Spiritual: An unlikely affinity exists between these two deities. As a goddess willing to do virtually anything to attain knowledge—including tricking Her father, Ra— She finds affinity with Odin, who was willing to sacrifice an eye to gain inner knowledge. Both deities occasionally assume disguises to achieve their needs. Isis takes the guise of an old woman to gain access to the island where the gods' debate over the throne of Egypt was underway, and also conceals Her identity while in the service of Queen Astarte during Her search for Osiris. Odin changes identities and appearances readily. Both hold titles claiming their influence over storms, thunder, and lightning; both can be hailed as deities of war.

ISIS AND CHRISTIAN DEITIES

Isis and Mary

Historical: Many temples of Isis were rededicated to Mary, and dozens of titles of Isis were also attached to Mary. Statues of Isis holding Horus have been renamed as statues of Mary holding Jesus. Statues of Isis also have been renamed as representations of Mary the Egyptian, a servant of Mary's, or of the third Mary, Mary Magdalene.

Isis, too, can be known as the Great Virgin. Marina Warner's book, *Alone of All Her Sex*, mentions a rumor current at one time in Alexandria accusing Mary of conceiving Jesus by an incestuous act with her brother, a curious echo of the brother-sister union of Isis and Osiris.

Joseph and Mary are said to have fled to Egypt for sanctuary, in a reversal of the Exodus from Egypt. All around them in Egypt would be images of Isis and Horus and Isis and Osiris.

Hundreds of titles used for Isis were also used for Mary.

Mythological/Spiritual: As mothers of divine children conceived in uncommon ways, Mary and Isis hold many affinities. Parallels of the Osirian mythos with that of Jesus are easy to draw.

Although the church limited Mary's power as an independent Goddess, she still was instrumental in maintaining the memory of other times when the supreme deity did not need to be male. As nurturing mothers, both Isis and Mary are said to be responsive to their worshippers and forgiving of flaws, as mothers are to their children.

Physical Portrayals: Representations of Mary share many details with images of Isis. Both are often shown with a crescent moon and in the company of stars. Depictions of Isis nursing Horus may have influenced the basic artistic concept of Madonna and Child. Several depictions of Isis holding the slain Osiris over Her knees bring to mind Michelangelo's stunning *Pietà*, though the existing Egyptian versions are considerably stiffer and less emotionally evocative.

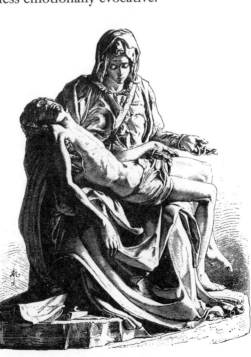

A nineteenth-century engraving of Michelangelo's Pietà.

Isis and the Black Virgin

Isis is behind many of the mysterious statues of the Black Virgin. A number of these were Egyptian statues of Isis who might be said to have "taken the veil," living on under this gauzy guise for many more centuries of worship. These Black Virgins are often considered to be much more powerful than conventional representations of the Virgin. Several modern apparition sites of Mary are at or near these Black Virgin shrines.[3]

Diane Stein suggests that the season of Lent in the Catholic Calendar is derived from Isis' search for and resurrection of Osiris.[4]

A major apparition of a Goddess figure took place above the dome of the Coptic Church in Cairo. Thousands viewed the appearance of a female being; not all identified her as Mary.

A number of saints trace at least part of their lineage to Isis. In modern Egypt, Coptic Christians still shake sistrums and have an Isis among their saints, though it is unclear whether she is named for the Goddess, a martyr, or another church celebrity.

☽ · ☩ · ☾

Chapter Thirteen
The First Hour of Night

THE EVENING RITE

A T THE END OF the day, when the sun is veiled by the horizon and the light slowly fades from the sky, the Evening Rite is celebrated. This misty time, when neither the solar, lunar, nor cosmic forces truly hold sway, is equivalent spiritually to the semi-lucid moments between waking and sleep. Both great clarity of thought and fantastic imagery of vision can occur. It is a time to reach for quiet and calm and to separate oneself from the challenges of the day hours. During the seasons when the dusk hour comes late, an Evening Rite or prayer can be a prelude to a mystical evening spent in spiritual projects or meditation.

NEPTHYS MEDITATION

Now is the hour of Nepthys, the Goddess of Sunset and Dusk, sister to Isis, sister to Osiris, sister also to Set, with whom she is locked in loveless marriage. Never far from her sight is the blissful union of her beautiful sister and handsome brother, the loving Osiris. But Nepthys is twin to Isis,

Her equal in beauty. And though she loves her sister, and fears her husband, Set, Nepthys desires Osiris, if only for an hour. Her womb aches for him. She yearns for his touch, the touch of Osar-Un-Nefer, the Beautiful Being, to heal her of the years of dry embraces with their brother Set.

It is not so difficult to go in the guise of her sister Isis to the couch of Osiris. Nepthys adorns herself with a garland of melilot clover. She finds Osiris alone in the darkness. Isis is elsewhere, attending a birth, visiting a temple—perhaps She is Herself in the arms of Min or Sobek, who in some places stands beside Her as consort.

Can she deceive him? Can Nepthys, the dark one, lady of dusk and sunset, put on her cheeks the joyful glow of Isis, who has known so many of Her lover's embraces? Can her own eyes be moist enough to sparkle, when she has had her very soul desiccated by the burning needs of Set?

But Osiris is unsuspicious. He murmurs happy words of surprise. She quells him with a kiss.

Like cool water in the desert is the embrace of Osiris. Like sunlight drifting through the fronds of his sacred palms is the embrace of Osiris. Like starfire his hands on her flesh; like the glow of the Milky Way he washes over her. Mist rising from the lotus pond, that is the emanation of Osiris. The shape of the sickle of the crescent moon, that is the white of his eye flashing in the darkness. And the flood of the Nile, the spill of the waters, that is the culmination of their combined passion.

Then from behind the Western Hills, thunderclaps and the staccato glow of lightning, a rare storm, a conjuring of Set. Nepthys rises from the couch, her hair in disarray, the fear returning too soon to her heart after being driven out by the love of Osiris. He protests her leaving, teases her for her fear of thunder, which is only their brother Set, after all. Nepthys must be provoking him! She forces a smile in replay, presses a last kiss on his firm moist mouth, escapes him with a bright promise. He turns back to sleep in the shadowed alcove, his face crushed against her forgotten garland of melilot.

Osiris.

An Evening Orison of Isis

Invocation by a priestess:

Hail Isis, glorious Goddess,
Day is done and the night is come,
The sun is set and the stars emerge.
This is the Evening Rite,
The rite to end the day of light.
Let Your instrument sound Your name,
Hailing You with all homage,
Isis, glorious Goddess.
To the candle wick the match I raise
On the altar set to You, Isis, glorious
* Goddess,*
And the nighttime incense rises,
* sweetly mixed,*
To put me in the mind of perceiving
* You,*
Isis, glorious Goddess,
Who rises behind me like a flame of
* gold*
And brushes my back with deft wings.
I make open the nape of my neck to
* You.*
Let Your portal welcome You, O Isis,
Great and glorious Goddess.
Up my hands rise and hold
The curved bow of exaltation,
And rise once more
To the sharp angle
Of invocation.
Come, oh great and glorious Goddess,
Come in the fullness of force and love,
Let Your garment for a moment clothe
* You,*
O Isis, Goddess great and glorious.

The Goddess will come in exact proportion to the priestess' ability to perceive and receive Her. This perception will grow and change and flow over time.

This rite can also be used as a moon greeting.

THE LUNAR MEDITATION

You may also wish to include part of this meditation in your lunar feast.

The rise of the moon is a visual exaltation of Isis. She is the moon, pearl of the night, magnified by the lens of the far horizon, drawing us up with Her as She rises to become a great white eye in the sky, wreathed by a circle of ice, wrapped in a rainbow on lucky evenings when conditions are right. In modern skies, a jet plane will occasionally trace a vapor trail across the edge of Her lunar aura, forming for a few moments a "Shen," the sign of eternity, drawn across the sky as if

Meditating upon the moon.

Khonsu.

proclaiming that these heavens are eternal.

The lunar initiation is very accessible. Women in particular are naturally in tune with the lunar cycles by the very physical manifestation of menstruation, which can be predicted by the passing of the moon. Groups of women who sleep exposed to the light of the full moon will soon bring their menses into the time of the full moon nights; it is artificial lighting which destroys this natural rhythm of the nights. The most cynical, least psychic member of a community will still acknowledge that there is something odd about the nights of the full moon, if only for its impact on others.

However, though the process of aligning oneself with moon energies may be less esoteric and more mundane for women, the lunar initiation is essential for men as well. Many cultures, including the Egyptian, regarded the moon as essentially male in nature, the home of Ihy, Thoth, and Khonsu. Frequently men will approach through love of, or fascination with, a woman who has undergone the lunar initiation, or who is about to undergo it. The moon is polarized in nature, showing only the bright face to us, the other side encased in darkness, visible only to the stars.

LUNAR ENERGY EXERCISE

On a night with a full moon, go to a room where the moon is visible through the window. Stand close to a lamp with its shade removed. Feel the quality of light, its heat, the way it changes the color of your skin and alters the colors you wear.

Turn off the lamp. Let the moonlight strike you. Feel its impact on your body and mind. As you grow accustomed to the difference you can feel the changes in the regions of your brow and the crown of your head. You will learn that, though the moon is associated with dreams and fantasy, its light induces a feeling of clear-headedness. Conversely, over-exposure to the sun, lord of rational thought, can raise the temperature of the brain and cause fuzzy thinking, sunstroke, and even permanent damage.

Now, light a candle and bring it to your face. Feel the mixed qualities of light play over your perceptions, the warmer light of candlelight, the iced light of moon. Meditate on these until you feel you have expanded your understanding as much as possible at that moment, and then end the exercise. You may want to continue observing the lunar light without the formal exercise.

In seeking lunar initiation, watch the lunar phases nightly. Make a special effort to see the moon in the morning and after midnight, and spy it out during the day. Actively seek out anything that reminds you of moon colors, foods, and fabrics. You don't have to purchase or consume these items; simply notice them. Note the phases of the moon and learn to imagine the moon in all its shapes and colors. Follow the tides, and make a special effort to watch the moon reflected on a natural body of water. Before or as you do these things, simply state, "I do this to learn more of Isis of the Moon. May it please You to guide and instruct me."

☽·◌☉◌·☾

Produce for offerings (in Egyptian perspective, more distant objects are placed closer to the top of the drawing).

Chapter Fourteen
The Second Hour of Night

— IN THE KITCHENS AND —
GARDENS OF ISIS

W E CONSUME FOOD IN order to exist. As human beings, we perpetually sacrifice other organisms—animal or vegetable, perhaps even mineral—so that we may live.

Since earliest times, human beings have perpetuated this sense of sacrifice in religious rites, offering foods to both deities and the dead, though how they draw nourishment from these offerings is obscure.

Food, then, is sacred. In the temples of Egypt, as in many other places, food offerings to the deities were a daily occurrence, often forming a part of the four main daily rites at dawn, noon, dusk, and midnight. At these times, foods were presented, reflecting the best of whatever a particular district had to offer. The temples were the storehouses, where foods were stocked against lean times.

Three examples of ancient Egyptian date palm motifs.

The temples were also the slaughterhouses, where sacrificial animals were examined and killed. In addition to relying on the offerings of the populace to feed the temple staff, the temples also provided food to the needy and to those living within the temple precincts.

Egyptian religious taboos on food were a source of confusion and wonderment for contemporary Greek and Roman authors. Generally, these writers made the same error here that they did in attempting to understand the modified polytheism of Egyptian religion. Although there were a myriad of gods, they fulfilled only a handful of roles, and each nome (or district) had its version of deity fulfilling those roles. As for restrictions on food, just about anything that was taboo in one district might be perfectly acceptable in a neighboring nome. Sometimes, in periods of political unrest or territorial rivalry, citizens of one nome who wished to irritate citizens of an adjacent nome would deliberately and with great publicity eat the sacred animal belonging to the other nome, often leading to violent conflicts.

For the Greeks and Romans, most of whom assumed that if a food was taboo in one nome it was therefore taboo throughout Egypt, the apparent dietary restrictions seemed enormous. In addition, taboos changed over time, so that what was forbidden in one temple in one century might be accepted later. Individual temples, depending on their location, access to food sources, and the inclination of their leaders, might violate taboos considered essential at another temple dedicated to the same aspect of deity.

SACRED FOODS OF ISIS AND OSIRIS

Isis, as an agricultural goddess and a Goddess of Fertility, claims nearly everything as a sacred food. As Goddess of Orchards, all fruits grown on trees are sacred to Her. Palms are sacred to both Isis and Osiris, as are dates and coconuts (an excellent lunar symbol food, by the way). Palm hearts, however, would not be an appropriate offering, since followers of Isis and Osiris were forbidden to destroy a cultivated tree, and the removal of the edible palm heart kills the palm.

Breads of all kinds were held in high esteem by the ancient Egyptians, and make ideal offerings. Frequently breads were baked in special shapes for offering purposes, and Isis Herself was said to bake offering loaves for the Great God (Osiris). One charming custom required flat, round loaves of bread with little human ear-shapes pinched into the center, to encourage the God or Goddess to hear the supplicant's prayer.

Although it offends modern whole-grain preferences, the Egyptians valued pure white bread above all other kinds, and prayed for an endless supply in the afterlife. Crescent-shaped rolls were also used as offerings. If your morning breakfast includes a croissant, you are eating a bread sacred for its lunar connotations. The Egyptians had dozens of different types of loaves, many with special ritual purposes that are, unfortunately, obscure to us today.

Chapter
Fourteen

*In the
Kitchens
and
Gardens of
Isis*

157

Date palm and fruit.

Onions were a staple food of the Egyptians, and workers were often partially paid in onions. Garlic and leeks were also widely consumed, and garlic was used in many medicinal compounds.

Lettuce was considered to be Sethian in nature—Set's garden was said to have contained a great deal of lettuce, which he valued for its supposed aphrodisiac properties. The clergy of the Temple of Isis at Philae were forbidden to eat lettuce. Another Sethian food plant was the watermelon, which was believed to have sprung up when Set, in the form of a bull, was pursuing Isis with the intent of raping Her. She escaped and Set, still in his bull form, spilled his semen on the ground. From this ejaculation the watermelon was created.

Honey was frequently used as an offering, as well as an ingredient in incenses and medicines. Both Isis and Osiris were associated with bees and bee-keeping. One of Isis' titles was Lady of the House of Bees.

Good, nourishing food of all kinds was sacred. Although some members of the priestly classes adopted vegetarian diets, this was not universal. Others abstained partially or completely from wine.

At Pompeii, the priests appear to have followed a plain diet, if the

remains of their last lunch are any indication. Buried in the ash after the eruption of Vesuvius in 79 C.E., the table at the temple of Isis held eggs, nuts, and fish.

Feasting was an important part of the temple services, especially at the temples of Serapis. His temples, which almost invariably had a shrine to Isis or were fully shared with Her, often maintained banquet facilities. These were used by guilds of lay worshippers, who met regularly in the temple precincts for a good meal and fellowship with other worshippers. The menus for these meals, based on surviving cost listings, were extensive (as well as expensive), but appear to have been very popular.

Wine and Beer

Wine was produced from very early times in Egypt. At first, it was almost exclusively produced on temple lands for the use of priestesses and priests, similar to the many Christian monasteries which still produce wine from their vineyards. The common, secular folk drank mostly beer. By the Greco-Roman period, wine was in general use throughout the Mediterranean region, frequently produced from vineyards established with rootstocks brought from Egypt.

Temples sometimes produced vintages for local distribution or international export. Terracotta labels designed to hang about the necks of wine vessels are often found with Isian symbolism, indicating temple use or use by worshippers at home. Not surprisingly, these artifacts are most frequently found in the rich wine-

A nineteenth-century illustration of a situla.

producing regions of France and Germany, which even in ancient times maintained renowned vineyards. Some of these are still producing today, and occasionally yield a statue or other artifact of Isis. A wine-cup belonging to a shrine of Isis on the island of Paos in the Aegean Sea has a long inscription to "Isis the Great" dated with charming precision to October 26, 73 C.E.

Later associations between Isis and Dionysus, god of wine and ecstasy, further strengthened Isis' role as Lady of Wine. Dark, sweet wines were traditionally held to be most sacred to Her. A wonderful modern wine which meets these requirements is Mavrodaphne, a Greek wine produced in districts where the worship of Isis existed from early times. It is created from vines which grew near Knossos in Crete, where Isis also found worshippers. Be warned, however: sweet wines are strong wines, and drunkenness was specifically forbidden in the temple rites of Isis.

Milk

Milk was also sacred to Isis (a cow goddess), and a recipe for the sacred "Milk of Isis" still survives. This pink-tinted, sweetened milk represented the healing, nourishing milk provided by Isis for her son Horus and to the pharaohs as Her divine sons. Milk was carried in Isian processions in a situla (a breast-shaped pail), which allowed a stream of liquid to spill onto the earth as a consecrated and consecrating offering.

A LUNAR FEAST MENU

Here are some suggestions and recipes which can be used for the "Lunar Feast" described in Chapter 10, "Festivals of Isis."[1]

Appetizers

blanched almonds

white cheese cut in circles

plain, light-colored, round crackers

onion dip

pomegranate seeds

"white" grapes

Main Dishes

crescent chicken dumplings (recipe follows)

bistillah with lunar symbols (recipe follows)

stuffed bread (recipe follows)

Side Dishes

small white potatoes, peeled and boiled

white rice

baked garlic with bread (recipe follows)

Desserts

lychees in syrup

white, round, lump cookies

white cake with silver sprinkles

Beverages

Milk of Isis (recipe follows)

lychee liqueur, ouzo, or other plain, clear liqueur, if desired (clear crème de menthe is also a good lunar beverage, as it hints of the "cold moon fire," with its chilly taste)

sparkling water

Crescent Chicken Dumplings

> 3 skinned, broiled chicken breasts
>
> 1 (5½–6 oz.) can water chestnuts
>
> 2 green onions, finely chopped
>
> 2 Tbsp. sherry
>
> 1 Tbsp. soy sauce
>
> 30–40 wonton wrappers

Chop together three skinned, broiled chicken breasts with a small can of water chestnuts. Add the finely chopped green onions. Marinate the ingredients with the sherry and soy sauce for one hour (most of the marinade will be absorbed). Place one tablespoon of filling on a wonton wrapper and fold it over diagonally, bending it into a crescent shape (if the wonton wrappers are stiff, try moistening them with a little water).

Steam the dumplings over boiling water for 15–20 minutes. Serves 10 as an appetizer or 5 as a main dish.

Bistillah with Lunar Symbols

> 1 (3-3½ lbs.) broiler-fryer chicken
>
> 2 medium yellow onions, chopped
>
> 3 (16 oz.) cans chicken broth (6 cups)
>
> 1 cup chopped parsley
>
> 1 cinnamon stick
>
> 1 tsp. ground ginger
>
> ¼ tsp. pepper
>
> ½ tsp. saffron threads
>
> 6 eggs
>
> 8 sheets filo dough
>
> 4 Tbsp. butter, melted
>
> 1 Tbsp. sugar
>
> 1 tsp. ground cinnamon
>
> ⅔ cup pine nuts (or ⅔ cup blanched almonds, finely chopped)
>
> powdered sugar and ground cinnamon
>
> stencil for design on top

Chop chicken giblets and place in a large (approximately 6-qt.) pot. Add the chicken neck, chicken, onion, broth, parsley, cinnamon stick, ginger, pepper, and saffron. Bring to a boil over high heat, reduce heat to a simmer, cover, and cook for an hour (or until meat is so tender it easily falls from the bones). Strain broth and set aside. Save chicken and discard chicken neck, onion, and cinnamon stick. Remove the skin from the chicken and shred the meat into small pieces. Set aside.

Preheat oven to 450°. Return the broth to a boil. Beat the eggs lightly and pour them slowly into the broth, stirring until curd-like masses form. Pour the fortified broth through a strainer placed over a bowl, working slowly so that the curds remain in the strainer. Let drain. Set aside the broth for later use in another recipe, or as a soup on its own.

Melt the butter and use some of it to grease the bottom and sides of a deep, 10"-round pie pan. Working quickly so that the filo dough does not dry out, place 6 sheets gently into the pan, working in a clockwise circle so that the pan is covered completely. Only about half of each sheet will be in the pan itself; the rest of the sheets of dough will radiate out from the pie pan like giant flower petals. Brush the filo dough sheets with butter, and sprinkle with the sugar and ground cinnamon. Put the shredded chicken into the dough-covered pan. Place the egg "curds" on top, and sprinkle with the pine nuts or chopped almonds. Cover the fillings with the filo dough "petals" by unfolding and tucking them in. Fold the extra sheets of filo dough in half and place on top of the pie so that the top is smooth.

Bake the pie in a 425° F oven for 20 minutes or until a light golden color. Shake the pan to loosen the pie and invert onto a baking sheet. Return the pie to the oven and bake for another 10 minutes. Turn over the pie once more onto a serving platter.

Using a sifter, sift cinnamon lightly over the top of the pie. Then, using a piece of clean paper cut in the shape of a lunar crescent, crescent and disk headdress, or other appropriate design, place this piece of paper on top of the pie. Sift powdered sugar over the top of the pie, covering the paper and all exposed areas. Gently lift the paper up by opposite edges and move it away to the side. Your design will be in dark cinnamon against the blazingly white background of the pie. Serves 8–10.

Creating this dramatic dish automatically provides you with an excellent chicken broth. You may wish to use it as a simple soup to include in your lunar feast. If you choose to serve the broth, before reheating it, add a can of drained water chestnuts which have been sliced into moon-like rounds.

Stuffed Bread (Chinese Baozi)

While making this recipe, think about Kuan Yin, the Asian Goddess of Mercy, who shares many attributes with Isis. Early representations of her may have been based on Greco-Indian statuary produced in the Gandhara region of India.

Among other attributes, she shares with Isis a merciful nature and love of children, as well as often wearing the looped Knot of Isis around her hips. She is also prayed to for help in the begetting and bearing of children, and for finding love.

Dough
- 4½ cups unbleached flour, unsifted
- ½ cup sugar
- 1 tsp. salt
- 1 package active yeast
- 1½ cups lukewarm water
- 1 Tbsp. melted shortening

Filling
- 2 cups cooked chicken, prepared in advance (see "Sweet Wine Chicken" at end of recipe)
- 2 Tbsp. hoisin sauce
- 1 Tbsp. soy sauce
- 2 green onions, chopped
- 2 Tbsp. parsley

Preheat oven to 350° F. Dissolve yeast in ½ cup of warm water. Sift flour, sugar, and salt together and stir in remaining warm water and shortening. Add yeast mixture and mix well. Knead for about 5 minutes. Let the dough rest for 30 minutes, covered with a slightly moist towel.

While the dough is resting, prepare the fillings.

Mix the chicken with the other filling ingredients. Squeeze off excess liquid, if any.

To make a *bao* (bun), take a golf-ball-sized piece of dough, press it flat, and place a tablespoon of filling in the center. Cover the filling with the edges of the dough, and press it down onto a 2 x 2 square of waxed paper. After all *baozi* (buns) have

been assembled, set aside to rise until doubled in size, about 1½ hours.

Steam *baozi* on a rack above boiling water, or in a bamboo steamer over a wok of boiling water. Serve hot, or allow to cool before freezing for later use. Makes approximately 25–30 *baozi*.

If you like, various symbols can be painted on the *bao*, using a clean brush and a little dark fruit juice (or, if you must, food coloring). Designs can be stamped onto the *bao* using a clean rubber stamp and juice or food coloring.

Sweet Wine Chicken

3 whole chicken breasts (or 6 halves)

3 green onions, chopped

½ cup sweet wine (such as Mavrodaphne)

2 Tbsp. soy sauce

¼ cup brown sugar

If you don't have any leftover chicken on hand, place 3 whole chicken breasts (or 6 halves) in a baking pan scattered with chopped green onions. Pour ½ cup sweet wine, such as Mavrodaphne, over the chicken. Add soy sauce. Sprinkle with ¼ cup brown sugar. Bake at 350° F for 40 minutes, turning once midway. For the *baozi* recipe, remove the meat from the bones, and cut into small pieces. This can also be served as-is as an entrée.

Baked Garlic with Bread

2 full heads (approx.) of garlic per serving

bread, French or sourdough

ground pepper, salt, and parsley flakes to taste

grated parmesan cheese (optional)

If you love garlic, once you've had bread prepared this way it will be hard to go back to the mildly herbed breads usually passed off as "garlic bread." Select about two full heads of garlic per person. The outer skins of the garlic should be intact and unblemished. Trim off the pointed tops so that most of the individual cloves are open at the top. Place them in a shallow baking pan filled with about ⅛" of water. Sprinkle water on top of the garlic. Add ground pepper, salt, and parsley flakes. Bake at 350° for 20 minutes, or until garlic is soft.

Squeeze garlic onto bread. Sprinkle with parmesan cheese, if desired.

Milk of Isis

1 qt. milk (4 cups)

6 Tbsp. almond syrup (recipe follows)

several large strawberries (or a red fruit juice)

Almond Syrup

1 cup sugar

1 cup water

2 Tbsp. almond extract

Prepare almond syrup by dissolving the sugar into the water. Bring to a boil, stirring occasionally, until syrup begins to thicken. Add the almond extract and stir. Let the syrup cool. This may also be made with vanilla syrup. Simply substitute 1 tablespoon vanilla extract for the 2 tablespoons almond extract.

To the milk add the almond syrup, stirring well (you may also use a blender if one is available).

Chapter
Fourteen

*In the
Kitchens
and
Gardens of
Isis*

163

A head of Isis-Demeter with a traditional Egyptian basket and two loaves of ear bread.

Squeeze several large strawberries into the milk for a light pink color, or use other red fruit juice. Serve chilled.

MISCELLANEOUS RECIPES

Easy Prayer Ear Bread

Using a can of ready-to-bake biscuits, separate each biscuit and flatten. Pinch up the dough to resemble a human ear. Bake according to instructions and offer on the altar to Isis, asking that She hear your prayer.

Sacred Cookies

Make your favorite cookie dough recipe, leaving out any additions such as chocolate chips or nuts. Select a piece of jewelry or a rubber stamp. Bake the cookies halfway and remove from the oven. Press the piece of jewelry or stamp into the cookie. If you draw well, you can also create a dotted image using a sharp toothpick. Finish baking.

Small cakes with the image of a hippopotamus were eaten to symbolize Isis' triumph over Set. Ankh-impressed cookies can be eaten to restore vitality, or an image of Isis on a cookie can be consumed to bring Her essence into you. You can color the images with food coloring, icing, or other decorations.

IN THE GARDEN OF ISIS

Ah, Isis, Lady of Green Things, Lady of Herbs, Lady of the Bees. Your temples are gardens as well as buildings. Here a stone well holds a stand of papyrus, though it grows a thousand miles away from the Nile. And here, at the edge of the desert, stands a long avenue of trees, some precious for the beads of incense they exude, some precious for shade, their fruit, the beauty of their flowers and leaves, each carefully planted in a ball of fertile earth set into the dry sand. Palms, sacred to Osiris and Isis, are not far away; they will grow readily in the sacred pools which, though long dry, still hold the remnants of rich mud that once supported lotuses and papyrus when the temple was still frequented.

And planted in containers, here are the richly-scented, night-blooming flowers, the blossoms that glow in moonlight. Alongside them grow mysterious medicinal herbs whose secrets You, Isis, alone know to the fullest. And with each drop of

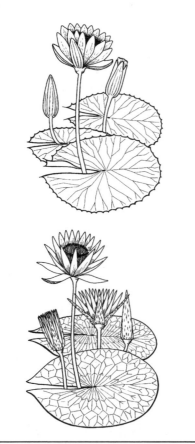

Above, *the white lotus;* below, *the blue lotus*

life-giving water that flows to the thirsty roots of these many plants, Your power as Lady of Moisture is reaffirmed.

☽ · � · ☾

Watering at night, under the moon, spraying the sky and letting the light-charged water fall back to earth, I realized that with a flick of the wrist, my garden could be blessed with a flowing Ankh, or a Shen, formed by the spray from the hose. The silver nozzle was not far from the silver aspergers once used in the temples, and the long, green hose pulsed like a living snake.

Moonlight and water have always shared a mystical union, and partaking of this power to ensure fertility for your garden is a simple yet powerful rite. Fountains or a lily pond are welcome additions to the temple garden. A garden to the Goddess is best designed as both lunar and solar, to be enjoyed by day and night.

One way to do this is to use finely crushed white gypsum for your pathways. This stone will glow in the daylight sun; however, even on the darkest nights your paths will take on a special luminance, reaching out to reflect every bit of available light. Under a nearly full moon, these pathways will seem lit from within, almost phosphores-cent. If space allows, you can form an ankh-shaped garden or lay out your garden in the configuration of a temple. Line these paths with flowers that love the night, such as gardenias, light-colored four o'clocks, nightblooming cactus, Japanese moonflowers, and light-colored roses.

Palm trees, both the finger-fronded and fan palm varieties, are welcome in the temple garden. They provide shade, a reminder of Egypt and the many Mediterranean ports where Isis made Her home, and can also be used ritually in decorations or divinations. The saw-tooth edge of the stem of fan palm fronds was used to count days, and was sometimes carried by Thoth as a symbol of his measurement of time. Watching the gentle swaying of palm fronds in any small breeze can be a meditation exercise.

Other appropriate trees are cypress, sycamores, and fruit trees. Citrus wood was sometimes used for ritual objects for the worship of Isis. Sycamores are particularly sacred to Isis when She is combined with Hathor as a goddess of love (who was sometimes called Lady of the Sycamore), and Her presence and blessing is easily felt in any wild grove of sycamores. Pine trees provide pine cones, which were sometimes used for ritual fires in the temples of Isis. Some varieties of pine provide a pitch that can be burned as incense for daytime or masculine rites. Dionysus, who shared many attributes with Osiris, was sometimes symbolized by the pine cone, and pine cones were offered to Osiris.

The laurel, or bay tree, was often used in divinatory rites such as those practiced at Eleusis. Its connection to Isis is attested to by the carrying of winnowing-fans made of laurel twigs in the Ploiaph-esia procession described by Apuleius.

Avocado trees, similar to the *persea* species which was sacred to Isis because of its heart-shaped leaves, may also be grown as an appropriate offering. Temples of Isis mated with Sobek rather than Osiris might prefer the alternate name, "crocodile pears," in lieu of keeping a live crocodile (not recommended!).

Roses were present in the rites of Isis and a later festival, the Rhodophoria, was celebrated for Isis at some of Her temples, particularly those in areas which grew roses for sale and export. Egypt grew many of the ancient world's roses, but these were the simple old roses rather than the many-petalled newer varieties.

Some newly-developed roses bear Egyptian names, such as a deep red, intensely fragrant rose called "Osiria," and the lavender-hued "Blue Nile."

Chapter
Fourteen

*In the
Kitchens
and
Gardens of
Isis*

165

The Goddess pouring the water of life from a sycamore tree onto the deceased and his Soul.

A popular lily, "Lily of the Nile" (*Agapanthus*), grows easily in many climates and comes in both dwarf and full-size varieties. These lilies flower in tufts at the top of long stems rising out of pale green foliage. Lavender, white, purple, and an occasional pink variety can be found at nurseries.

Fragrant four-o'clocks are easy to grow, and bloom abundantly in the late afternoon, remaining open into the early morning. All the varieties are beautiful, with some variegated varieties producing individual pure red, yellow, and pink flowers on the same plant, often on the same stem. These flowers have a delicate fragrance which has never, to my knowledge, been captured as an essential oil or used in fragrances.

Jasmine blossoms (both day and night-blooming varieties) are excellent offertory flowers. One variety of Arabian jasmine has small, cuplike flowers which are perfectly scaled as miniature lotuses for offering to statues, or to float in tiny bowls of water.

Incantation to Plants

An "Incantation to Plants" attributed to the Greek physicians of Alexandria follows.[2] This would be an excellent incantation for watering, or while collecting plant materials. The mention of "resin" probably refers to incense, which could be frankincense, copal, myrrh, gum, or any other resin-type incense.

You were sown by Cronos
Made welcome by Hera,
Protected by Ammon,
Born of Isis,
Nourished by Zeus of the Rains.
You have grown by favor of the Sun
and of the dew.
You are the dew of all the gods,
The heart of Hermes,
The seed of the high gods,
The eye of the Sun,
The light of the Moon,
The dignity of Osiris,
The beauty and the glory of the sky,
The soul of the Daimon of Osiris, who
feasts in all places,
The breath of Ammon.
Rise up, as you caused Osiris to rise up;
Lift yourself up like the Sun.
You are as tall as the zenith;
Your roots are deep also as the abyss.
Your virtues are in the heart of
Hermes;
Your branches are the bones of
Mnevis; [3]
Your flower, the eye of Horus,
Your seeds, the seed of Pan.
I purify you with resin even as the
gods,
For my good health;
Be purified also by my prayer and be
powerful,
For our sake, as Ares or Athene.
I am Hermes.
I pick (or water, or tend) you with
good luck, and with the Good
Daimon,
And at the propitious hour,
On the day which is right and propitious for all things.

Chapter Fifteen
The Third Hour of Night

ISIS THE DANCING GODDESS

ISIS," THE EGYPTIAN WOMAN said to me, "was a belly dancer." The exotic, confident woman in front of me, also a belly dancer, proudly claimed the Goddess as a member of her own tradition and attested to following the Goddess' tradition as well. All around me at the convention of belly dancers Isis was evident: adorning pictures and jewelry imported from Egypt; taken as a dancer's name; recalled in the titles of dance songs on tapes and records; evoked from images of Her priestess, Cleopatra. And rightfully so—dancers' finger cymbals and tambourines have been excavated from Her ancient temple sites; the sacred sistrum is a compelling addition to the drone of Middle Eastern dance music; the multi-colored veils are attested in ancient literature as appropriate garb for Isis. A

Priestess of Isis and bellydancer, Daniela Gioseffi, in her book, *Earth Dancing*, points out the use of the veil as a symbol of the crescent moon, and suggests that the cow horns of Isis were associated with the swirling veil as well.[1] The opening and closing of the dancer's veil, she believes, was nothing less than a reminder of the Veil of Isis and the mysteries which could be revealed or concealed.

THE VISIT OF THE GODDESSES

In the following tale, entitled "The Visit of the Goddesses" in Lewis Spence's *The Myths of Ancient Egypt*, Isis Herself dances and plays music on the occasion of the birth of three sons of Ra who are destined to become Pharaohs.[2]

Court dancers performing before the Pharoah.

Now when the sons of Ra and Rud-didet were born, that deity requested Isis, Nebhat, Meshkent, Hakt, and Khnumu to go to her, and taking the form of dancing girls, all except for the god Khnumu, who followed them as a porter, they descended to earth and approached the house of the priest Ra-User, Rud-didet's husband, and played before him with their instruments of music. They endowed the children with various attributes, and called them User-ref, Sah-ra, and Kaku. They then quitted the house and bade Ra-user rejoice. In return for their good wishes he bestowed upon them a bushel of barley, which Khnumu placed upon his head, but as they were on the way back to their divine abode Isis said unto the others, "Would it not have been better had we done a marvel for these children?" To this the others assented, and they there and then fashioned a likeness of the crowns of Egypt, of the crown of the Upper Land, and of the crown of the Lower, and hid them in the bushel of barley. They then returned to the house of Ra-user and requested permission to leave the barley in a closed chamber, which they sealed up, and then took their leave. A few weeks afterward Rud-didet asked her handmaid if the house and all that was in it were in good condition and the handmaid replied that all was satisfactory except that the brewing barley was not yet brought. Her mistress then inquired why that had not been done, and the servant answered that their store had been given to the dancing girls, who had arrived on the day of the children's birth, and that it now lay in the closed chamber under their seal. Rud-didet then ordered the maid to use it for the present, saying that Ra-user could replace it before their return. The girl opened the chamber and, entering, was surprised to hear people talking and singing, music and the sound of dancing, and such sounds as one hears in the palace of the king. She quickly returned and acquainted her mistress with what she had heard. Rud-didet then entered the room herself and also heard the sounds, but could not locate them. At last she laid her ear to the sack which held the barley, and found that the sounds proceeded from it ...

These sounds were taken as token that the three sons would all become rulers of Egypt. The story continues, but the ending is lost.

In the mythological tale of the contendings between Set and Horus, the son of Isis, the sun god Ra grows bored as he presides over the legal battles between the two contenders for the throne. Ill-tempered, he abandons the proceedings. The assembled pantheon of Egypt, needing Ra's presence to settle the matter once and for all, calls on Hathor, goddess of love, dance, and beauty, and a near-twin to Isis. She goes alone before the sun god Ra and performs an erotic dance for him. Restored to cheerfulness, Ra returns to the legal proceedings, and eventually Horus is recognized as the rightful heir to Egypt.

Both Bast, the cat goddess intimately associated with Isis, and Hathor, the goddess of love and pleasure who is often identified with Isis, are goddesses devoted to dancing, music, and joy. Osiris is particularly fond of music and dancing, and this is credited as one of the reasons his civilizing missions to other nations were so successful. Later, this love of dance and music assisted the equation of Osiris with Dionysus.

Whether danced as a birth rite, or as a rite to provoke desire, belly dancing and all other types of dance are excellent forms of worship for Isis, for both men and women. Singing and dancing were performed every day in honor of Isis and Osiris in some temples. Murals showing dancers performing during the sacred rites of Isis still survive.

Dancing for the gods was common in the ancient temples. In Egypt, pharaohs danced before gods and goddesses during the performance of sacred rites. The Priestess of Isis, Omm Sety, described how

Chapter
Fifteen

*Isis the
Dancing
Goddess*

169

Dancer with finger cymbols.

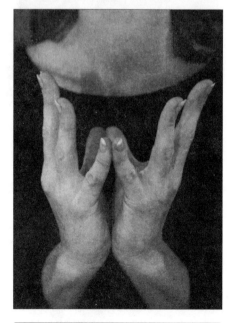

Top, *glyph of arms held in* ka
position; middle, *Closed Lotus Bud
hand position;* bottom, *Open Lotus
Bud hand position.*

the Pharaoh Sety the First danced
for her when he appeared to her in a
vision.[3] Instructing her to beat out a
rhythm of ten rapid beats followed
by a forceful beat and a brief pause,
Sety spun around with his arms
stretched out sideways, jumped up
and down with his arms bent up to
represent the symbol of the *ka*
(soul), ran in place and brandished
an imaginary war axe and finally
finished with a jump and a shout.
This vigorous account of male
dancing is consistent with the
evidence we see in temple paintings
and reliefs.

Some writers believe that the
ghawaji dancers of modern Egypt
are descended from a caste of sacred
dancers employed in ancient times
by the pharaohs and at the temples.
ghawaji music is haunting, using
droning instruments and drums that
make it very easy to slip into
dancing trance.

MAGIC MIRROR DANCE

This rite can be used for many
purposes. At its most basic, it is a
dance of worship and thanks for
possessing a body to use in
expressing dance. At its next level, it
is a way of generating and releasing
energy for a specific need. Finally, it
is (most fully in the version for
women) a way of contacting and
combining with the divine essence
of Isis.

Attire yourself in clothing that
inspires you to dance and move.
Add scarves or jewelry, belts or
bangles. Stand in front of a large
mirror, preferably one that shows
your full body.

Light two or more candles and
set them at the end of the room

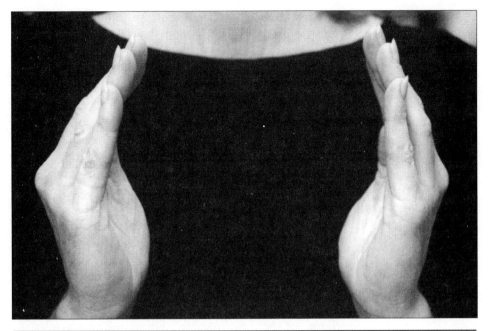

Horns of Isis hand position.

Chapter
Fifteen

*Isis the
Dancing
Goddess*

171

opposite from the mirror. Shaded electric lights can also be used—try draping them with a transparent scarf. The lighting should be dim, with the mirror appearing to float in the near-darkness. If you have appropriate music, start it before beginning. If you have no music, let the sistrum, finger cymbals, rattles, or your own voice or clapping hands be your accompaniment.Taking a stick of incense, light its tip and draw a body-sized ankh over your image in the mirror. See this ankh as sealing out all negativity and preparing a clear mirror for the use of the Goddess. Watch the image drawn by the glowing tip. It will stay in your eyes; let it fade. Set aside the incense into an appropriate container. Gather into your mind your image of Isis as a dancer, one who dances to create, to welcome, to awaken, to enlighten, or whatever is appropriate to the mood of your rite. Offer to the Goddess a lotus bud formed by your hands at the

level of your heart, then raise your hands as high as they will go, letting the "lotus" open. Hold the position for a moment, then let your hands fall down in an arc.

Pick up a sistrum or rattle. Shake it thoroughly in either a circle or to each of the eight directions, as well as above your head and below your feet. Let the shaking of the sistrum move your entire body. As you move, watch your image in the mirror. Look at the reflection of your face in the dim light, swirling against the mirror. Who is this powerful priestess? What face of Isis does she show? What will her dancing bring into being? Perhaps this swirl of skirt or scarf evokes the wings of Isis, that dark veiling the mourning Isis, this gesture of arm or hand the crescent of the moon or the globe of the sun.

As your energy and activity peak, offer them to the Goddess and to your purpose in dancing. Then dance until you tire or enlightenment pauses your movements. Don't overdo—exhaustion is not useful to this rite. Stand before the mirror and let your breath settle. Form the sign of the horns of Isis above your head. Hold this position for a few moments, then let your arms drift down to your sides. The rite is ended. Turn up the lights, drink some water, and bring yourself fully back to normal consciousness. You may want to eat a light snack or take a shower.

ISIS AND MODERN DANCE

One of the greatest avatars of modern dance, considered at once scandalous and mesmerizing, bears an Isian name. Isadora (which means "Gift of Isis") Duncan swept away convention with her free interpretation of the human body in motion, reinventing classical themes in her dances and greatly expanding the horizons of those who followed her in the new world of dance which borrowed much from the Pagan temples. No longer would dance be considered in the Western world a trivial entertainment; under her inspired guidance the art of dance regained some of the sacred qualities which had been lost in the Western world.

Nor was Isadora the only woman dancer to draw inspiration from the Egyptianized atmosphere of the late nineteenth and early twentieth century. Ruth St. Denis, inspired by an Isis-like goddess depicted in an ad for Egyptian cigarettes, decided to recreate the dances of ancient Egypt for her audiences. She had to wait a number of years before she found the funding to present her Egyptian

tableaus, but the names of performances in her *Egypta* are evocative: "Invocation to the Nile"; "The Palace Dance"; "The Veil of Isis"; "The Dance of Day"; and "The Hall of Judgement." Surely dances with these titles would not have been out of place in the temples of times past, especially when one is reminded that temples of Isis were so often found in close proximity to the city theaters, sometimes even sharing a wall with them.

MUSIC IN THE TEMPLE

On cool desert evenings or at the hours of the daily rites, the walls of the great Isian temples resounded with jubilant chanting and singing. Contemporary authors noted that Temples of Isis could be located simply by listening for the sound of the daily rites pouring out into the open air.

In the Greco-Roman period, the priest in charge of the musicians and temple choir was called the *precentor*, who guided the *paeanistai*—singers of the paeans of praise to Isis. Musicians accompanied the processions and played during the ceremonies. Some of these are described by Apuleius in his account of the Ploiaphesia festival:

> Then came the charming music of many instruments, and the sound of pipe and flute in the sweetest melodies. They were followed by a delightful choir of the most select youths, radiant in snow-white festal tunics; they repeated a captivating song which a skilled poet had written for music with the aid of the Goddesses of Song, and the theme of this from time to time contained musical preludes to the solemn vows

Playing the great harp.

Chapter
Fifteen

*Isis the
Dancing
Goddess*

173

to come. There came also flautists dedicated to great Sarapis [sic], who repeated through a reed, held sideways towards the right ear, a tune traditional to the temple and its deity …

Another account of a procession in Alexandria mentions musicians playing lyres, citharas, and tambourines. Singing and chanting by the assembled congregation was also apparently practiced, at least in Greco-Roman temples.

Sistrums and hand-cymbals have been found at many temple sites. From paintings and reliefs, we often see *oloi*, a set of flutes played simultaneously; pan pipes are also mentioned. Harps were common in Egyptian temples, and were used in Greco-Roman sanctuaries as well. The African harp, or Nubian lyre, was also played in Her rites. Finger cymbals and paired temple bells have also been found in Isian sanctuaries.

Musical notation of any form was rare in ancient times, so historical records of the Isian temple music are lost to us today. Some songs may have persisted for thousands of years, particularly those that follow minor and other less common modes. Putting new lyrics on old tunes is an ancient practice; the Akkadians put new words to Sumerian music in 2800 B.C.E. Some musicologists believe the present Christmas carol, "The Holly and the Ivy," is a survival of an imperial Roman tune. Like sacred sites, music survives and transcends religious fashions.

Isis in Classical Music

In modern times Isis has not been neglected by the great composers. Wolfgang Amadeus Mozart created brilliant music for his opera, *The Magic Flute*, which was first performed in France in 1791 under Mozart's direction. Originally, the opera bore the title *The Mysteries of Isis.* It tells the story of two young lovers protected and guided by a benevolent Priest of Isis.

Statue of female playing oloi.

A century later, the composer Verdi created his most beautiful music for the similarly-themed *Aida*, another Egyptian-inspired romantic opera taking place in and around a Temple of Isis. Both operas are still widely performed today, and may have contributed to the modern recognition of Isis as a living spiritual force.

PURIFICATION WITH SOUND AND MOTION

The purifying properties of sound are not often recognized, but they are invigorating as well as cleansing. The purifying effect of many musical vibrations is one reason why attending concerts and listening to music is so pleasurable. The high-decibel onslaught of rock and roll concerts, while damaging to the ears and jarring to the brain, may at one level shake loose negativity from the audience. This emission of negativity, while cleansing to the person experiencing it at the time, when multiplied by thousands of tightly-packed people in a less than spiritual frame of mind may account for the violence sometimes associated with public performances of some modern music.

Wendy Buonaventure, in her excellent book, *Serpent of the Nile: Women and Dance in the Arab World*, quotes an apparent survival of ancient dance and sound purification from the memoirs of Armen Ohanian, a well-born Armenian woman born near the turn of the century who later pursued dance as a career. The prospect of an unhappy marriage plagued her with nightmares while she waited in her future husband's home for the

Chapter
Fifteen

*Isis the
Dancing
Goddess*

175

Sistrums from the author's collection. Left to right: *modern African, northern European, Greco-Roman, and Egyptian.*

marriage to occur. Her screaming at night required the services of holy men, who advised a dance ritual to cleanse her of the evil spirits believed to possess her. Talismans to ward off evil were hung about her and she was forced to dance through the streets to the tombs of saints. The dancing and noise of the finger cymbals she wore were to force the evil spirits out of her body, and the talismans would then act as sacred seals to keep them from returning to plague her. However, because her fears and anxiety were not caused by supernatural forces, but by a very real unwillingness to participate in an arranged, loveless marriage, the rite did not work. Ultimately dance was her salvation and purification, which she turned to after a suicide attempt, and she lived on to become

an articulate defender of Arab dance and its performers.[4]

All types of music can be cleansing. Music, like scent, has a subtle effect which is both physical and spiritual. Certain songs or styles of music can bring great release. The ancients knew this, and were certain to include music and sound in their temple rites.

The sacred rattle of Isis, the sistrum, can be used in purifications. The clattering or jingling sound of this instrument functions in the same way as the rattle of a modern-day shaman, shaking up the atmosphere and clearing out lingering negative influences. Ordinary rattles, tambourines, or belly-dancing zills can also provide a burst of purifying energy.

Sistrum Purification [5]

Traditionally the sistrum is said to have been shaken in groups of three shakes in each of the four directions. You may also add the four additional compass points of northeast, southeast, southwest, and northwest. Do this to start your own purification by clearing the area around you. Then begin shaking the sistrum or rattle about three to four inches away from your body, moving from head to toe and then back to your head. Shake the sistrum under each foot and under your groin. Repeat this sequence as many times as necessary, and feel free to improvise. Obviously, you are moving during this purification, and it may evolve naturally into a sacred dance offering.

Sound purification using the sistrum or rattle can also be done for another person who stands in front of the sistrum-shaker as she or he performs the rite. In this situation, the priest or priestess should cleanse him- or herself with sound prior to beginning the procedure for another. If sistrums and rattles abound, this can be used as a group dance purification rite. Anybody can shake a sistrum and use it to emit purifying noise; because of this, it is a good group-participation rite.

In selecting or creating a sistrum or rattle for sound purification, listen for a fairly harsh, clattering sound rather than one that is high-pitched or only sweet. Small drums can also be used in purification, though these are more difficult to use effectively when purifying oneself.

Finally, purification by sound can be accomplished by using nothing more than your own rapidly clapping hands, accompanied by your voice. You don't have to sing to make sound; simple noise will do as well, and can be powerful in freeing old, internalized energy. The seven vowel sounds were chanted in Isian temples during ceremonies, possibly similar to the intoning of "AUM" by some groups today to open consciousness and begin a rite.

☽ · ☉ · ☾

Chapter Sixteen
The Fourth Hour of Night

ISIS AS LOVE GODDESS

ISIS-ASTARTE. ISIS-INANNA. Isis-Aphrodite. The worship of Isis dances with sexuality, passion, and romance, first drawing near, then pulling away, then reuniting. Isis and Osiris are said to mate within the womb, magnetized by irresistible desire. They marry and enjoy a union of great love and erotic joy, offering a model of perfect marriage to the early Egyptians. Working together, they provide to their people all the arts and crafts of civilization: agriculture, music, weaving, brewing, writing, building. Torn apart by tragedy, Isis and Osiris maintain a bond even through death.

The story of Osiris' death and dismemberment would seem to negate the sexuality of their union, but instead only provides the opportunity for resurrection and, specifically, phallic restoration, a sharp contrast to some other stories of mother goddesses, such as Cybele, who can appear to require the sacrifice of flesh for the sake of spiritual blessing. The actions of Isis after the death of Osiris, when She brings him back to life long

Above, *Osiris and Isis;* below, *Cybele,
an ancient sacrificial Mother Goddess.*

enough to impregnate Her with Horus, are taken by some writers to indicate that Isis urged Her followers to be as sexually aggressive. That the outer courts of Her temples were sometimes criticized as places where lovers could meet privately also attests to the blessings that Isis can bestow on those in love. At the same time, however, some of Her followers and clergy were expected to be sexually chaste for extended periods. One priestess vowed to Isis that she would remain celibate for life, while many women observed a ten-day sexual fast during one festival.

A search of general mythology reveals very few divine couples passionately in love with one another, especially in the Western world. Egyptian mythology reveals many strong individual gods or goddesses, but no coupled pair of the same strength of emotion as Isis and Osiris. In contrast, we have the pain-ridden couple of Set and Nepthys, Isis' own twin sister, who is unloved by her husband and yearns for Osiris.

ISIS AND LOVE SPELLS

There is no question that Isis hears and answers the prayers for love presented by Her worshippers. By asking Isis to send you a happy relationship, you are putting it in Her hands. But what about desire for a specific individual? Love spells that are aimed at an individual are obviously unethical, because they almost always tamper with another person's free will. Should everyone avoid doing this type of love spell? We're supposed to. If you are standing in front of your altar doing a "generic" love spell, yet simmering just below the surface is the desire that this general spell work on that specific individual, you are still doing a love spell aimed at that person. You may be able to pretend that was not your intention, but, in effect, it was.

Here are two love workings, one a prayer and the other a simple rite, that avoid the moral problems with the approaches mentioned above.

Prayer Regarding Unrequited Love for Another

Great Isis,
Lady of Love,
Goddess of Romance,
Isis-Aphrodite!
Isis-Inanna,
Hear my prayer.
Know that in the recesses of my heart
Burns a flame of love for _____.
The ways of the heart are mysterious,
*   Lady,*
And I ask Your guidance in this path.
If my love for _____
Weighs true in Your hands
Let _____ know that
I welcome (his/her) glance.
Let (him/her) know I delight in
*   (his/her) conversation.*
Let (him/her) know that I yearn for
*   the touch of (his/her) hand*
And desire that we should love one
*   another happily.*
If my attention is not welcomed by
*   _____,*
Let my heart release all desire for
*   (him/her);*
If You find this love unworthy,
Cleanse my heart of it.
Take its power
As an offering.
Bring forth new joy

And free me of sorrow.
Great Isis,
Hear my prayer!

Love Spell

Assemble together some objects, photos, pieces of writing, or other items that remind you of the person you love (or believe you could love). These can be of a real person known to you, images from history, a past romance, or motion pictures, or drawings or sketches you have

A nineteenth-century engraving of the famous Venus de Milo. Venus/Aphrodite is often correlated with Isis.

made. These do not all have to be of one person; in fact, it is best if they are from at least three different individuals.

Look over the items. Decide what aspect of each image attracts you the most. Perhaps a photo of a movie star represents your ideal physical form, while an excerpt from the love poetry of Kalidasa represents the ideal way you would like your love to express feelings. A souvenir from an old romance may remind you of the best moments of falling in love, a feeling you would like to enjoy again. Perhaps you admire the honesty in a casual friend, or the sports ability of a coworker or teammate. Ask for

anything and everything you would desire in a mate. If you have someone in mind that meets most of these criteria, use his or her image to represent these qualities, but always specify that you seek an individual *like* that person, not that specific person.

Select a scent for incense that represents to you something of the type of person you desire. Then select a scent to wear that makes you feel your most attractive. Bathe or shower, and dress as if preparing to meet this perfect person. Apply the scent. Light a candle and use the flame to light the incense you have selected. Stand in front of the objects and items you have selected. Inhale deeply several times, slowing the inhalation of breath each time.

Eros and Psyche.

Isis,
Goddess of Love,
Holy Spouse,
You who cause lovers to embrace one
    another,
I ask You
In Your vast power
To look over the lands
Under Your holy sight
And make known to me
The one who welcomes my love,
[select the following appropriate lines
    here]
Who resembles _____ in form,
Who possesses the _____ of _____,
Who will return to me the feeling of
    love I knew with _____,
Who can _____ like _____.
[add additional lines as needed]
Goddess,
Gaze into my soul and heart.
Let me know what will truly bring
    me joy,

Let me desire whoever will bring me
my truest fulfillment,
Let me embrace the one who will find
greatest joy in my love,
And return to me the same.
Great Isis,
Hear my prayer!

THE STORY OF EROS AND PSYCHE

The myth-cycles of Olympus are rife with lust, rape, and marriages of convenience, but have few love stories of the gods. An exception is the tale of Eros and Psyche, which, significantly, was placed in association with the Isis cult by Apuleius of Madaura when he wrote of his initiation into the mysteries of Isis and Osiris. In this tale, lovely Psyche becomes the wife of the unseen and mysterious Eros, who embraces her nightly but only in the dark, warning her that she must not see him "unveiled." For some time Psyche lives with Eros in perfect bliss, but eventually her jealous sisters convince her that she is married to a hideous monster who will eventually do her harm. They convince her to slaughter her husband. On the fateful night, she holds a lamp to see the monster beside her, but instead the beauty of Eros makes her weak, and her lamp quivers, accidentally sprinkling a few drops of scalding oil upon him. Eros rises up in horror and pain, sees the knife she holds, and flees from her.

Eros returns to his mother, Venus/Aphrodite, who tends his wounds and harasses Psyche. Ultimately, Psyche must go to the Underworld and confront Persephone to fill a box with a magical beauty unguent for Aphrodite.

What Psyche does not know is that Venus intends that the dangers of the journey will destroy Psyche. But Psyche is guided through safely with the help of a friendly talking tower and a reed. After obtaining the ointment from Persephone, Psyche,

Psyche returning from the Underworld
with the box of beauty which
Venus/Aphrodite had commanded her to
obtain from Persephone.

believing that she will win Eros back by use of the unguent, opens the box and falls into a corpse-like sleep.

Eros, now healed from his wounds, misses his sweet Psyche and seeks her. He wakes her with a prick from one of his arrows of love. He then flies off to persuade Jupiter to take his part against the still-angry Venus. Venus is placated, Psyche and Eros are joined together as husband and wife, and eventually Psyche bears a daughter whose name is Pleasure. For the full text of the story, along with a revealing commentary, see Erich Neumann's *Amor and Psyche: The Psychic Development of the Feminine.*[1]

ISIS AND EARLY ROMANCE NOVELS

Religion and romance novels may seem to be strange bedfellows indeed. The romantic love between couples, however, was a cornerstone of the faith of Isis. This theme is revealed by a number of ancient action/adventure/romance novels starring a devoted couple forcefully separated by pirates, kidnappers, robbers, barbarian chieftains, violent acts of nature, interfering relatives, and other trials. Steadfastly maintaining their faith and love, these storm-tossed lovers finally unite under the blessing of Isis and proceed into a presumably happy ever-after. With only a few changes, these novels could unspool as a modern movie, or take a place beside the latest bodice-ripping novels on the bookstore shelves.

One example of this type of novel, Xenophon's *Ephesiaca*, is largely devoted to the efforts of the heroine, Anthia, to preserve her chastity for her beloved Harbokrames. Anthia is so lovely that she is considered to be a manifestation of the Goddess Artemis, who is here treated as identical to Isis. Anthia fiercely defends her chastity against unwanted mates, while Harbokrames is nearly crucified on the banks of the Nile. When they finally reach safety and are united under the blessing of Isis, Anthia embraces Harbokrames in a ritual mating similar to the actions of Isis in reviving Osiris. The time for chastity has passed, and we are told that now "their life is one long holiday."

Anthia is the one who takes the sexual initiative. As quoted by R. E. Witt in his *Isis in the Greco-Roman World*, "She fastened her lips to his with a kiss, and through the lips all the thoughts that were in their minds were transmitted from one soul to the other." Witt suggests that Anthia is doing no less than imitating Isis in Her resurrection of Osiris.[2]

The Isian Novel of D. H. Lawrence

In his last book, *The Man Who Died*, D. H. Lawrence combined and contrasted the themes of the Isian resurrection faith with that of the Christian. Lawrence was essentially a Pagan and an advocate of the ancient mystery faiths. Into a particularly sterile time in the Western world he brought an antidote of sacred sexuality.[3]

In Lawrence's novel, Christ has survived the crucifixion but finds himself mentally and spiritually very detached from all that has gone before. He leaves behind all those who knew him and travels, finding by chance a woman dedicated to Isis who maintains a tiny temple to the Goddess. For a long time she has especially reverenced Isis in Search, seeking Osiris. In the survived Christ she finds her Osiris, and brings him to knowledge of the spiritual graces to be found within the flesh. He undergoes another resurrection, this time a joyful conquest of the trials of life, not death. They conceive a child. Although opposition by her family forces them apart, he promises he will come to her again. (The Christ-Osiris-Isis link is explored from a different perspective in Clysta Kinstler's novel, *The Moon Under Her Feet*, where the author posits that Mary Magdalene was a priestess of Isis. She also explores the Set-Osiris conflict as a corollary to the Jesus-Judas opposition.[4])

Lawrence was not the first writer on Isian themes to find his works reviled for their sexual content and at the same time widely distributed for the same reason. The most complete account we possess of an Isian mystery initiation, that of Apuleius, owes its existence in modern times to the sexually explicit passages in the manuscript. Because of the erotic content of its early chapters, Apuleius' *The Golden Ass* was a popular document in the scriptoriums of monasteries throughout Europe, and the many copies made assured its survival to the present day.

Although this is not the place for an extensive literary examination, Dion Fortune's magical novels were influenced by Lawrence's novels of the relationships between men and women. In her mystical novel, *The Winged Bull*, she subtly

acknowledges this influence in her choice of names for her main character, Ursula Brangwyn, the same name Lawrence used for a character in his novel, *Women in Love*.

The Magical Novels of Dion Fortune

The magical novels of Dion Fortune, particularly *Moon Magic*, *The Sea Priestess*, and *The Winged Bull*, deal extensively with the magic that can arise from a fully developed polarized relationship.[5] The relationships she depicts are "romantic," but it is romance stripped of sentimentality, where love and passion are not ends in themselves but the means to greater spiritual development, leading partners to the ability to function as fully-realized human beings. Her characters fulfill the roles of priests and priestesses, initiating each other and teaching each other the worship of the Great Goddess Isis.

Fortune intended that reading her novels would form a kind of literary path of initiation. Because of her intention, they are not summarized here. They confirmed me on my path to Isis, and I urge any man or woman interested in the faith of Isis to spend the time it takes to read them. For me, re-reading them is almost an annual event, and I always discover new insights that I missed or was blind to during previous readings.

The path of the polarized, functioning priestess-priest pair is not an easy approach by any means; relationships are frail enough without the additional burden of magical and spiritual development. But the goal, a united pair of human beings capable of furthering their own

evolution as well as that of humankind, is well worth pursuing.

How does one set off on this pursuit? Not, as one might expect, by seeking out one's perfect mate, or by searching through endless relationships to discover the right person. The ability to function effectively in a polarized relationship relies on each individual's having first attained the ability to function well separately. The projective and receptive potentials in each of us need to be acknowledged, because they will express themselves regardless, and often in ways that we would prefer to modify. Ignoring either pole of the human battery results in short-circuiting, which may manifest itself in many types of illness, both mental and physical (though there is, from a spiritual standpoint, no difference between the two), sexual perversion, violence, depression, job burn-out, and creative paralysis.

It is also true that persons who are very active and successful in the material world may be withdrawn and faltering in the spiritual world. Women may feel an echo of this conflict played out in their monthly cycles; some researchers believe that many symptoms of PMS and other disorders can be eased simply by the woman getting more sleep at certain times during the month. In men, being constantly projective and rarely receptive frequently manifests itself in physical illnesses, which may also follow a timed cycle.

POLARITY DEVELOPMENT EXERCISE

Picture yourself as being or embracing your ideal image of a person of the opposite polarity to what you normally manifest. If you are quiet, imagine the most dynamically active individual you can. If you are always too busy, creating so many new projects that the idea of a vacation is stressful in itself, imagine a contemplative individual who is always serene.

Watch the figure you create in your mind's eye. What are they wearing? What is their expression? What are their surroundings? Do they seem to know you? If not, introduce yourself to your "creation." Tell them you admire their qualities and want their advice from time to time. Listen to what they say to you. Think through some situations where you would like to draw on your "other half." Take notes or draw sketches if you wish.

You may find that you feel the need for more than one character. In this situation, you may need to expand both opposite aspects of yourself, and these individuals will help you to achieve this. In my own mind, I have at least two: a dynamic, ethical male unafraid of righteous conflict and a gentle, dark-haired priestess who is as mysterious and cool as the lotus pool I visualize behind her.

Perfect balance, by the way, is not the goal. You want to attain an awareness that allows you to alternate from one mode of approaching existence to the other, letting circumstances and experience dictate what aspects of self you allow to predominate at a given time.

INTO THE COILS OF THE LABYRINTH

Behind all acts of love and fertility is the Earth. Isis of the Earth, a darker aspect which holds both sex and death, must be met, recognized, and integrated. The brighter aspects of love and polarity will be unknowable unless the deep richness of Isis of the Earth is understood. Here is a meditation to lead you to the beginning of that understanding.

The Earth Meditation

Rock-hewn at the roots, many of the Egyptian temples stood over subterranean rooms and passages where the temple structures were put in direct contact with the primal earth forces. Remember, for this meditation, that on the other side of the earth lie starfields, and deep inside the earth boils a hot, molten core, an internal sun.

We are of the earth: our atoms, our tiniest components, are all formed of the dust that has wandered together into the bright, blue sphere we call home. What forms our Earth came from the stars; to the stars it will one day return, feeding the conflagration which will occur when our local star transforms itself into a nova—a "newness" in the sky.

As with all initiations, the final passage is an eruption into another sphere. With Earth, we enter into the sphere of the stars; with the fiery Sun, we find the strength to make and face malleable, watery changes; with the initiation of the stars, we find the solid, unifying fabric of the universe; with the initiation of the waters and tides, we find the structure overlying chaos and the flows of motion contained even in random action.

Isis of the Earth is a black goddess, charred by subterranean torches, dark and fertile as both Nile mud and the sky which will hold the stars that shall appear in the heart of the Earth initiation. She is mighty and terrible; not life, but existence is Her motive; all things that exist, that are material and have solid form, are in Her domain. To Her are sacred the crystals, the stalagmite pillars, the dry lichens— all that is ancient and solid, slow except in the moments of creation or destruction.

Her lovemaking is raw union; later, much later, are the subtleties of polarity which will unite Her bright priestesses and priests. Yet without Her, She of the Dark, there is nothing. She has taken form out of the rock, out of the lava, from the great frozen waves of stone, and emerges, bound still by Her backbone to the inner earth, taking on the beginnings of line and form.

From early beginnings such as these the children of Earth carved what their higher senses whispered would come to be a harkening forth of the Glorious Goddess, who would preside over the civilizations of the Earth. But not now, not yet; She presides silently over survival, over the deep primeval beauty of a young planet. Later She will have a brighter guise who adopts humankind as Her children. Now Her sacred things are those which to us seem soulless and lifeless. Life and death are one to Her—there is no sorrow, no lamentation. One day we will know a guise of this goddess who has learned to love and to lose; She is many millennia away, as are

those who could recognize Her. No prayers for this goddess; only the injunction: Exist; Endure. Sense the whirl of the stars above and feel the inner workings of the planet itself.

Go beneath the temple, then, for this meditation.

In seeking this understanding, explore dark, hidden places, even if this is just the crawlspace below your house. Walk along high cliffs. Dig in the ground with your hands and observe the particles that make up soil. Spend a day at a natural hot springs or mud bath. Plant one seed each day and note the action of the phases of the moon and the heat of the sun. Make objects of clay. Carve a rock.

View videotapes of volcanos exploding. Simply state before or as you are doing these things, "I do this to learn more of You, Isis of the Earth. May it please You to guide and instruct me."

Chapter Seventeen
The Fifth Hour of Night

— Isis as Divine Midwife —
and Mother

I N THE POPULAR STORY of Isis and Osiris, Isis fled from the imprisonment of Set to the swamplands, where She endured a difficult labor and gave birth to Horus. Because of Her own travails in childbirth, Isis became a special patron of women about to give birth. At many Egyptian temples, there was a building called the Mammisseum, where mystery plays portrayed the birth of Horus and, sometimes, the sacred birth of the ruling pharaoh, who was always identified with

Horus. These birth houses were covered with scenes from the Isis story, and it is possible that they were also used as birth houses for local women.

Ancient temple records show that sanctuaries of Isis frequently arranged for the hire of wet nurses to aid women who did not have sufficient milk of their own to nurse their children. The "Milk of Isis" was considered to be a powerful charm, and could be symbolized by a sweetened, pink-tinted milk dispensed from breast-

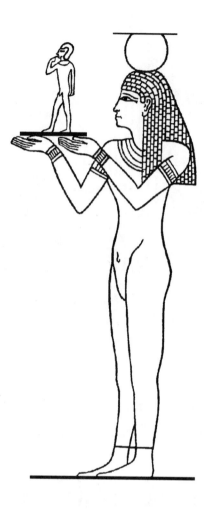

shaped pails, which dribbled onto the earth when carried in processions (see the situla illustration on page 158 in Chapter 14, "In the Kitchens and Gardens of Isis"). Milk of Isis may also have been used as a substitute milk for abandoned infants or those whose mothers had no milk. Pharaohs were often depicted as nursing at the breast of Isis, Her tender hand guiding them to Her nipple.

Although the motherhood of Isis is often the first aspect discovered by the modern worshipper, Isis was originally revered more as the Throne Power, the Great Sorceress, and the Divine Inventrix of the essentials of living, than as specifically a mother goddess. But, as with many other things, once motherhood was associated with Isis, She did it grandly. Isis is usually thought of as the mother of Horus, Her son by the posthumous coupling between Herself and Osiris. However, a number of other deities were considered to be Her children as well. Bast was called Daughter of Isis; Merul, a deity worshipped in the Philae area, was considered to be Her son. The pharaohs, as incarnations of Horus, were all sons of Isis, and many of them were depicted seated on Her lap, suckling Her breast. Representations of Isis suckling Horus became very popular in the last years of Egyptian power. As She grew more powerful in the Greco-Roman world, Horus was often called Harpokrates instead of his Egyptian birthname.

Above, *the goddess Nut holding Harpocrates;* below, *Isis suckling Horus as Her consort Serapis stands nearby.*

A RITE FOR PROTECTION OF CHILDREN

The protection of our precious children is a concern of any parent and, indeed, of anyone who loves a child. Placing your little ones under the protection of Isis accomplishes two things: it calls the attention of the goddess to the children, and reinforces a parent's own commitment to the safety of his or her children. It creates a psychic lifeline between goddess, parent, and child that can pull power to the child in time of need.

This rite can be accomplished with or without the child present. If the child is absent, you may place a toy, photo, or other object representing the child on the altar surface. Simply praying with intent to Isis will accomplish the same results.

Great Isis, Holy Mother,
You who see all,
You who hear all,
Guard the child _____.
Keep him or her safe,
Near or far.
May the seven scorpions
who guarded You in Your wanderings
protect my (this) child on his or her
    daily paths.
Soothe his or her fears
In all hours of the day and night
May _____ be safe within Your care.[1]

PARENTING DEDICATION

Raising children is an offering to the gods. Isis' fierce motherhood and thorough training of Horus, as well as Her fights on his behalf before the gods, show her commitment to her son. The challenges of parenting are spiritual and initiatory as well as mundane and troubling.

Stand in front of your altar or shrine, on which an image of Isis as

Chapter
Seventeen

Isis as
Divine
Midwife
and
Mother

189

The goddess Mersekert (an aspect of Isis) suckling Horus.

a mother figure has been placed. Light incense and white or pink candles. Place your hands over your heart. If your child is present, place one hand on your heart and the other in contact with your child. For a babe in arms, hold the child in your arms in front of you.

"I, _____, parent of _____, dedicate my parenting to the glory of Isis. May You grant me wisdom, patience, and all other skills I need to raise my child, a strong and happy individual, who will glory in the joys of life and be unafraid of the challenge of death.

Enlighten and empower me, Isis, that I may be a good guide of souls to my little one, that I may teach by example and not by harsh correction, and that I may learn as well from the small being placed in my care, for the age of a soul is ancient and in my arms I may cradle my long-past parent and hold my future mother.

As You nurture me, may I nurture my children. As You are patient with me, may I be patient with them. As You give me love, may I give love as freely. As You help me grow, may I help them grow.

Great Isis, grant this my prayer!

Stand and meditate for a few moments. Leave the candles burning if possible.

AN ISIAN LULLABYE

May the Wings of Isis enfold you,
Safe may they always hold you.
Near or far,
The Great Mother
Will hear your call.
Isis watches
Over us all.

The sparkling stars are spinning—
Listen and you hear them singing—
May your dreams be of wondrous
*   things;*
Now sleep gently within Her wings.

☽ · ☉ · ☾

Chapter Eighteen
The Sixth Hour of Night

Isis and Alchemy

D URING THE ROMAN EMPIRE, Isis was renowned as an alchemist. Both physical and spiritual transformation using alchemical practices and philosophy came under Her domain. Her benevolent patronage of the scholars at Alexandria, which was the foremost scientific city of the Roman world, doubtless enforced Her reputation as a goddess skilled in alchemy as well as other sciences.

The association of Isis and alchemy, with its paired focus on the production of gold and spiritual immortality, was a natural one. The myths of Isis credited Her with the resurrection of Her husband Osiris and creation of the rites of mummification. Her reputation as a magician in possession of the secret name of Ra was longstanding. Add to this Her renown as an inventrix of divine medicines, and it is obvious why She and the alchemists joined forces. Through a fascinating document where Isis is instructing Her son Horus in the alchemical arts, we get a glimpse of the high regard in which Isis was held by the early alchemists. These documents, carefully guarded and passed through generations of alchemists, also preserved the memory of Isis, and may even have played a role in the development of the theme of courtly love, since the spiritual/chemical symbolism is often expressed in sexual and romantic terms in these documents.

The preservation of these manuscripts also promoted the

Above, *the Ouroboros*; below, *Thoth was hailed as a god of alchemy.*

equality of women, both through the presence of the wise, active Isis instructing Her son and by the documentation of a number of prominent women alchemists active during the Roman empire. Several of these have come down to us. One shared a name with Cleopatra, and left behind a widely-reproduced diagram of the *Ouroboros*, a snake biting its own tail, often used as a sigil for eternity.

Maria the Egyptian, another female alchemist, worked with Zosimos, a famed alchemist from Akhmin (Panopolis) who wrote a twenty-eight-volume encyclopedia on alchemy, but was commonly considered to be his superior in the art of alchemy.

Even during medieval times male alchemists often had female assistants, who were regarded as essential to the successful completion of the work. One source suggests that persecuted witches sometimes found asylum with the slightly less persecuted alchemists, who recognized and respected their knowledge of herbs and compounds.

The words "alchemy" and, later, its refined offspring, "chemistry," are said to come from the Arabic word for Egypt, *Al-Khem* or "out of the Black Land." The Black Land was the fertile dark mud deposited by the Nile's flood. From earliest times, Egypt was thought of as the home of alchemical practices and philosophies. Thoth, as well as Isis, was hailed as a god of alchemy and a divine instructor in the art.

Alchemy is a science of transformations, and as such its results appear to be magical. It could be equally termed the magical element of science, with tangible results in

Medieval male and female alchemists.

all phases of human behavior, intellectual, psychological, spiritual, and physical. Its study can easily occupy a lifetime; its mastery will require many incarnations. The instructions on oil blends and incense are only the doorstep to the hall of alchemy and science.

ISIS AND THE ANGEL AMNAEL

From the *Codex Marcianus* we have the curious document entitled "The Prophetess Isis to Her Son Horus," which details an adventure experienced by Isis and its final result. The tale is told in the first person, as Isis recounts the story to Her son. She explains that during the time Horus went to fight for his father's kingdom against the wicked Set, She retired to Hormanouthi, a city sacred to Thoth and the capital of the alchemical community of the time. She describes that a certain time had passed and then an angel "who dwelt in the first firmament" noticed Her and desired Her, approaching Her in a great hurry to consummate his desires. Isis refused him because She wanted to first ask

him about the methods of preparing gold and silver. This stymied the angel, who apparently would not or could not answer Her, so he put Her off until the next day, when a greater angel, called Amnael, could come with him to answer Her questions. The first angel told Her that Amnael could be recognized by a ceramic vessel full of shining water which he would bear on his head. (This is intriguing, since a sign of Osiris was also a vessel of water which was borne by priests in procession and also presented in the temples for worship.)

The following day Amnael appeared alone and was also seized with a passionate desire to unite with Isis. However, Isis was adamant that he answer Her questions. Finally he showed Her his sign (the vessel of shining water) and told Her all the secrets.

The text has him show Her his sign and tell Her the mysteries a second time (or perhaps expand on them). He made Her swear a binding oath that She would never reveal the knowledge to anyone other than Her son, Horus, and Her "closest friend," although the grammar is so ambiguous on this point that it may refer again to Horus.[1] From this comes the final phrase, "so that you are me, and I am you." In other words, they are made identical by sharing this knowledge. Again, the phrasing is vague, and may refer to Isis and Amnael as well as to Isis and Horus.

The next section shifts and becomes for a moment a pastoral farming scene. Horus is told to "go and watch and ask Acheron the peasant" and to learn from him who is the sower, who the reaper, that whoever sows barley will harvest barley and that whoever sows wheat will harvest wheat. Isis elaborates on this and further tells Her son that "a man is only able to produce a man, and a lion a lion, and a dog a dog." Isis adds that anything occurring contrary to this is a miracle and cannot survive for long, "because nature enjoys nature and nature overcomes nature." She then goes on to say, "Having part of the divine power and being happy about its divine presence, I will now also answer their questions about sands, which one does not prepare from other substances, for one must stay with existing nature and the matter one has in hand in order to prepare things." Once more She asserts that wheat begets wheat, a man begets a man, and that gold will harvest gold.

An elaborate alchemical recipe follows, probably with the intent to produce the "Philosopher's Stone," the stone that will continuously beget gold. Isis closes this part of the text with the sentence, "Now realize the mystery, my son, the drug, the elixir of the widow."[1]

EVERYDAY ALCHEMY

Transforming matter, whether it is cooking together ingredients to form bread, burning incense, or forging an alloy of silver and gold, is all, in broad terms, a form of alchemy. The transformation of matter also acts as a catalyst to psychological and spiritual transformation, and this effect is specially strong when dealing with scents and odors. Because the human sense of smell is so primitive, stimulating our olfactory nerves cuts through many civilized defenses and emanates almost directly into the brain. A scent can trigger buried emotions and memories; it can attract, arouse, or repel; it can heal and inspire.

Sweet odors of all kinds are sacred to Isis. Sweet white flowers, such as gardenia or plumeria, are excellent to aid in the contact of the feminine and lunar aspects of Isis.

When mixing together ingredients, all of your vessels should be clean. Boil empty glass vessels, if necessary, to sterilize them. Cover and let cool before using. Keep droppers separate to avoid contaminating one oil with a trace of another. Write down on a card all information regarding your blendings. At a minimum, this should include the date, moon phase (and/or other pertinent astrological information), type and amount of each ingredient, and the manufacturer or source of each scent or substance.

Essential Oils

Particularly potent are the highly refined essential oils of plants and flowers. These oils are powerful and can be intoxicating. If you have never experienced a true essential oil, you may not realize what a scent can do to your consciousness. Most oils available today, including many whose labelling seems to indicate that they are essential oils, are partially or wholly synthetic, many with petroleum bases or by-products. Put bluntly, old dinosaurs do not smell like roses, especially when burned as incense.

If you choose to use essential oils, buy aromatherapy-quality oils from a reputable supplier. It is well worth the expense and trouble.

Caution: please remember that true essential oils are often caustic and can burn; *do not* use undiluted essential oils directly on the skin.

An essential oil can be placed in a diffuser to spread its scent throughout an area. An alternative is to heat some water and allow a drop or two to fall on its surface. Maintain a gentle heat, and the aroma will fill your house. A drop of essential oil left to evaporate on a rounded crystal can also substitute for altar incense, though the scent will not travel as far (nor as quickly) as it will when using a diffuser or warm water.

In Dion Fortune's *Moon Magic*, the priestess of Isis, Lilith Le Fay Morgan, discusses her use of scent to establish mood and alludes to what she calls the "psychology and theology" of scents. She lists her use of sandalwood, cedar, galbanum, and frankincense, as well as the essential oils of geranium, jasmine, and attar of roses.[2]

Plutarch mentions that on a daily basis the morning incense in the temples of Isis is resin and the noon incense is myrrh, while the evening scent is the complex scent kyphi. Kyphi is a rich, deep scent perfect for nighttime rites. It is highly evocative, and makes it easy to see dim images of the ancient temples. It can be an effective incense to burn for scrying and other divinatory work.

Plutarch lists a version of the ingredients for kyphi, noting that while the unguent makers compound it, sacred writings are read out to them, and that the order of the ingredients added during mixing is also crucial. He lists honey, wine, raisins, the round cypherus, resin, myrrh, camel's thorn, hartwort, mastic, asphalt, rush, monk's rhubarb, greater juniper, lesser juniper, cardamom, and sweet flag. Different recipes vary in both the number and kind of ingredients, ranging from a minimum of ten (from Dioscorides) to fifty or more separate ingredients listed by other writers.

Dioscorides' recipe, a version of which is quoted in Lise Manniche's *An Ancient Egyptian Herbal*, is relatively straightforward.

Dioscorides' Recipe for Kyphi

½ pt. cyperus (a type of bulrush used as a thickener)

½ pt. juniper berries

12 lbs. of stone plum raisins

5 lbs. of resin

1 lb. of aromatic rush

1 lb. asphalatus (Cytisus lanigerus, Genista acantho-clada—a thickener)

1 lb. Iuncus odoratrus (Cymbopogon schoenanathus)

1½ oz. myrrh

8½ pts. old wine

2 lbs. honey [3]

Stone the raisins and grind them with the wine and myrrh. Holding

back the honey, pound and sift the remaining ingredients together with the raisins. Let sit for a day. Boil the honey to thicken it, strain, and mix with the other ingredients. Store in an earthenware pot or jar.

This type of complicated incense tends to improve with age, and is intended to be burned over charcoal. The exact quantities are difficult to estimate. As for the wine, try a deep, sweet wine such as Mavrodaphne, or a good port, or a port-like wine such as Malmsey.

Kyphi was also added to wine as a flavoring and used as a purge by physicians. It induced trance states and promoted sleep.

An Oil to Attract Love

> 30 drops light musk oil
> 5 drops true essential oil of lavender
> 10 drops true essential oil of ylang-ylang flowers

Place the light musk oil in a container, then add the lavender and ylang-ylang. Shake together and let rest, tightly capped, for several days. Adjust the amount of lavender and ylang-ylang to suit your personal taste.

This may be used as an offering or anointing oil, or, sparingly, as a perfume.

An Oil to Remember What You Are Told in Dreams

A present-day Middle Eastern tradition repeated by the manufacturers of Talisman oils suggests placing a drop of jasmine oil on the outside of your ear to better recall what you are told in your dreams.

SCENTS SACRED TO ISIS

These can be used in their fresh form as flowers or leaves, or in extracts or essential oils.

Earth Aspects

Cedar
Myrtle
Oppopanax
Pine

Lunar/Feminine Aspects

Gardenia
Jasmine
*Kyphi
*Lotus
*White/Light Musk
Rose

Sea Aspects

Lavender
Mugwort
Rosemary
*White musk

Solar Aspects

Honey and beeswax
Lemon
Myrrh
Orange
Osmanthus

Stellar Aspects

Benzoin
Frankincense
Sandalwood

indicates blends which may be acceptable for some uses.

☽ · ✹ · ☾

Chapter Nineteen
The Seventh Hour of Night

RITE OF NIGHT

NOW THE STARS ARE brightly wheeling across the sky. The astronomers make careful notes of their passing from vigil points on flat temple roofs, sighting along sticks to focus their vision on individual stars. The alchemists mind their alembics, monitoring temperatures on delicate compounds. Soon the temple bakers will begin preparing bread for the morning offerings. A few patients and penitents lie half-awake, seeking after magical dreams of the Goddess, and near them are the physician priests and priest-esses. Scholars squint against the light from their oil lamps, peering at ancient documents.

But for most, it is past time for sleep. The clothes of the statue of the Goddess are removed, the doors to the little shrines shut and sealed. And so we shut and seal ourselves, in this Midnight Rite.

MIDNIGHT RITE

Before going to bed, stand before a lit candle at your altar, or in front of a window where you can see the sky and stars. Consciously release all the tensions that have tied themselves to you during the day, and offer up the energy locked in them for the use of Isis. Let the energy rise up in the heat from the candle, or feel it being pulled from your body into the fiery stars far away.

I hail You and praise You,
Glorious Goddess,
At the end of this day which You
granted me.
May my actions within its hours be
judged to be justified,
And my words within its hours found
to be true.

Hipparchus in the Observatory of Alexandria.

Drain from me all ill intent and
action;
I offer to You all energy I have locked
in unworthy action or reaction;
May tomorrow by Your grace find me
wiser and my joy in the universe
still greater.
I ask Your welcome now in the
Temple;
Accept me this night for rest, for
study, and for worship;
Grant me dreams of meaning and the
memory to recall them.
Hail to You, Goddess of the starry
pathways;
Hail to You, Goddess of the Deep
Black,
Hail to You, Goddess of the Shining
Sun at Midnight,
May I partake of Your glory forever.

Add whatever other prayers are needed for yourself or others. Extinguish the candle and go to bed.

Another Nighttime Prayer

From the ancient Egyptian, translated by Padiusiri:

Great Isis,
I call out to You against the eyes of the
Lords of darkness.
Great are You of all the Gods, beau-
tiful in Your dwelling,
Lady that sets protection against the
fiends in the land.
Hail to Thee whose beneficial spirits
are the Gods of Your Land conse-
crated from within the Other
World.
Beautiful are Thy manifestations in
the realm of the Lord of Life who is
Thy protective brother.
Give to me Thy spirit and power in
Heaven,
Great Power of Isis, protect me!

MEDITATION ON THE MIDNIGHT ISIS

Black Isis is chaos. Until recently, even science has thought of chaotic behavior as an evil anomaly in the divine order, something to be eradicated by the imposition of tighter and increasingly microscopic order. All existence once seemed predicated on order; randomness was to be ferreted out and rejected.

Chaos, however, is the fount of our existence; pure order is a largely artificial and deadly concept. Eastern philosophy has offered many insights in this area. Although on the surface the Asian cultures seem even less accepting of disorder than those of the West, the symbol of yin and yang allows each side to hold the seed of the other. An overabundance of order automatically creates chaos.

This can be seen at work in political systems throughout history. Generally speaking, it is not excessive license that leads the people of a nation to make war on a neighbor. Rather it is the result of its opposite, repression and excessive order, which leads a nation to work out some of its frustrations on its neighbors, or gives rise to an attempt to purge its borders of any group which professes to be different. Hitler's Third Reich was a very orderly government, and in orderly fashion led the world into chaos.

An old saying about initiates is that they must have their feet in hell and their heads in heaven. This illustrates the truth that to be fully functional, anyone who seeks to advance spiritually must have an understanding of both chaos and order. Another traditional way of presenting this truth is that a spiritual initiate must be like the lotus or water lily. While roots spread in the undifferentiated mud, the stem fights to rise through dark water. Then it floats on the surface, gathering nourishment from the air and light, before pressing its accumulated energies into the bud that will burst forth as a bright, fragrant flower unfolding in an apparently orderly manner. Uproot the bulb from its bed of chaos, however, and the flower will have nothing to nourish it, and it will die.

A world without lotuses, without life, would be a very orderly place. The atmosphere of dead planets shows much more order than our turbulent Earth. We are in a world inheriting the legacy of too much order which has turned into chaos. We have discovered, with naive surprise, that destroying our planet may destroy us. We have also learned, to our horror, that the ability to break an ecosystem does not presuppose an ability to fix it. We see species becoming extinct without new ones rising up to replace them. We destroy organisms that give us oxygen, which we need to live, by using machines which create poisons, which can kill us. This is truly chaos.

As one drives a skid-locked car in the direction of the skid to regain control of the vehicle, we need to return to a purer sense of chaos to remedy the results of an overabundance of order. This is the call to the great potential of Black Isis.

Black Isis is ancient and primeval, concerned with necessity and primary survival, whereas Bright Isis is concerned with enhancement and resurrection. Each needs the

other, feeds off the other, but Black Isis is the more ancient. Black Isis makes it possible for Bright Isis to be born from the bones of Her black mother.

Black Isis is the heat of caves, the light of the luminescence of stones and of decay, the harsh heat and unnatural light of flowing lava that runs like the blood of the planet. She is oceanic, volcanic, large, and great. Her tides are too vast to be perceived, far from the hourly and daily solar and lunar tides of which the Bright Isis, in all Her aspects, is mistress.

No priestess or priest is one without the other, and no attribute belongs alone to one aspect or the other. Bound by the Earth of which She is a part and a manifestation, a priestess firmly rooted in the traditions of Black Isis will never lose

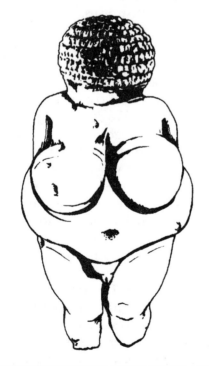

Ancient fertility goddesses speak of the raw power of Black Isis.

sight of necessity and practicality, and may be much more human—kinder—than an ungrounded priestess who has cut herself off from her dark roots and flown off on airy flights of spirituality which nourish only herself. Likewise, the priestess of Dark Isis who does not acknowledge her starry self will find it difficult to allow the free flow of the Goddess' power through her when it entails empowerment of another or allows the use of primal energy for apparently superficial things.

Black Isis and Bright Isis are, ideally, bound together. Bright Isis may stand tall as an obelisk in the sunlight; Black Isis is the rooted stone concealed in the earth which gives stability and permanence to the manifestation above. Bright Isis reflects and emits light; Black Isis is the welcome shadow behind Her. Like day and night, sleep and wakefulness, both are needed.

In the daily workings of the human race, it will be Black Isis who breaks through the habits and outworn taboos of convention and creates the stage where Bright Isis, now in the outer guise of Aphrodite or Hathor or Sarasvati, will entice another to love and joy.

It is the Dark Isis, with Her warm waters and deep, slow tides, who will guide the child of love to birth. And dual-breasted woman will nurse such a child and would-be initiate with both bright and dark, reprimanding, guiding, teaching, and refining until the child is capable of finding and maintaining its own inner contacts. If both Bright and Dark are in balance, this will not be a wrench for either creatrix or offspring. Though here the metaphor has been one of child-bearing, the same processes are equally true of any endeavor. It will be Black Isis who sees and exploits an opportunity, for She is aware of the precariousness of all manifestations of life and knows the most efficient ways to improve chances of survival.

Bright Isis will gather to Herself the resources necessary for creation, whether through people attracted by Her light or information flowing to Her. Material essentials will come from the Great Dark Mother, and so will the tenacity—the rock-hard patience—that it takes to see an endeavor to fruition. To glorify, expand, and detail such an activity will fall to Bright Isis; the ongoing nurturing will be shared by both aspects. And sometimes the fullest measure of a Priestess or Priest of Isis is in their knowledge of which aspect is appropriate, and in their ability to allow either aspect full play in the psyches of those involved.

Black Isis is the most difficult, and yet most powerful, of the aspects of Isis. Revealed in Dion Fortune's novels, the priestesses devoted exclusively to this aspect are generally loved and hated with equal force. Men are especially enchanted with these women; like fast sports-cars, they combine the attraction of both sex and death.

Black Isis combines aspects of the pure force of the Isis of Nature, with whom She is often combined. Priestesses of this aspect are often aligned with the element of fire with its attributes of sharp change and volcanic explosions, rather than the lunar, watery types of change found in priestesses of other aspects. However, if change, alteration, or re-creation is needed, there is none better fitted to do it than a priestess of Black Isis.

Fire-priestesses routinely leave a trail of ashes behind them; before judging them too harshly it is wise to remember there are some plants whose life cycle is such that they can only sprout on charred earth, and others whose seeds must burn to germinate. In these cases the actions of a priestess of Black Isis can be cleansing and revivifying, but she is definitely not the aspect of Isis for those who revere the status quo. Her action is for good, but it is good on a cosmic scale and may override human sentiments and feelings without remorse.

For persons in need of liberation, either the men with whom the Black Priestess consorts or the women who become Her priestesses, Her liberating power may be the only opportunity for freedom or fulfillment available. Those for whom the actions of the gentler processes are sufficient will probably find their own initiations on slower paths. Those who need the actions of the black priestesses may never break through otherwise, and instead only recede farther and farther from their own true natures.

The great mystery here is that it is the priests and priestesses of the Black Isis who become the great priestesses and priests of the evolved Bright Isis.

THE BLACK RITE

To understand the meaning of the term "The Black Rite," remember that to the Egyptians the fertile earth was dark and black. Their land could be called *Al-Khem*, or, "the

Black Land." Their "black rite" was not dark in the sense of evil, but in the sense of the spiritual, physical, and mental fertility it evoked.

At midnight, in the concealed chambers behind the Osirian chapels in common use, the Resurrection of Osiris would be performed, and the "Sun would shine at Midnight," perhaps in the form of the phallus-like obelisk which was used as an image of a solidified ray of Ra. With this rite was associated Khepra, the sun-beetle who flies in the heat of noon. At the opposite hour, the solar power was in ascendency as the "Sun Behind the Sun," said by some to be the star Sirius, far away and perhaps a distant homeland for humankind.

Deep in the night, it is believed priests and priestesses would take to themselves the spiritual forms of Isis and Osiris and embrace one another in their names. Through sexual power a spiritual fertility was attained. Even pharaohs were said to be born of these sacred matings, though nothing, not even the fragments of the rites we speak of, has been confirmed by literature or archeology. The initiates through the centuries are silent or evasive.

☽·⚭·☾

Chapter Twenty
The Eighth Hour of Night

─── ISIS IN THE STARS ───

Henceforth I spread confident wings to space;
I fear no barrier of crystal or of glass;
I cleave the heavens and soar to the infinite.

Giordano Bruno[1]

ISIS' STELLAR LINEAGE IS well attested in ancient sources. From the beginning She was the sparkling of Sirius in the early morning, beckoning the Nile to flood forth. Many other stars have been associated with Her or called by Her name. One reason the name of Isis was so frequently attached to various stars is that astronomy was actively practiced in Her temples. Astronomer-priests watched the skies nightly from the flat rooftops of these temples, and made regular observations. In the Osiris chapel at Denderah, the Egyptian zodiac (upon which our modern one is based) was depicted on the ceiling. One prominent Greco-Egyptian astronomer, Ptolemy (not one of the

The star gods near the North Pole. Note the hippopotamus goddess Tauert-Isis at the far right with a crocodile upon Her back. They correlate with the constellation we know as Draco. The Meskheti, *at top center, was the Egyptian equivalent of our Great Bear.*

pharaonic Ptolemies) made his observations from the roof of a temple of Serapis and wrote several treatises which have survived to the present day.

Among the stars named after Isis is Antares, which was associated with Selkit, the scorpion goddess who was sometimes depicted in the Isian headdress. Antares was associated with Isis in the ceremonies conducted in conjunction with the great pyramid complex at Giza, where She bore the special title of Lady of the Pyramids. The early astronomer, Kircher, called the Scorpion constellation, of which Antares is a part, by the name *Isias*, or *Statio Isidis*, because of its ancient associations with Isis.[2]

The constellation of Taurus, the Bull, was sometimes called by Isis' name because of the cow horns frequently shown in images of Isis, which symbolize Her role as Mother of the Sacred Bull.

Isis was considered to control the stars in the constellation of Ursa Major, or the Great Bear. She exerted domain over the other constellations of the north which were believed to project an evil force over the sun during the spring. This may be connected with the belief that Isis could change the courses of the stars and transform negative influences into positive ones.

The figure in the constellation of Virgo was sometimes viewed as Isis holding wheat, which She was said to have dropped to form the Milky Way from the individual grains, or as holding Her son Horus. This constellation was also sometimes identified with Fortuna, who in turn is frequently identified with Isis.

Pliny, an astronomer from classical times, stated that the planet Venus was also called Isis. Isis was frequently associated with both the goddess Venus and the similar deity Aphrodite; She also shared identity and titles with Ishtar, whose sacred planet was Venus. The following Sumerian prayer to Inanna (an early form of Ishtar) is quoted by E. C. Krupp in his book, *Echoes of the Ancient Skies*, and may be used to greet Isis as well.

The Egyptian zodiac in the Temple of Denderah.

PRAYER TO INANNA

The pure torch that flares in the sky,
The heavenly light shining bright like
the day,
The great queen of heaven, Inanna, I
will hail …
Of Her majesty, of Her greatness, of
Her exceeding dignity,
Of Her brilliant coming forth in the
evening sky,
Of Her flaring in the sky—a pure
torch—
Of Her standing in the sky like the
sun and the moon,

Known by all lands from south to
north
Of the greatness of the holy one of
heaven
To the Lady I will sing.[3]

The moon was often called Isis, and the two were considered to be manifestations of the same greater cosmic energy.

As Isis Myrionymos, the Goddess of Ten Thousand Names, She was identified with the constellation Virgo. As Goddess of the Sacred Throne, Isis can be found in Cassiopeia and her Chair.

The January Ploiaphesia cere-mony, taking place in the month of Aquarius, tied Isis to that constella-tion as well. The zodiac in the Cathedral of Notre Dame in Paris shows Aquarius and Isis jointly launching a ship for the *Isidis Navigium*.

By her birthdate, Isis can also claim the sign of the Crab, Cancer, or of Leo, depending on the calendar preferred.

The classical poet Ovid, whose mistress was a devotee of Isis, states that offerings were made to the dolphin constellation Delphinus as stars sacred to Isis.

A double star, designated by the Greek letter *mu*, in the constellation of Canis Minor was known as Isis. In the constellation of Draco, another double star was known as Isis or Tauert-Isis; it marked the head of the figure (which ancient Egyptians saw as a hippopotamus, and would later be called "the Dragon").

Above all, Isis' special star was Sirius. This star, actually the most visible entity within a complex twin (and possibly tripled) star system, was known as the "Home of the Soul of Isis." Sirius is a sparkling gem rising in the eastern sky in winter time, preceded by the Pleiades, and then Orion, the great hunter who was thought to be Osiris. With two other bright stars, the red Betelgeuse in the left shoulder of Orion, and Procyon to the left, Sirius forms a great inverted triangle in the sky. Follow the row of stars in Orion's belt east-ward, and you will find the tremu-lous light of Sirius, known also as Sothis. It scintillates with flashing colors, especially just after rising, when the atmosphere refracts its light. This star invites worship.

The Sirius star system is also associated with Anubis, Osiris, and Nepthys. The complicated and fascinating interrelationships within this multiple star system are exam-ined in detail in Robert Temple's *The Sirius Mystery*. While the extra-terrestrial premise he discusses may be difficult for some to accept, the documentation he provides should be of interest to all.[4]

The goddess Isis-Sothis.

Sirius was also known as Isis Hathor, Isis Sothis, and Isis Satit. Two other titles applied to Sirius which may also have been applied to Isis Herself were The Brightly Radiating One and Fair Star of the Waters. At Denderah, in the small temple of Isis which was once oriented toward Sirius, it is titled Her Majesty of Denderah.

Canis Major, the constellation of which Sirius is now a part, was visualized in the heavens later on. The association of the dog with Sirius was made or at least known by the Egyptians, who used a dog-like hieroglyph for the star.

Argo Navis, the Ship constellation, has associations with Isis and Osiris and their sacred boats. It is also associated with Isi and Iswara, two Hindu divinities who may be additional aspects of Isis and Osiris. Canopus, a prominent star in Argo Navis, was sometimes called the Star of Osiris.

Here is a praise-poem which speaks of the energy of Isis of the Stars:

Into the stars I will take Your name,
O Goddess of the desire of my nature.
On my soul it will be emblazoned in
    letters of light and life.
I will seek Your resting places among
    the stars
And I will make lights to You that
    will not grow dim nor flicker out.
To You I will make altar lights of
    lasers
And dance holy circles in space with a
    chariot of steel and plastic.
Step on my back
And let me be
The Boat of Millions of Years
To carry the gods

Through the evernight of space to the
    places of days.
I will make for You a temple
Measured with galaxies for cubits
And call each altar-star
By one different of Your myriad
    names.

Recently, a number of major asteroids have been given names. One of these bears the name of Isis, restoring Her to official status in the heavens of the Western world.

THE STELLAR MEDITATION — ISIS OF THE HEAVENS

Simultaneous with the Dark Goddess residing within the earth, Isis of the stars—Ast of Astra, perhaps better termed Isis of the Cosmos—touches this planet again with another burst of divine energy, from without rather than from within. As tenuous and all-encompassing as Isis of the Earth is bound, restrained, and solid, Isis of the Stars is a great fluid energy animating the spaces between the thrones of space as well as those "thrones" or "stations" themselves which are the planets, suns, and cosmic concretions of all kinds.

Isis of the Stars is the mysterious reason why quantum physics postulates that all particles once in contact with each other will forever behave as if still influenced by that long-past touch; as with atoms, so with us. She is the Cosmic Connector without restriction; ultimate communication and access without loss of individuality. Like light, Isis of the Stars teaches that it is possible to be many things and at many places at once; Her diaphanous, starlit web spreads into many other dimensions as well.

Go above the temple, then, out onto the roof, out under the night sky, to prepare for this meditation. Seek also on the astral for the full initiation of the pathways of the stars.

In seeking this initiation, study the stars with the help of a guidebook. Use binoculars or a telescope, if you have them. Go to a local planetarium. Drive to the mountains to visit an observatory or simply to view the stars away from city lights. Identify Sirius or other stars associated with Isis. Stay up all night watching the sky, particularly on a moonless eve. Choose a star and note its placement at the same time every evening. Put the constellations on your bedroom walls with glow-in-the-dark paint. Imagine yourself flying among the stars. Watch videotapes on the creation of the cosmos, travel to the stars, or related subjects. Read about astronomy and astrology. As you begin or do these things, say: "I do this to learn more of Isis of the Starry Heavens. Guide and instruct me, Goddess, as it pleases You."

Chapter Twenty-One
The Ninth Hour of Night

— ISIS AND THE WORSHIP — OF THE HANDS

THE ONE WHO CREATES. The Maker of All Things. The Fashioner of Humankind. The Producer of All Life. These are just some of the titles we know for Isis as a supreme creator-goddess, and the deep nighttime hours are perfect for creative work if sleep evades us.

Every religious path which is devotional ascribes to their own form of deity the power of primal creation, of bringing into form the planet, the race, even the universe. And humanity, to a much

greater degree than any other species, is a creative breed. We make and change our environment, sometimes for better, sometimes for worse. Our curiosity leads us to develop new things. We do not settle, as a species, to accept things the way they are. Whether in crafts and sciences or in magic, we take what the universe has presented to us and transmute it into new things.

Small wonder, then, that the holy servants of virtually every race have also been artisans, craftspeople, and scientists as well as priestesses and shamans. To create a new object is to imitate the creative forces of the gods we worship; to do it well is to make an offering to those essential forces of creation. These are prayers of the hands, a meditation that has physical as well as spiritual results. The action of creation requires a focused yet relaxed state of mind which promotes spiritual harmony.

Anything which you lovingly do or make can be designated as an offering. A fine meal, a rebuilt engine, a restored antique, a hymn of praise, even a well-played sport

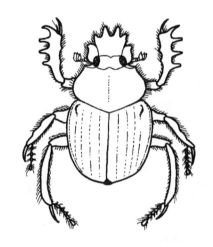

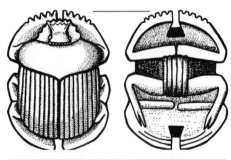

Top, *a frequently-used species of scarab beetle*, Scarabaeus sacer; below, *the top and bottom of a Middle Kingdom amulet which realistically renders this beetle.*

can be consecrated as an act of worship. Even thoroughly cleaning or repairing objects used in your rites can be an appropriate and calming offering. Restring a fraying Isian necklace; polish the silver-plated candlestick; dust the temple statuary; alphabetize the library of sacred books. Accomplishing these mundane chores can be particularly helpful if your are feeling "off your contacts" or spiritually out of touch.

The projects given here are of course designed for worshippers of the Isian tradition, but they can be adapted to many deities. If you are feeling stressed and in need of immediate benefit, choose a project which can be completed in one sitting.

Above all, when working on sacred objects, be focused, relaxed, and joyful. Many spiritual insights and accomplishments are kept from us merely by the act of striving after them. Think lightly and brightly on your concept of Isis while you work. This lightness of mind will enhance the aura of the completed project and make it more useful to you.

SACRED SCARABS

Time: 1–2 hours
Difficulty: Easy

These scarabs can be placed on the altar as decorations, carried as amulets for luck and protection, or used in divination as a set of Egyptian runestones.

The scarab beetle has been sacred in Egypt since predynastic times. It was thought of as a symbol of the solar energies, since the beetles took flight in the hottest part of the day, when the sun was strongest. These bright, metallic beetles with the unmistakable whirr of wings demanded attention.

Later, other types of beetles were also considered sacred, such as the "dung beetles" who would deposit their eggs in a ball of mud or dung and roll it along the ground. This was seen as a metaphor for the rolling of the sun across the sky each day. One of the earliest sun gods, Khepra, was pictured with a scarab beetle in place of his head.

Representations of these beetles abound in tombs and temples. Scarabs of stone, with sacred inscriptions, were placed in mummy wrappings to guard the soul in the afterlife. Pharaohs issued large inscribed scarabs to commemorate important events.

An Ancient Scarab Spell

Idries Shah, in his book *Oriental Magic*, gives the text of a scarab consecration rite. This "Rite of the Beetle" in the worship of Isis indicates ancient connections between Her worship and that of Khepera, who by one version of the genealogy of the gods would be Her great-grandfather.

Place the sculpted beetle, place it upon a paper table. Under the table there shall be a pure linen cloth. Under this place some olive wood, and set on the middle of the table a small censer wherein myrrh and kyphi shall be offered. And have at hand a small vessel of chrysolite into which ointment of lilies, or myrrh, or cinnamon, shall be put. And take the ring and place it in the ointment, having first made it clean and pure, and offer it up in the censer with kyphi and myrrh. Leave the ring for three days, then take it out, and put it in a safe place. At the celebration let there lie near at hand some pure loaves, and such fruits as are in season. Having made another offering on vine sticks, during the offering take the ring out of the ointment, and anoint thyself with the unction from it. Thou shalt anoint thyself early in the morning and turning towards the east shall pronounce the words written below. The beetle shall be carved out of a precious emerald; bore it and pass a gold wire through it, and beneath the beetle carve the holy Isis, and having thus consecrated it, use it.

The spell in question was "I am Thoth, the inventor and founder of medicine and letters; come to me, thou that art under the earth, rise up to me, greater spirit." It was further stated that only on certain days could the process take place: the 7th, 9th, 10th, 12th, 14th, 16th, 21st, 24th, and 25th days, counting from the start of the month.[1]

Scarab beetles are an easy shape to mold. In Egypt, they were often carved of stone or molded from faience, a kind of clay with a high quartz content. They are still made in Egypt in large quantities today, sometimes allegedly mixed with the feed of turkeys or other fowl to give them an appropriately "ancient" appearance when later retrieved after the birds have digested them.

Instructions

For our purpose, any type of modeling clay which will dry hard or can be baked is ideal. Bread dough is also very suitable for this project. The Egyptians were very aware of the sacred qualities of bread, and

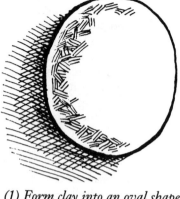

(1) Form clay into an oval shape.

(2) Gently press to flatten bottom.

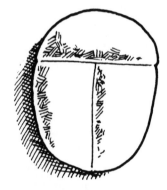

(3) Inscribe back of scarab with a "T".

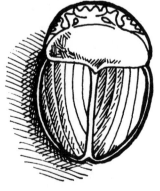

(4) If you wish, add more detail.

they frequently made images of the resurrection-oriented gods, such as Osiris or Sokar, out of bread dough mixed with sand and incense, along with other ingredients.

One of the most successful clays I have found for molding amulets is easily available, pleasant to work with and something many of us already have experience using. In addition, a very decent faience-like color can be created with little effort. This magical, bread-based substance is Play-doh™. By mixing together roughly equal amounts of the blue and white colors with a small amount of yellow, a good turquoise faience color can be achieved. If you like, a small quantity of beach sand or powdered quartz can be added, or a little salt. This gives a slightly rougher texture and the crystal substances allow the object to take and hold a "charge" better than mere dough or clay alone. Fimo™ and Sculpey™ also work well, but their textures are smoother and less like the ancient clay.

To form a scarab, take a piece of dough or clay about the size of your thumb tip. (1) Form this into an oval or egg shape and gently press it down onto a flat surface, so that the bottom is flattened (2) but the top of the scarab is still rounded. Using a pen, knife, or toothpick, inscribe the back of the scarab with a "T" (3) to indicate the separation between the head and the wingcase. You can add more detail (4) or leave it highly stylized. Turning it over, you can inscribe the flat bottom with a symbol or hieroglyphs. For some of these, please see the section entitled "Divination with Scarabs" in Chapter Twenty-Two, "The Oracles of Isis." You can form each scarab individually or allow the first one to dry, press it into moist clay, lift it out, and then harden the resulting mold. Press clay into the mold, then lift each scarab out and decorate it individually. You may find it helpful to powder the mold to help the scarab release.

Feel free to be very creative. Scarabs were also occasionally made retaining the basic scarab body shape but adding heads of different animals and even human faces.

PALM DIVINATION STRIPS

Time: 1 hour

Difficulty: Easy if using parchment paper; moderate if cutting a palm frond.

To divine with these strips, gather up the strips, cast them onto the ground in front of you, and then remove them pair by pair. The single strip remaining holds the answer to your question.

Palm Frond Method

Take a palm frond, either from a fan palm or a feather-like palm. Using scissors, slice twenty-nine equal strips from the frond. Trim off any sharp ends. Using a felt-tip black marker, inscribe on each piece a hieroglyph or symbol of a deity. Use any of the symbols listed in Chapter Twenty-Two, "The Oracles of Isis."

Parchment Paper Method

Take a sheet of parchment or other thick paper and cut out a single long, narrow triangle to represent a palm frond rib. Use this as a template to cut out twenty-eight more pieces. Mark each piece with a symbol.

SISTRUMS

Time: 8 hours or more
Difficulty: Hard

The sistrum was a widely recognized attribute of Isis, and was used in many of Her temple rites. Ancient authors described several kinds, one with a sweet, tinkling sound and the other providing a harsh, clattering noise. Sistrums were also used in rites to other gods and goddesses, particularly Bastet and Hathor.

Two methods for making a sistrum are given here. The first requires access to metalworking tools; the second can be formed more easily.

Making my first sistrum was truly an initiatory experience. I had never worked with metal before, but the home I was sharing at the time offered metalworking tools and a patient instructor.[2] The creation of the sistrum forced me to confront and overcome my own fears about using tools such as bandsaws and power drills.

Tools Needed

metal drill
bandsaw
hammer
power sander
metal chisel
protective eyewear (essential!)

Materials Needed

thin sheet copper or a 20" length of ¾"-wide copper stripping

24" of ⅛"-diameter copper wire

13 (1") copper disks, brass washers, or very small, inexpensive belly dancer finger cymbals

6" length of 1½"-diameter wooden doweling, polished or smoothed citrus wood, or driftwood for the handle

large flat headed nail or screw

pencil

(optional) woodcarving tools and/or paints for decorating the handle

If this is your first metalworking project, please keep in mind the following guidelines:

1. Always wear protective eyegear. Metal particles fly everywhere. Also be careful not to touch your eyes if you may have metal particles on your hands. If a piece of metal falls in your eye, get medical attention immediately.

2. Tie back long hair and remove all jewelry.

3. When using the drill or bandsaw, always be aware where your fingers are. Keep them away from the drill bits and saw edge.

4. Measure everything twice.

Instructions

If you are using sheet copper, mark off a strip 20" long and ¾" wide. Use the bandsaw to cut the strip from the sheet. Sand or hammer off the rough edges until they are smooth. Using the hammer when necessary, shape the copper strip into a tented shape as shown.

Make sure the sides of this form are even. On the outside of the copper strip, mark three holes on each side. This is where the bars of the sistrum will be inserted, so it is important to leave enough room between the bars for the disks to hang freely without touching the disks on the other bars. If you have very small disks or washers, you may want to add another row to the sistrum. Both three- and four-bar sistrums were common.

Drill the holes you have marked. Fold over the ends of the sistrum where it will join the handle. Mark your attachment point or points and drill holes at those spots also.

If you are unable to find copper disks or brass washers, you can create disks by using the bandsaw to cut small squares of metal and then sand off the corners using the power sander. This is how I did it, but it is time-consuming and surprisingly difficult. Preformed disks which only need to have a hole drilled in the center are much easier to use. Washers, whether brass or other metal, are also fine, but their tone is not as sweet as copper.

Measuring across your sistrum frame, cut your copper wire, allowing an inch extra on each side of the sistrum. This is where you will bend the wire to hold it in the sistrum framework. Bend or pound the last inch of wire so that it holds a right angle. Thread this through the hole. This can be cut using the bandsaw or a metal chisel.

At this point, your basic metal work is done. If you want to carve the sistrum handle, do so now. If you prefer to paint it, you can complete assembling the sistrum first.

Attach the framework to the handle using either a nail or screw. A screw is preferable, since the sistrum will be enthusiastically shaken during rituals. If you do use a nail, start the hole in the handle, add a little white glue, and then

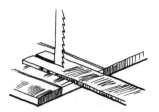

(1) Use bandsaw to cut strip.

(2) Bend strip into tented shape. Let flat bottom ends overlap so that a hole can be drilled for a nail to attach framework to the handle.

(3) Mark holes for sistrum wires. Drill holes.

(4) Attach framework to handle before inserting wires.

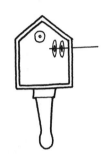

(5) Insert wire, add disks, thread wire though opposite hole.

(6) Bend wires at right angles.

(7) Other possible shapes.

Illustrated steps for making your own sistrum.

finish nailing the framework to the handle.

Now thread the wires, one at a time, into the holes on one side of the framework. Add three or four of the disks, then slip the wire into the other side of the framework. Bend or pound it so the end forms a right angle with the framework. Repeat this with the other wires. Your sistrum is finished.

Traditional decorations for the sistrum include cats and images of Hathor. Feel free to give the sistrum your own new interpretation. There were many types and styles in use, and these all differed in size, appearance, and sound. Some sistrums had no disks and produced sound merely by the action of the wires slamming against the metal framework. These diskless sistrum wires were carefully made so that each wire would sound a different musical note, emitting a balanced chord of sound when shaken. Several miniature sistrums have been found in Isian tombs in England.

For my sistrum I departed from tradition by using a piece of rough driftwood in the shape of a cat's head for the handle. Another wonderful sistrum employed by a woman shaman used a forked deer antler for the framework and handle. Two modern sistrums in my collection come from Kenya and are simply constructed of a forked branch strung with wires and holding dozens of disks cut out from tin cans. Although roughly crafted, the sound and action is cleansing and exhilarating.

A TRADITIONAL ISIAN FESTIVAL DECORATION

> Time: 1 hour (not including time required to find a palm tree and cut a frond) or as long as you want to spend on decorating or making decorations for it. If using a woven fan, 30 minutes to gild it and let it dry.
>
> Difficulty: Moderate

Isis, in her role as a supreme mother goddess, brought forth a Sun-child, Horus, at the time of the winter solstice. His birth was synchronous with the return of lengthening days, the end of the decline of the hours of light. What better symbol of hope and the eventual arrival of Spring than the birth of a child? Many other faiths placed the birth of a new infant-god at this time of year, including Christianity, Mithraism, and many others in the ancient world.

Throughout history there has been much sharing between religions which celebrate similar holidays at similar times. For this reason we now find "Hanukkah Trees" in some Jewish households, derived from the tradition of "Christmas Trees," which were in turn derived from the tree-decorating rites of many Pagan faiths.

In the faith of Isis and Osiris, followers were forbidden to cut down a living tree, and the ceremony of the "Raising Up of the Djed Pillar" may have originally been tied to tree worship and the decorating of the sacred object. For those who might enjoy adding a symbol with Isian associations to the Solstice-time observances, here are instructions for creating an Isian Solstice Frond using a fan palm branch, gold paint, and Egyptian-inspired ornaments.

The ancient worship of Isis included many public processions in which sacred objects were carried to be displayed to the masses which lined the pathway of the procession through the city, much like modern parades or Mardi Gras celebrations. Gilded palms and winnowing fans were sometimes carried to symbolize rich harvests or, possibly, the life-giving breath of Isis. Isis was said to have gathered together the dismembered parts of Osiris onto a winnowing fan. Palm trees were sacred to Isis and Osiris and frequently grew in the temple gardens, providing shade and fruit. The multirayed form of the fan palm is also symbolic of the rays of the sun, appropriate here at the time of its return.

Instructions

First, find a fan palm frond or, if this is not available, a large decorative winnowing fan woven of fiber. These are frequently available in basket or international shops, and are usually flat and shaped like a leaf. If you do use a fan palm frond, try to use one which has fallen naturally or has dried on the tree. By all means avoid harming the tree from which it was taken. If you must cut a living frond, repay the tree with a gift of fertilizer and water.

Once you have selected the frond, use scissors to trim off any flimsy portions. Be careful doing this, as some fan palm fronds have unexpectedly sharp serrations along their edges. Trim it down far enough so that when it is held upright, the frond tips do not flop down.

Cut the stem down to about an 18" section. In the case of very woody palm stems, you may need to use a small saw. (Note: Depending on the size of your palm frond these measurements may differ. Also, if you are using a ready-made winnowing fan, you should be able to simply gild it and hang it on the wall with a nail.) Depending on the overall flatness of the fan palm, there are two methods for preparing the frond to be displayed. If you have a straight, flat frond, simply drill a hole in the middle of the fan portion about 8" in from where the individual "fingers" separate. Paint the frond using gold or silver. Then attach it to a wall, using a nail through the hole.

Another method for displaying your frond is to take a wide-mouthed vase filled with sand or glass pebbles and insert the palm frond stem into it. The Solstice Palm can then be set against a wall if the frond is too heavy to stand alone using this method.

Once you have gilded the palm, you can paint additional designs on it or create separate ornaments to hang on it. Ordinary Christmas ornament hangers can usually be used to pierce the frond to attach decorations. Small glass baubles are pretty, or you can create ornaments incorporating Egyptian symbols. Suitable signs would be the Isis knot, the ankh, and the Shen, symbol of eternity. These can be painted onto store-bought ornaments or made of almost any material. Metallic chenille wands can be bent into almost any shape. Other symbols include the crescent and disk headdress of Isis, the cornucopia which She often carried in classical times, and the lotus. Garlands of small glass beads can also be added, and beads strung on wire can be formed into the symbols mentioned above.

As you make your Solstice Palm, remember that in the temples of ancient Egypt the higher clergy were almost invariably accomplished, skilled artisans. Whether their talents were directed toward the creation of sacred statuary, the building of temples and shrines, or the compounding of the oils and incenses used in the temples, work of the hands was regarded as a sacred act of worship, emulating the primal creative forces exerted by the gods and goddesses themselves. Any act of creation is an act of worship, even more so when the effort is directed at creating an object to be used in festivals of the god or goddess with whom you are allied.

Use of the sacred frond which you create does not need to be restricted to the festival of the Winter Solstice. It is also intended

for display at the time of the *Isidis Navigium* on March 5, when the launching of the Ship of Isis opened the season of navigation in Greco-Roman times. Due to the palm's rayed star shape, a silver one would be appropriate to display at the time of the rising of the star Sothis (also known as Sirius), which has long been sacred to Isis worshippers as the "Home of the Soul of Isis." This rising time, when the star is again visible in the sky after long absence, will vary by latitude, but it occurs in modern-day Egypt around August 1. A call to a local observatory can tell you when Sothis is visible in your area.

Whenever or however you display this symbol of Isian faith, remember that the faith of Isis was renowned for its religious tolerance and support of divergent viewpoints. This frond can, from the Isian viewpoint, share space with the symbols of any other faith and need not supplant any.

☽ · ⊕ · ☾

Chapter Twenty-Two
The Tenth Hour of Night

THE ORACLES OF ISIS

ISIS, AS A DIVINITY considered to be "beyond Fate" and free to change the maledictions of the stars if She pleases, has a unique relationship to the art of divination. To "divine" is to speak of what has been set in motion by the "divine" beings, the gods and goddesses themselves. In the ancient world, the predictions of the soothsayers were usually taken to be true and permanent, beyond modification by gods or humans.

But with Isis, no fate is considered to be fixed if She wills otherwise. Divination in this light becomes a convenient way of determining patterns and possibilities and assessing physical and spiritual conditions. Tarot readings and other fortunetelling methods are subjective guides to be used when needed, but their predictions are not final. They can be a dynamic method of communicating with the Goddess, and are also excellent tools for meditation and inspiration.

219

Many temples of Isis functioned as oracle centers, and virtually every temple provided some method of divination. At Socnaipou Nesos, a major Isian temple site, questioners would write down two possible outcomes to a problem, or two answers to a question, and the "correct" one would be returned to the worshipper after the appropriate priestly conjurations. Another method used at one temple of Isis used twenty-nine leaves from a male palm tree frond, each inscribed with the name of a deity. The palm strips were mixed together and set aside two by two. The remaining palm leaf would be interpreted as the answer to the question, positive or negative depending on the deity inscribed on the leaf. A method for creating a set of these is included in Chapter Twenty-One, "Isis and the Worship of the Hands."

Divination has always been a holy activity, ideally entrusted to the trained members of a temple or others genuinely in touch with the spiritual forces of the universe. In ancient times, as now, secular fortunetellers were suspect and frequently the subjects of restrictive legislation. Although some of this was simply political oppression of those who did not support the current government or religious hierarchy, in other cases this was a genuine attempt to protect people's lives, by preventing their exploitation by the unscrupulous.

Correctly employed, divination is a diagnostic tool which can reveal and examine trends in a person's life, and, if necessary, help amend negative patterns. Like any tool, it is dependent upon the skill, experience, and dedication of the person employing it, the participant's state of mind at the time of the reading, and the strength of the spiritual contact made.

Very few events are irrevocably predetermined, but the likely reactions of a person, or even of a state or nation, are often so rigidly ingrained that long strings of events can be predicted with great accuracy without any special psychic insight.

There are thousands of methods of divination which have been used in many places and circumstances. Frequently these divinatory methods accumulate vast bodies of ritual necessary for their use and practice. Like anything else, the methods and accompanying rituals are tools, ways of instilling an insightful psychic trance state in the diviner. Many trained psychics need to do nothing more than turn their attention inward to obtain the information needed.

Several modern methods have antecedents in the Egyptian temples. One school of thought believes that modern tarot cards can be traced back to hallways lined with painted images which were said to be found in some temples of Serapis, the aspect of Osiris who was paired with Isis in Greco-Roman times. In these hallways, twenty-two images faced each other in pairs, suggesting to some modern researchers the twenty-two cards of the major arcana. Intriguingly there is also a French tradition, mentioned by Voltaire, that the Gypsies were actually Isian priests and priestesses who fled from persecution, carrying with them their sacred teachings in the form of pictures which evolved into the tarot.

Yet another authority believes that the original tarot designs were derived from the Bembine Tablet, or *Mensa Isiaca*. This beautifully crafted "tablet" or "table" was apparently the top of a Roman altar to Isis. On it are figured literally dozens of mystical symbols and figures. Certainly images similar to some tarot cards can be found on the altartop, but it is impossible to say if the *Mensa Isiaca* inspired the tarot cards we use today.

Whatever the true origin of divination by tarot cards, card reading is a valid method of divination and can be used in conjunction with the worship and service of Isis. Here is a short and very basic listing of some of the Isian symbolism found in many tarot decks. As with almost any mystical language, the meanings are open to interpretation, change, and new insight in keeping with your own experience. In general, when reading for insight into intensely spiritual matters, it can be beneficial to read at random, shuffling the deck until it feels right and then drawing as many cards as seem appropriate. However, in times of emotional or spiritual distress, using a pattern can be comforting (and, perhaps, more accurate) since it imposes a structure on the reading. You may also prefer to shuffle loosely and read only the cards that jump from the pack.

Occasionally you may receive the answer to the question that you *should* have asked, rather than the one you actually asked. You may also receive a reading for someone else close to you. If a reading seems far removed from what your own true (not wishful) instincts tell you, it may not be your reading.

For those who prefer to use a fixed reading pattern, the Egyptian-inspired "Lotus Pattern" is presented on page 230. This a basic reading pattern which is helpful in seeing general trends and issues, and is a good "first reading" for yourself and others.

If you do choose to read for others, never be afraid to curtail a reading if you discover that an unrelated question is being addressed. If you have recently read for yourself, and find that many of the same cards are coming up in a reading for someone else, consider that your original reading may be continuing. You may wish to try "clearing" the cards by sorting them out into the Major Arcana and the individual suits, consciously erasing any remaining influences over the cards. Then try the reading again.

Above all, remember that divination is sacred. It is a ritual and should never be done frivolously or "just for fun." At the very least, divinatory rites should be preceded by a thorough washing of the hands and a brief prayer or invocation to the Goddess.

SOME ISIAN INTERPRETATIONS OF THE MAJOR ARCANA

For the purposes of this brief introduction to possible Isian interpretations of the tarot, I have referred to the classic Waite deck, from which many modern packs have been derived. While some tarot readers have substantial disagreements with Waite's depictions of the forces associated with each card, the designs do perpetuate the spirit of decks centuries older. The artist-executrix of the deck, Pamela

Coleman Smith, has provided simple renderings which do not intrude on the interpretations as harshly as some modern packs do.

Virtually any deck can be used to read using the following Isian interpretations.

0 – The Fool

This card, showing an innocent soul walking cheerfully at the edge of a high cliff, accompanied or warned by his faithful dog, can indicate the astral journeys guided by the godform Anubis, the jackal-/dog-headed psychopomp or guide of the soul.

Playing the fool, or "making an ass out of oneself" can also evoke images from Apuleius' Isian novel, where the hero, turned by dark magic into an ass, finds salvation and rebirth by the grace of Isis.

The Fool can also represent the newly cleansed and initiated soul who has been through the ordeals of the sacred mysteries and is open to follow without fear whatever path Isis may delineate for Her new worshipper, confident in the guidance that She will provide.

1 – The Magician

Behind a square altar that would have fit perfectly into many temples of Isis, an enrobed and empowered priest prepares for a rite. His wisdom is dynamic but not yet solidified. He may indicate someone who will act as an initiator into further mysteries.

The Magician represents the functional, rather than the bureaucratic, priesthood of the temples. His work, though ritualized, is still not far removed from the ecstatic conjurings of a tribal shaman.

This card can also represent an active or potential Priest of Isis. In conjunction with the High Priestess or another of the Goddess cards, he can indicate a magical working or relationship.

2 – The High Priestess

In some early decks this card is named Isis, and in most packs the symbology of the woman figure is clearly Isian. The general iconography is that of a seated woman between two pillars, a cloth with cut pomegranates hung behind her. This may veil an unseen statue or conceal an empty space, both of which were employed in the ancient temples to symbolize the Goddess. An Isian crescent and disk headdress crowns the priestess, and a crescent moon is washed by the watery folds of her robe. A half-hidden scroll speaks of further mysteries to be revealed.

This card can indicate the Goddess or one of Her priestesses, and is always a good indication that there is sacred work involved in the matter being divined, although this may not be obvious. This card may also act as an "alarm clock." If you have felt out of touch with the Goddess, this card may appear to call you back to your time of "temple service," and is usually followed by a variety of small mystical tasks which come into your hands to be accomplished.

3 – The Empress

This card has strong associations with Isis as Goddess of the Grain, through the garden of wheat growing at the feet of the enthroned Empress. Since the throne was the very emblem of Isis' name in the original Egyptian hieroglyphics, any throned figure can be interpreted to be drawing on or supported by the essence of Isis. The heart-shaped shield joins the image of the Empress with interpretations of Isis as supremely loving wife and mother.

The Empress can represent a different type or period of priestesship, one which works through the home environment rather than that of the temple. Dion Fortune called this "the path of the hearth-fire." This path contains its own vital and dynamic magics, and the relaxed figure of the Empress contains a vast reserve of potent and fertile power.

4 – The Emperor

The Emperor, grave and determined, can represent Osiris or Sarapis in his role as King. The Empress and Emperor cards form an exoteric, worldly couple in counterpoint to the esoteric, mystical couple formed by the Magician and High Priestess. In one sense, one pair abides or functions within the temple and the other pair works out within the world.

The presence of the Emperor card in a reading can indicate an Osirian influence on the matters at hand, particularly as it relates to divine authority or "The Will of the God."

5 – The Hierophant

Although seemingly a strongly Christian card, the Hierophant originates in Isian symbolism. The High Pontiff's headdress for both religions derives from the double crown of ancient Egypt. The Hierophant's association with the temple of the High Priestess is indicated by his similar placement between two pillars. Other minor priests attend at his feet, and their tonsured crowns are similar to the shaven-headed priests of Isis. His

face, compared with that of the High Priestess, shows that he may be a brother to her, which recalls the sacred marriage between the siblings Isis and Osiris.

Ritualism itself is important to the Hierophant; the bureaucracy of the temple is in his hands, and may keep him from the ecstatic mystical heights attainable by the Magician—or he may have had his fill of them, and retired in order to guide the temple in more mundane ways. His presence in a reading may indicate either a lack or an overabundance of attention to ritual detail. He may also represent a senior priest or mystical teacher, though generally a very demanding one.

6 – The Lovers

Blessed by a fiery winged angel, the primal lovers look perplexed, a feeling often shared by their modern counterparts. Whether love and sex are sacred, secular, or sinful is a question which has no single answer. The worship of Isis can entail periods of chastity and abstinence as well as periods of romantic and passionate sexuality. Neither is automatically required or condemned by Her.

This card can be a bellwether of an intense mystical relationship integrating the independent male and female forces. The lovers represented may not be Adam and Eve, but instead Isis and Osiris in human and undeified form. Some older decks show a second female, Lilith, offering an extra-union temptation and echoing the actions of

Nepthys, who seduced Osiris illicitly but out of genuine love for him.

7 – The Chariot

Although most early decks use horses instead of sphinxes to draw the cart, ancient coins showing Isis sometimes depicted Her riding in a chariot drawn by sphinxes, an image which may have been familiar to Waite and Smith when they designed the deck. Crescent moons and stars bring Isis to mind, although the figure in this chariot is male. Carriages much like the chariot here were used in sacred processions for Isis, and were the forerunners of the floats used in modern parades.

The presence of this card usually indicates a time when opposing forces are successfully drawn together to move forward in a dynamic harmony. Because of its association with the festival processions, it can also act as a reminder of a necessary celebration to be observed.

8 – Strength

The conquering aspect of Isis was represented by an image of the Goddess with a chained hippopotamus, representing the vanquished and controlled Set. Although Isis had the power and right to slay Set because of his murder of Osiris and

his attacks on Horus, She chose to show him mercy instead. A similar concept is shown here by the infinity-crowned Goddess shutting the jaws of the lion.

This is a very positive card, reminding us that the strength of Isis is available to draw upon when we need it, and that this same strength can be cultivated in our own natures. Its presence in a reading may also indicate a demanding period ahead which will require peaceful but firm actions.

9 – The Hermit

Does he hold his light high for others to follow, or is he searching for someone or something? The lone figure seeking in the darkness has strong associations with the dark-cloaked Isis in Search, wandering Egypt, searching for the scattered parts of Osiris so that She may "re-member" him and assure his immortality.

Many times priests and priestesses may find it necessary to retreat within to recharge their spiritual batteries and gain new insight into themselves and their faiths. This card can suggest that silent, solitary seeking is necessary to restore internal balances and gain new perspectives on difficult subjects.

10 – The Wheel of Fortune

This is the card of Fate, of situations beyond normal control, either in everyday or mystical life. Fate can sometimes be seen as the manifestation of the Dark Isis, who deals with human concerns very impersonally. However, Isis in Her brighter aspects is known as The Goddess Above Fate, who can rewrite the stars' forebodings if it suits Her to do so. Statues were often dedicated to Isis-Fortuna or Isis-Tyche. Part of Isis' wide appeal in the Greco-Roman world was due to Her renown as the only Goddess who could conquer Fate.

Isis also rules over cycles and tides, both symbolized here by the turning of the Wheel. In Waite's version, a type of Set-beast is approaching the top of the Wheel for his moment. He, like everyone, will both rise and fall repeatedly. But the wheel is not merely rotating over and over again; it is also moving forward. We are not going in repeated circles, but always into new spirals. These may bear a resemblance to previous rotations, but we are actually inscribing an entirely new part of the pattern.

11 – Justice

Isis often wears the ostrich plume of Ma'at, the personification of the principle of justice who was worshipped as a goddess in Egypt. To be *ma-a kheru,* or "true of voice," and so at one with Ma'at, was the aim of every Egyptian. To be "justified" meant that the afterlife would be a pleasant, harmonious existence, whereas those whose actions in life were "unjustified" would suffer great torments.

Justice is rarely applied blindly by Isis, though She can be a vengeful Goddess if deliberately or frivolously betrayed. As noted above, though well within Her legal rights to do so, Isis refrained from killing Her brother Set even in the midst of a battle between Set and Her son Horus. (Horus, more hotheaded than either of his parents, is said by some texts to have sliced off Isis' head in anger at Her act of mercy to his bitter enemy. Thoth restored Her head.)

The sacred nature of true justice is shown by the figure sitting between the pillars of the temple also depicted in the cards of the High Priestess and the Hierophant. The headdress, seen as a city wall, was worn by many goddesses in ancient times, including Isis in some later representations.

The presence of this card indicates a need for balanced thinking and actions. It can indicate there is karma to be paid off, either from a past existence or, much more commonly, from the present one.

12 – The Hanged Man

This card symbolizes the myths of the dying and resurrected gods and goddesses, particularly those who have been hung, such as Odin, Inanna, Jesus, and Osiris, who was entombed inside a tree after his death at the hands of Set. Generally it is a card of submission to other forces, responsibilities, or commitments, and can indicate that action for the general good rather than for personal gratification is necessary. Self-sacrifice and the enlightenment which can follow on submission to the divine is the key theme of this card.

The tree on which the figure hangs may also represent the Djed pillar of Osiris, and brings to mind the tree-pillar in which the coffin of Osiris was entombed at Byblos.

13 – Death

The Death card is a disturbing one no matter how often it is encountered. Although any experienced reader knows that this card rarely, if ever, predicts true physical death, the harsh medieval imagery of the armored skeleton is difficult to ignore or explain away cheerfully.

And this is as it should be. The Death card signals profound change, with an existence that will be different once it has passed. It is always a card that demands a decision, either to accept or fight against the changes to come. It is also a card of initiation, long-sought or unexpected, and of the "Death" that must be transcended to know the holy mysteries.

Isis is an underworld goddess as well as an earthly and cosmic one. Her presence was important in many of the rites conducted for the dead in ancient Egypt, and She Herself was said to have invented embalming, with the help of Anubis, the god who bore a dog- or jackal-headed mask and was said to be the illegitimate offspring of Osiris and Nepthys.

14 – Temperance

A winged angel pours water between two vessels in an action which recalls the purification rites depicted in the Egyptian temples. In these images, two gods, usually Anubis and Horus or Thoth, pour two streams of water in a double arc around the subject of the purification, usually the deceased or the pharaoh.

The image of angels as winged beings may have been derived, at least in part, from the many images of Isis as a winged goddess, folding Her wings protectively around statues of the pharaoh, or using Her wings to waft life-giving air to revive Osiris. One Isian priestess' religiously-conservative family interprets her Isian religious jewelry as representing guardian angels, though they are aware that she

ascribes a different meaning to them. This peaceful compromise probably pleases Goddess and angels alike.

The Temperance card is also related to the concepts of male-female polarity and of working with opposite forces. It's important to remember that the ultimate goal of Temperance is not stagnant balance but a dynamic alternation of forces, controlled but not destroyed.

15 – The Devil

The personification of evil which enables the dark sides of all deities to be safely separated and suppressed by human worshippers always presents difficulties, no matter what the faith. Although it is tempting to assign an instant correspondence between the Devil, especially under the name of Satan, and Set, Osiris' "evil" brother, it is not always accurate. Set's role as the Opposer was a late one, and the earliest texts we have referring to the death of Osiris seem to indicate that his death was by accidental drowning, not homicide.

There were definite political disputes between followers of the faith of Set and followers of the faith of Horus, but while sometimes bloody, these may not be considered spiritual battles in any real sense. As a sign of unity in later times, a single god image was occasionally provided with two heads, one of Set and one of Horus, and some royal names reflect the same acceptance of a dual-natured god.

This card carries with it a warning of contention and quarrels, and of problems caused by our own willing bondage to forces that are not beneficial to us. It can also be a caution against arrogance and pride.

16 – The Tower

This is a card of "lightning from Heaven," sudden changes shattering old ways. It is tempting to associate this card with Alexandria, a sacred city of Isis, and especially with the Pharos lighthouse. The Pharos lighthouse was the greatest of its kind, with a blazing beacon that stood so tall critics feared that captains would mistake its beacon light for a star and be guided off course rather than led to the safety of the Alexandrian harbor. One of the Seven Wonders of the ancient world, the Pharos stood for nearly eight hundred years before falling into ruin, partially toppled by an earthquake.

Many old ideas were certainly thrown down and smashed to pieces by the exhaustive research of the scientists and physicians who labored, under the patronage of Serapis and Isis, at the Museum and Medical School of Alexandria. The Library, part of which was housed in the Serapeum, boasted hundreds of thousands of volumes and survived more than one fire. Scholars still debate whether the Library was finally destroyed with the rise of beliefs hostile to pagan viewpoints, or if the previous volumes were sold or scattered through the Arabic world as the library fell into neglect.

17 – The Star

An eight-pointed star, sacred symbol of Ishtar, has risen behind a naked goddess flooding the land, pouring water into water. The star may be Sothis, also known as Sirius; the figure may be Isis, the great fructifier and goddess who causes the flooding of the Nile when Sirius rises again after its long absence. From a tree behind her a bird gazes at us, perhaps Tahuti, god of wisdom, in his guise of an ibis; or perhaps it is the Bennu, the phoenix-like symbol of the resurrection of Osiris.

The Star shines brightly and is a good omen for success in a venture. The abundant moisture points toward opportunities for growth now present: wait too long and the flood will have passed, the tide will have turned. But the very abundance of the life-giving moisture reminds us of the need to store and channel these fertile forces so that they can be effectively used long after the flood has ceased.

18 – The Moon

The lunar associations of Isis are vast. Simply gazing at the moon will teach many of these concepts without recourse to books.

Isis in many senses *is* the moon, particularly in Her role as mistress of tides and dreams. The Gates of the Land of Moon are sometimes encountered in visions by seekers after Isis.

The Moon card signals mystical work is at hand. Because lunar influences can be amorphous and ephemeral, it is easy to be deceived about one's own needs and motivations, and even more so about those of others. At the same time, there is a brilliantly enlightening quality about full cold moonlight, which can be invigorating and inspiring.

Since the moon is visible to us by the interaction of its reflective surface and the reflected light of the sun, this card can also indicate any situation which requires duality to function. This can refer to the delicate interplay between lovers, co-workers, or family members. Its presence can also indicate high emotional tides which may need to be carefully managed to avoid discord.

19 – The Sun

The Waite deck Sun card depicts a golden sun-child on a white horse. The presence of the horse may be an Egyptian-style word pun on the name of the solar child, Horus. As a powerful Sun goddess, Isis at Her most radiant is symbolized by this card.

In a reading, the warm light of the Sun is a positive influence on almost any situation and as an "outcome" card usually indicates a very positive conclusion to any

matter. In its simplest sense, the Sun is a card of energy and positive power.

If you are unfamiliar with the mystic dynamism of the solar influences, you may want to practice the daily Noontime Rite to Isis to better understand this variety of spiritual potential.

20 – Judgement

Once more an angel appears (see "14–Temperance"), this time to summon the dead from their graves. The keynote of Judgement is accountability. The Egyptians expected to encounter in the afterlife a kind of trial where they would be required to recite the so-called "Negative Confession," asserting that during life they had not stolen, mistreated widows or orphans, and so on. There were a variety of different "Negative Confessions," which usually numbered forty-two. Apparently the Egyptians, ever a pragmatic people, were uncertain of their purity after death and also relied on a spell to keep their own hearts from telling of their transgressions during the judgement!

Taken at face value, this card may token that good judgement will be essential to resolving a situation. It can also indicate that a situation will arise where the participants will be judged or called to defend past actions, associations, or beliefs.

Chapter
Twenty-
Two

*The
Oracles of
Isis*

229

THE WORLD.

21 – The World

Isis dances to keep the world in motion. This is a jubilant card of celebration. Although still slightly veiled, reminding us that Isis always has greater secrets to reveal, the naked goddess is joyful. This is a card of the Hilaria, the Finding of Osiris and the reunion between God and Goddess.

The World is an excellent card to receive as an outcome token, as it indicates that the questioner will literally "have the world in their hands." The circlet surrounding the Goddess is a reminder of the Wheel of Fortune, here turning in the most positive way for all.

Isis in the Minor Arcana

Isis is present in many places in the Minor Arcana. As a Queen, she can be identified with the Queens, particularly of Cups, and provides the throne for all the Kings.

The Knights and Pages can be considered to represent various aspects of Her son Horus and the resurrected or living Osiris. In particular, the Knight and Page of Wands appear against an Egyptian background of pyramid-like hills.

The undiluted forces of the Aces recall Isis' power as Lady of the Elements.

Pentacles: The five-pointed star was sacred to Isis, and formed an element of Her name as Isis-Sothis. Circled, it formed the ancient Egyptian symbol for the Duat, or Underworld. Here the suit of Penta-cles is identified with the Earth.

The Nine of Pentacles is a strong Goddess card complete with Isian falcon.

Swords: The Two of Swords may be the High Priestess outside the temple, maintaining the delicate and dangerous balance of the cosmos.

Osiris can be seen, waiting for resurrection, in the figure of the knight on the sarcophagus in the Four of Swords.

The Eight of Swords may recall the betrayal of Osiris by Set and the many cuts which dismembered him, and the Nine of Swords can refer to the imprisoned Isis after the death of Osiris.

Cups: The Two of Cups, with its snake-entwined caduceus between its mated, dedicated pair of lovers, hints at the sacred magic of love and all enlightened or divine unions, such as that of Isis and Osiris.

The Seven of Cups offers many choices, but the only illuminated choice is to select the Veiled Goddess, Isis, rising from the central cup.

Wands: As a symbol of green growing things, Wands relate to Isis as a goddess of fertility, growth, and increase. Isis often carries wands, either the lotus-wand of beauty or the Set-headed scepter of domination. The Ace of Wands can symbolize the resurrection of Osiris, the "Green God."

THE LOTUS READING

A popular mystical metaphor compares a true initiate to a lotus. The lotus has its roots in the mud, nourished by decaying matter in the darkness. But it sprouts blindly.

Filled with faith in a light it can only dimly perceive, it sends up a green stalk, travelling through the dark waters until it finally breaks through the surface, climbing into the light and air. Its leaves may float on the water, between the worlds of light and dark, wet and dry, nourishing a bud that will soon burst into bloom like a small vivid sun, fragrance permeating the air around it.

Because of this association between the lotus and initiation, this tarot layout uses a lotus motif. This pattern is very good for initiatory or mystical readings.

Shuffle the cards thoroughly. Lay them out one at a time, face up, starting with a single card as the "root" of the lotus. This card represents the basic influences on the present. Often, it is a card of past events, either from the recent past, childhood, or past lives.

The next card, which begins the lotus' "stem," shows more of the present, particularly your own place in it. Sometimes this position may be covered by the card of a person who is close to you or otherwise exerts a strong influence over your life.

The third card reflects your present environment. This can mean your workplace, your home, or your internal mental environment.

The fourth card, the last on the stem, shows the beginning of the culmination of these influences. This will be the situation just starting to unfold if no action is taken to change it.

Next, lay out three cards at the top of the "stem," setting down the middle card of the triad first. This forms the bottom of the lotus and will usually represent two opposite (but not necessarily opposing) forces

at play in the near future. The center card is the "key card," and represents the core of the near future, which the adjacent cards modify. For example, if the key card was the High Priestess, you could anticipate many opportunities for mystical work in the near future. If one of the adjacent cards were the Moon, this would strengthen the key card because the Moon and the High Priestess have a natural affinity; you might expect a period of increased psychism as well. However, if one of these cards was the Five of Wands, a card of quarrels, you might anticipate that focusing on your mystical work

Lotus pattern for tarot card reading.

could cause problems with those you live or work near.

The next row consists of five cards, and expands on the near future in more detail. Set out the cards as indicated in the diagram, starting with the center card. Again, the most crucial card is the middle one, with the outside cards modifying the key card's influence and each other.

The final row consists of four cards, representing two possible solutions to or progressions of the present reading. Read the left-hand pair as one outcome, and the right-hand pair as another.

After laying out the entire Lotus Reading, you may find that you would like further clarification of a particular card or sequence. If so, you can add one or more "Lotus Buds" to your reading. Shuffle the remaining cards again and lay out three of them near the area that needs further information. Be cautious, however, not to over-read. The insights you seek may already be in the cards you have previously selected; you may simply need to meditate on their possible meanings after the reading is over. Major readings can be written down and the cards laid out again later for further study.

EGYPTIAN RUNESTONES

One night I had a dream of an old temple. With only minor changes for the sake of narrative, here is what I dreamed. Perhaps memory or just wild fancy, divination by a net full of scarabs to me rings true; possibly it will for you as well.

☽·◈·☾

Just beyond the dark shadows of palm trees, desert sands gleamed below a full moon. It was early evening and the temple was crowded. A cool breeze rose from the Nile. Music was playing and the young men and women who studied at the temple were enjoying a rare night of cautious freedom. Sweet wine was allowed as a special indulgence; musicians played harps, flutes, and drums.

A young priestess saw a boy she fancied, not of the temple but a foreign guest joining in the secular festival, who seemed to fancy her, too, by the way he would smile at her. But she was a priestess and might yet seek the higher degrees; marrying a foreigner who would worship strange gods and take her far away—what would that do to her and her faith? She turned away from him but glanced back under her eyelashes. He was still smiling at her, thinking her coy, his odd pale eyes bright against his tanned face.

Now one of the elder priestesses, so ancient her hair had gone to white and she refused the artifice of a wig, came forward. She was the strictest and most demanding of teachers and it was obvious what an effort it was for her to unbend in front of her charges. The young priestess shuddered. Was she imagining it, or was the high priestess glaring in her direction? She glanced again at the young man. He, too, had felt the chill of the high priestess' gaze.

The young priestess sighed. Well, that was that. No boy would have the courage to thwart the high priestess just to flirt. Once more she looked back at him, to confirm his lack of courage. He winked at her and her heart beat fast.

The elder priestess had turned her attention to other concerns. In her hand she held a finely woven net filled with dozens of small scarabs of different sizes, colors, and shapes. Some, to be sure, were ordinary scarab-beetles; others had the heads of animals or gods, and a few were human-headed.

"Gather close and sit down, everyone," she said. "Now it is time to see the future on the wings of the sacred scarab. We honor Khepera, grandfather of Isis and Osiris, caught now in this net but soon to be released. When the scarabs fall, catch one or snatch up whichever one touches you or falls nearest you, for that will be your future. Bring the scarab to me and I will tell it for you."

The high priestess began to swing the net containing the scarabs back and forth, back and forth. Finally she began to raise the net, swinging it faster and faster until it was swinging in an arc around her head. Suddenly she let go of a corner and the scarabs sprayed the room, falling everywhere with a clatter on the stone floor. The foreigner, jumping to catch a scarab, just missed and batted it over at the young priestess; it hit her shoulder and disappeared into her robe. He sprang to follow it and laid hands on her shoulders long enough to steal a kiss in the confusion; at the base of her spine, she could feel the hard lump of the lost scarab for an instant before the elder priestess was by them.

"What are you doing?" she demanded.

"His scarab …"

"… fell down her robe."

"Then stand up and let it fall!" The young priestess obeyed. The scarab slid through her clothing and plunked onto the floor. "Pick it up!" the high priestess ordered the boy. He bent, smilingly, and retrieved the scarab, holding it out to the woman.

"Where's yours?" she asked the young priestess.

"That's the only one I touched."

The elder priestess took the scarab from the boy. "It's one for the both of you, then." She frowned with annoyance and turned over the red scarab to read the inscription on the bottom. She read it over more than once, then sighed with resignation and an arch look at them both. "The Union of Isis and Osiris," she said at last. "Generally foretells a marriage. Just as well—you never could remember all the words to the invocations!" The young priestess and her new love smiled as the elder priestess returned their scarab and dismissed them, moving on to interpret somebody else's scarab.

☽·☉·☾

The dream above gave me the inspiration to create a system of divination using scarabs as the basic unit of interpretation. Priests and priestesses of Isis often have an interesting affinity for scarabs and the beetles they represent. The first time I ever saw one of the large, metallic scarab beetles which are similar to the ones first recognized as a symbol of a god in ancient Egypt was on the day of my ordination in the Fellowship of Isis. One flew in to join us during the ceremony, and stayed happily through the reception, being passed hand to hand by the participants until it finally flew away. Another priestess of Isis has a similar story to tell of a beetle visiting her initiation ceremony as well.

Ancient texts provide a complicated "Rite of the Beetle" performed as an Isian ceremony. Khepera also participated in the rite of the Midnight Sun, which he represents (despite the fact that these beetles do not fly at night).

At the present, there are no ready-made scarab runes available, so you must create your own, or modify existing ones. This gives you the opportunity to personalize the system and make it uniquely your own. If you feel a particular attraction to a symbol, object, or deity of ancient Egypt other than those described below, find an appropriate divinatory meaning for it and include it. The number of scarabs is arbitrary; you can reduce or increase their number. As a "party game" such as the dream itself seemed to describe, several sets of scarabs could be mixed together in the net, but be sure that they are of durable materials if you intend to throw them very hard. Also be sure your guests are of at least equally durable materials!

DIVINATION WITH SCARABS

Gather together or make a number of scarabs of approximately the same size (though they don't need to be of the same color or material). Paint or inscribe one symbol on the bottom of each scarab. You can also draw the symbols on paper and then cut them out and glue them to the flat sides of the scarabs.

Obtain a net to carry your scarabs. This should be of a small enough mesh that it will not let the scarabs fall out. A loosely-woven scarf can also be used.

When you want to divine, sit on the ground or floor, take the scarabs in their net, and swing it rapidly in a small circle in front of you. Let free one corner, and when the scarabs drop, pick up the one closest to you. If one bounces and touches you, choose that one instead. This will answer most simple questions and act as a keystone to a more elaborate reading if necessary. Sometimes I let them fall, randomly pick up three of them as quickly as I can, and read from those.

There are no "inverted" scarab interpretations such as those sometimes provided for reversed tarot cards. Positive and negative qualities of any force are always present in different degrees. It's wise to remember this in your readings, no matter how positive or negative a reading may seem on the surface.

Here are some suggested scarab symbols and meanings. Feel free to change them if you wish. These can also be used for the palm strip divination.

Suggested Scarab Symbols

The Lotus: Spiritual unfoldment, love, beauty, peaceful resolution of difficulties. A good time to meditate and study. In health readings, a positive outcome, particularly when new health awareness is created, because then "the lotus is carefully tended."

The
MYSTERIES
OF

ISIS

234

In romantic readings, a positive outcome indicating long-term happiness.

The Crocodile: Dangerous forces or those difficult to control. Unexpected mishaps or accidents. Unseen forces beyond casual control.

The entry of new individuals into one's life, with negative or difficult results. In a reading pertaining to health, it may indicate the need for strong or sudden intervention measures. Can also indicate an individual you have never before noticed suddenly emerging into your consciousness, like a crocodile rising from the water.

Be alert and divine often to prevent difficulties.

However, if the reader is in resonance with the complex deity Sobek, a consort of Isis at Soknaipou Nesos, this scarab may be interpreted as a positive presence of the god force, well adapted to the surrounding environment and capable of fierce defense rather than predatory attack.

The Palm Tree: The sacred palm oases of Osiris offered sanctuary, rest, and cool water to inhabitants and travellers in the desert. This scarab can denote travel and vacation. It is a scarab of fruitfulness and plenty. However, it can also denote isolation, as the distant oases were sometimes used as places of exile from the richer worlds of the cities along the Nile. In health readings it can indicate convalescence or the need for retreat. In romantic readings it generally denotes solitude, but can also advise of the need to retreat from the world with your loved one.

Isis: The throne headdress of Isis is a powerful and positive scarab for those in resonance with Her. If cast in answer to a question, this generally denotes a positive outcome. For followers of Isis, it may also indicate a need to get out of the way of the Goddess and let Her create the resolution She desires for you.

In readings pertaining to health, this is a healing sign. In readings of love, it is also positive. As with all the godform scarabs, the presence of the scarab of Isis may indicate that the reader is fulfilling a portion of the Isis mythos.

Osiris: The presence of the Osiris scarab speaks of initiation and of non-physical concerns. If cast in answer to a question, this scarab can indicate that the answer is still unresolved, unknowable, or not yet appropriate to be revealed. In readings pertaining to health, it usually means that rest and convalescence are required and that recovery may be slow. In love readings, it is a positive sign. Again, the presence of a godform scarab may also indicate that the reader is fulfilling or interacting with one of the portions of the Osiris myth cycle.

The interpretation of the Osiris scarab also depends on the relationship of the reader to the different aspects of Osiris. Since most of the surviving inscriptions concentrate on the important funerary and initiatory aspects of Osiris the common conception him is a tombbound, gloomy one. But just as Isis can be perceived as perpetually in search of Osiris' body or perpetually mourning him, Osiris can also be perceived as continuously alive in an eternal moment where the attack of Set has yet to occur. In this mode of perception, Osiris is a lively lover, exhilarated by music and dance and the intoxication of the love he shares with Isis.

Seshet: Seshet is the sacred goddess of writing and of measuring. The presence of this scarab can indicate that it is time to take action before opportunity is lost. There is also an implied caution to be certain that work is begun on a solid, well-measured foundation.

In health readings, this scarab can advise to search for more information or confirm results of exams or tests. In romantic readings it can advise you to quantify relationships or perhaps write down how you feel. Ask and answer questions to make sure there are no misunderstandings. In financial readings, check record-keeping and be sure it is accurate and complete, especially if it is kept by others.

The Shen: The Shen is the sign of eternity, of endless cycles. It is often shown clutched in the talons of Nekhebet, the vulture-goddess sometimes associated with Isis.

The presence of this scarab in any reading usually means a delayed outcome.

The Ibis (Tahuti/Thoth): The god Thoth or Tahuti represents wisdom and discernment. In a reading, this scarab indicates that the reader is to seek more information, to strive to act wisely and justly, and to seek imaginative answers to problems. It is an excellent scarab to receive in relation to any educational concern or question. In health matters it can indicate that a specialist's opinion should be sought. In romantic readings, platonic friendships are indicated, as well as positive alliances of all kinds.

Again, as a godform scarab, the presence of Thoth may indicate that the reader is working through the Thoth mythos.

The Cat (Bast): Cat goddess of joy, Bast was sometimes thought of as the embodiment of the "Soul of Isis," since the words *Ba-Ast* translate to that phrase. Bast was revered as a loving mother goddess and a less bloody form of the lioness goddess Sekhmet, a powerful defendress and goddess of war and destruction. The essential and sometimes changeable independence of the cat makes this scarab subject to many interpretations, depending on the reader's own personality. Bast is usually positive in romantic readings, particularly those where sexuality, rather than romantic love, is desired.

The Ankh: The Ankh is the foremost symbol of life. Various explanations of its form have been presented, varying from its likeness to a sandal strap (and therefore symbolic of the motion of life), to the outline of the female genitals, or the union of the male and female organs. One of the more logical explanations is that it derived from a stylized African fetish-doll carried to promote fertility. These round-headed dolls with short arms and straight sticks for bodies strongly resemble the Ankh form. However, the origin of the Ankh symbol was probably different from any of these and may remain unknown. In addition to being a symbol of life, the Ankh is also a transmitter of force, which is life in another form. Its presence in a reading is positive in virtually all circumstances.

The Temple: The high pylon gates leading to many of the temples of Egypt announced the beginning of sacred space, of enclosure. The presence of the Temple in a reading may indicate that the reader is in or about to begin a period of "temple service," where esoteric duties must be discharged. It can also refer to other "sacred enclosures," such as the home or workplace. Explore any sacred aspects of the matter at hand to be sure you have examined the spiritual as well as the material sides of things. It can also be a reminder to take a necessary retreat from mundane concerns, and to work on refining your soul rather than merely earning your paycheck.

The Nile: The Nile river is the source of Egypt. It is the guiding thread of Egyptian culture, bringing life in all its forms to what would

otherwise be barren. Its presence in a reading is generally positive. The Taoist approach to resolving difficulties by flowing around them like water may be suggested by the Nile scarab. Look for less aggressive solutions to problems, including simply waiting for events to unfold. Eternal or cosmic flows, tides, and seasonal changes are also present in the Nile scarab.

Nepthys: The scarab of Nepthys indicates darker sexuality, desperate actions, and strife in marriage and other relationships. The presence of her scarab, as with the other godform scarabs, may indicate that the reader is fulfilling or interacting with her myth.

Nepthys can also indicate a person whose motivations are unclear or uncertain, or whose actions may more or less innocently bring harm. This scarab also indicates times and periods of transition, just as Nepthys is symbolized by the dusk, the time between night and day. In readings for both love and health, Nepthys indicates a difficult outcome. However, if Nepthys can be equated and balanced by her twin, Isis, her influence will be much more positive.

Nepthys, shadowed by Isis, oppressed by her brother-husband Set, and unable to entice her beloved Osiris save in the guise of Isis, can personify victimization and

alert the reader of this potential or leaning. However, Nepthys grows to defy Set and allies herself with Isis, uniting with Her in the resurrection of Osiris. In this sense, Nepthys frees herself, redeems her actions, and achieves a balanced goddesshood as a twilight deity, underworld goddess, and maker of dreams.

Set: The presence of the Set scarab indicates great strife, unjust dealings, and prolonged litigation. Here is an oppressor in all senses, tolerable only as a controlled force to be used against greater or unknown evils. His nature is fiery, dry, and destructive. As a bringer of utter chaos, he can in some cases be liberating to persons or things caught in stultifying bonds. His presence in a reading for health indicates feverish conditions and/or injuries which will be difficult or time-consuming to heal. In romantic readings, he indicates unhappy or abusive relationships and harsh sexuality unmitigated by love.

All these implications are different for followers of Set, who consider him the oppressed, rightful heir to the throne of Egypt cast aside in favor of a child suspiciously begotten on a dead king. His own legitimacy for the throne of Egypt was favored over that of Osiris in some early mythologies.

The Starry Sky of Nut: Nut is a primal goddess, whose body is the star-flecked sky. She gave birth to the five gods Isis, Osiris, Nepthys, Set, and Horus. Her nature is cosmic, and her presence in a reading indicates that there are great matters at hand, possibly beyond ordinary human control. In this sense, this scarab indicates a concept close to inexorable Fate. This scarab is a positive influence on any creative endeavor or new beginning, and is also positive for love and health.

Khepra: A visit from the grandfather of the gods, Khepra, is always positive. This scarab can indicate positive divine intervention in the matter at hand, and can indicate that the reader is on track with their instincts and should proceed. With his associations with midnight, this scarab can also be a messenger of initiation and of receiving concealed or protected knowledge.

The Sistrum: The sistrum is a symbol of Isis and especially of Isis-Hathor, goddess of love and pleasure. It is a sign of religious observation and also of music, dance, joy, and lovemaking. This scarab is very positive in both romantic and health readings. However, for a sistrum to be of use, it must be shaken into activity. The presence of this scarab may exhort you to take action, break free, and embrace joy.

For those attuned to the Hathor godforce, this scarab can also indicate that the reader is fulfilling or interacting with the Hathor mythos.

Anpu: Anpu (also known as Anupu or Anubis) is the great Guide, not only of the dead but also of the astrally projecting, dreaming, and those who are on the threshold of initiation with its attendant death-like experiences. His presence in a reading for health is ambivalent; he may guide to a cure during sleep or may guide the soul into and through the underworld, perhaps to return to the world of the living.

This scarab is an alert to pay attention to dream content, or to actively invoke the help of dreams in approaching a problem. When found in romance readings his presence may indicate that the relationship is in fact initiatory rather than strictly or only romantic. Anupu, as a godform force, indicates to those in resonance with him that they may be performing or interacting with the mythos of Anubis. He leads one to new knowledge and is a strong protective force.

Horus: Horus is a complex godform embracing many aspects. He is probably most easily approached as Horus the Child, the sacred offspring of Isis and Osiris. His predominant symbol is the hawk, a high-flying, circling bird of prey and strong solar symbol. Horus is also the reborn Osiris, and contains within himself the dynamic aspects of Osiris and the potential for his Underworld aspects. In readings dealing with conflicts, particularly those over property or career, this scarab indicates eventual but hard-fought triumph. He is a positive force in health readings, and can represent a lover in romantic readings. He can also, because of his role as a divine child, represent children and concerns relating to children.

The Cobra: The Cobra symbolized the divine and is one way of writing the name of a goddess in the hieroglyphic writing. Both Isis and Osiris are sometimes depicted as crowned cobras. As a symbol of the kundalini force, the cobra can call attention to sacred sexuality and the pursuit of enlightenment. Cobra venom may have been employed in initiatory rites, and may also have been used by the pharaohs to assist their transitions into the afterlife.

In readings, the cobra scarab can indicate sudden change and activity, particularly when such changes lead to greater personal knowledge and wisdom.

The Solar Barque of Ra: The scarab symbolizes the energy of the sun and the powers of Amon-Ra, considered by some to be chief of the gods and as such a symbol—as all gods and goddesses are—of the Oneness behind the millions of deities perceived by humanity. This scarab gives both complex spiritual information as well as mundane day-to-day prognostication. Osiris and Isis are both forms of Ra in the heliocentric literature of Egypt; equally, Ra can be considered a form of either of them.

As a vessel, the Barque of Ra can also indicate travel. It is benevolent but indicative of change in love, health, and financial readings.

The Crescent of Isis: Isis frequently is depicted wearing the horns of the crescent moon along with what is often incorrectly identified as the moon itself. Actually, the round disk she wears is the "Sun Behind the Sun," not our familiar, local Sol but the twin suns of the Sirius star complex. This scarab speaks to us of the cycles and rhythms of time, both short-term and long-term, as well as hidden influences.

Although the association of Isis with Sirius is very ancient, recent astronomical research is leading some scientists to suspect that our own sun is half of a twinned star system with a twenty-six million year cycle which reflects the perplexingly regular cycles of mass extinction observed in our geologic record. It is possible that we do not need to look to the distant Sirian star system to discover the "Sun behind the Sun" represented on the headdress of Isis.

The Pyramids: The Pyramids represent aspiration, stability, and the slow passage of time. Their appearance usually indicates that an event will be long in coming or in duration. The Pyramids also hint at mysteries concealed in the mundane casing of the outer world. We are used to seeing pyramids in ruined forms. Originally, some were glazed with crushed white gypsum, inscribed with hieroglyphs, and then crowned with golden capstones which glowed in the sunlight. As such, in their ruined state, they also are beacons which hearken back to older, more golden times. In a reading they can indicate a need to turn back to the past to restore, re-examine, or re-experience our formative experiences.

The Union of Isis and Osiris: This scarab indicates the essential polarity between Isis and Osiris, and implies all aspects of union, from physical to alchemical and divine unions. It is a scarab of culmination and balance, but in a dynamic, not a static form. This scarab is sacred love in all its forms, and creative power at its most primal. In romantic readings it indicates balanced energy and positive resolutions.

The Frog: Heqet, the Frog Goddess, is a symbol of fertility and birth. Associated with Hathor, this sign is positive in health and romantic readings. In financial readings, it indicates a sudden windfall or funds from an unexpected source.

Min: Powerful god of sexuality, the presence of this scarab in a reading indicates vigor in all areas of health and finance. In romantic readings, it may indicate that the attraction is primarily sexual rather than emotional.

The Ushabti: The Ushabti figures were small images placed in tombs to "answer" for the dead if they were called upon to work. In a reading, this scarab indicates unexpected or unwarranted help from friends or family. In health readings, it can mean a period of being unable to be very active and reliance upon the help of others. In romance, it can indicate undue dependence on another. In finance, it can be positive or negative, and may mean a pick-up in business that requires additional help.

The Incense Bowl: The Incense Bowl was a common offering to deities. Its presence in a reading indicates that it is necessary to pay attention to the spiritual and communication with your deities. By itself, it is neutral in most readings. Turn to the gods for the specific answer.

The Sphinx: The Sphinx, enigmatic lion lying on the desert, concealing its age and true origins, has been a symbol of mystery for thousands of years. In a reading, it can mean that no answer is available or revealable at this time.

☽ · ☉ · ☾

Chapter Twenty-Three

The Eleventh Hour of Night

ISIS AND DREAMING

IN DREAMS, IN THE night when the soul may be cold and dark, Isis comes to Her worshippers and answers their needs. Here, a dream of healing; there, a dream of love to assuage the loneliness of waiting; for another, the solution to a puzzling problem; and to one more, a dream of initiation or intuition.

But there are those who lie blinded while they sleep, uninstructed in the art and science of dreaming; when the Goddess comes to them She finds a mind closed and barred to Her and all divine forces, and against these gates She will not choose to pass until welcomed. Simply requesting Her presence and guidance as you fall asleep will eventually bring Her to your dreams.

THE JOURNAL OF THE DREAMTIME

If you are fortunate enough to already enjoy a rich dream life, begin a dream diary. This journal, best kept in a blank book by your bedside, will become a uniquely personal record of experiences and thoughts that might otherwise go unnoticed. You will be able to determine subtle trends in your life based on long periods of time, such as dreams that you tend to have in spring, or a dream that regularly occurs near your birthday, or in conjunction with a holiday.

Ideally, your dream journal should include a brief assessment of conditions in your waking life, written down after you have recorded your night's dreaming. If you keep a regular journal, the two records can be easily compared. As often as possible, note down other external conditions, such as the weather or moon phase. The more detailed your dream record, the more valuable it will be to you.

However, don't let the need for detail keep you from simply writing down your dreams in any way you can. This is the most essential purpose of the dream journal.

If you do keep other records with your dreams, always write down your dream material first and leave the mundane details for later. Dreams are ephemeral, and important material can be swiftly lost. This is particularly true if you have dreamed of word-oriented material, such as a poem, factual information, or a name. Scribble down this type of information as quickly as you can.

Here is a sample dream journal format and example.

Dream Diary Entry Format

Description of dream(s):
Day and date:
Time of day or night of dream:
Phase of the moon:
Moon sign:

Weather:
Health:
Mood:
Time of day or night dream was recorded here:
Food/drink/medicine(s) consumed before sleep:
Events in real life that may have affected these dreams:

The dream journal was recognized as an important tool by the priestesses and priests of the Egyptian and Greek temples of Isis and Serapis. The writing-down of nightly dreams was required of novices. We have a series of twenty-seven dreams written down for this purpose by a man named Ptolemaeus, who chose sanctuary at the Serapeum of Memphis to avoid punishment for a misdeed that had gotten him in trouble with the secular authorities. Ptolemaeus' dreams, which resemble in every respect modern dream chronicles, were set down in a matter-of-fact style, simply describing the dream action. Among dreams of everyday occurrences, such as encountering a friend on the street, he also finds himself dreaming of Isis.

These holy dreams were carefully scrutinized by the dream-interpreters among the priesthood. Often, these dreams were submitted as evidence that a student or novice was ready for additional training or corrective study.

LEARNING TO DREAM

The dynamics of dreaming are very precise and functional, attested by many sources and the experiences of thousands. Yet as a whole, we are

led to believe that dreaming is an unreliable, irrational activity over which we have no control. Dreaming is sometimes regarded as a kind of subconscious mental scribbling which may be merely the random discharge of our electrically-based brains, as devoid of meaning as the purely rationalist scientist would have us believe we are devoid of souls.

Fortunately, this is not the case. Dreaming is a communion both with our own souls and with the universe, as well as with the deity or deities we choose to ally ourselves.

Isis has always spoken through dreams, whether to alert a potential initiate to an impending initiation or to bring a cure to the mind of a sleeping patient undergoing the "temple sleep" within the walls of Her sacred precincts.

Yet dreaming without attentiveness is a little like switching on the television and randomly watching stations, not knowing if the programming is a factual documentary, pure imagination, or fact and fiction mixed together in a docudrama. You may watch another remake of a story that has always fascinated you, even if you have become very familiar with the plot. You may come across a station with a weak signal that you can barely make out, or one in a foreign language. Every once in a while, you may see a program which affects the way you live, opens you to new possibilities, and changes you in an essential way.

All of these experiences have parallels in the world of dreaming, sometimes mixed together haphazardly, sometimes revealing a careful order beneath the apparent chaos of imagery.

As you learn to dream, the chaos recedes, and meaningful, reliable dreams increase. Dreaming well is an acquired skill, obtainable by all and easy to master. Learning to dream can be a lifetime study, or a pastime to which you return now and then. It can also be a powerful magical and spiritual tool, which can ultimately grant communion with Isis.

Many cultures place great emphasis on the content of dreams, as prophetic tools and as instruments of self-revelation and inspiration.

A belief held by some Buddhists is that portions of one's karma can be erased in dreams, because the reality of the emotions experienced are equivalent to actually undergoing the experience in waking life. In the Western world we have the phrase "I'll sleep on it," which can indicate that, consciously or unconsciously, the seeker expects to explore the problem in ways that can only happen during sleep.

Many important inventions and discoveries have been achieved due to insights received in dreams. Among those unwillingly admitted to by scientists include the invention of the sewing machine and Kerkule's understanding of the chemical structure of benzene, whose circular nature was revealed to him in a dream of a snake eating its own tail (also an old alchemical symbol) which for the dreaming scientist exploded into the realization that a circular structure was the answer.

Two excellent books by Dr. Patricia Garfield, *Creative Dreaming* and *Pathways to Ecstasy*, provide

Chapter
Twenty-
Three

*Isis and
Dreaming*

245

novice dreamers with a wide variety of methods and material to stimulate dreaming. Garfield studied the sophisticated dreaming techniques of the Senoi, a peaceful, cooperative tribe living in Malaysia. Their well-organized society actively teaches dreaming techniques to its members on the basis of three essential rules, which can be used successfully by any dreamer. As Dr. Garfield summarizes, the first rule is to "confront and conquer" any dangerous situations or beings encountered in nightmares. The second rule is to always move toward pleasurable situations, whether these are emotional or sexual, and even when they violate waking taboos. Finally, the dreamer is advised to dream through to a positive result or the completion of a positive action within the context of the dream. Dreams that taper off to nothingness or that end without the dreamer achieving the maximum positive potential from the dream scenario are to be avoided.

The Senoi also emphasize the need to request or require gifts from the dream person encountered, whether these are attacking monsters or dream lovers. These gifts must be beautiful or useful, and may be a poem, song, or helpful new technique of accomplishing a daily task.

The Iroquois of northeastern North America also used advanced dreaming techniques, and based many political actions on the content of dreams. As they were a complex, successful society, the guidance they received was apparently accurate. Their dream knowledge coincided with sound psychological principles. For example, they recognized that desires may be distorted in dreams, and that one object or person may be substituted for another. Needs expressed in dreams were taken very seriously by the entire tribe, who as a group would attempt to provide the dreamer in reality with what they needed to fulfill their dreaming wish.

DREAMING EXERCISES

Simply creating a strong intent to dream more dynamically can often provide immediate results in your dream life. I usually begin to have more frequent dreams, lucid and otherwise, when I am reading or writing about dreamwork. Dreams also seem to grow on each other, and one outstanding dream will often carry several other interesting ones in its wake. Once you have established a dream diary, reading back over the entries on a particular type of dream before going to sleep may invoke additional ones.

On an evening when you wish to dream well, start thinking of the dreamtime ahead at various times during the evening. If you are fortunate enough to be surrounded with supportive individuals, mention that you intend to work on dreaming tonight. Be alert for dream material that you would like to include, perhaps expanding on a theme from a movie or television program, or a book you are reading. Ask for suggestions from those around you. Write down a brief list of things you would like to dream about, and go over it several times until you know the contents well. This can be used as a tool during dreaming to expand

and control your dream content. Stay up a little later than usual, so that you are feeling distinctly tired when you go to bed. However, try not to stay up more than a half-hour to forty-five minutes past your normal bedtime. Much more than this may trick your body into thinking you are staring another waking cycle, which will make it more difficult for you to get to sleep. Sometimes physical labor or exercise can also help prepare you for dreaming.

If possible, try to arrange your waking time so that it is later than normal. It is widely documented that most individuals have the majority of their dreams in the hours between about five and eight A.M. Lucid dreams are also much more likely during this period. Some researchers, such as Dr. Garfield, experience their lucid dreams only during this period. Bed time or amount of sleep may have little to do with this phenomena; it may be a function of human biorhythms.

When going to bed, allow yourself more time than usual to prepare to go to sleep. Expand every part of your nighttime habits, and allow time at every step to contemplate the opportunity for dreaming which is approaching. Beside your bed set a notepad and several writing instruments. You may prefer pencils, since they do not run out of ink and can write at once, without twisting or clicking. Remember that you will want to write very quickly, before you lose your dream; any sort of action or delay can cloud your recollection of the dream.

POSTURE FOR THE TEMPLE SLEEP

This positioning of the body promotes effective dream and trance work.

Select a pillow which will enable you to lie flat on the bed with your neck supported. Your head should be at a natural angle with the rest of your body. Piles of pillows distort the body's natural line and interfere with dreaming, as well as being bad for the spine. Priests and priestesses at the healing temples who used dream incubation were aware of this and frequently had only a half-round of polished wood to use as a pillow. This may sound ascetic and uncomfortable, but the technique contributed to a varied and powerful dream life—and probably fewer back or neck aches!

You may find it comfortable to use a small pillow that fits just under the back of your neck and lets your head rest directly on the mattress. This can be made more comfortable by adding another little pillow under the small of your back.

Lie still for a few moments, letting your eyes adjust to the darkness. Your room should be dark and still. Breathe slowly and deeply. Think around the ideas you had for tonight's dreaming. Don't try to force a particular image. You may find a sudden fantasy taking off from one of the ideas. Let it flow if this happens; this is akin to dreaming, and may lead seamlessly into dream.

Press your eyelids together very lightly. Watch the colors you see. They may start to coalesce into images. If this happens, it is an excellent sign that your night's dreaming will be especially rich.

Chapter
Twenty-
Three

*Isis and
Dreaming*

247

About this time you may feel an urge to turn onto your side, generally the right. Go ahead and make yourself comfortable. Sleep will come soon.

If you wake during the night, hold still for a moment. Search your mind for fragments of dreams. If you remember any, write them down at once. If nothing comes to your conscious mind, turn over in bed. This will sometimes stimulate a memory of a nearly-lost dream, but as it can also erase faint traces of dreaming, move only after you are certain that nothing is arising in your consciousness. Also try sitting or standing up to retrieve additional details after you have written the initial impressions down. And *write them down*. What seems unforgettable and life-shaking at 3 A.M. will have dissipated like mist by dawn.

BANISHING RITE FOR NIGHTMARES AND THEIR AFTERMATH

An Isis ritual for banishing the negative influences of a bad dream was used by the Egyptians. Here is a modern version of it.

Isis,
Great Goddess,
Mighty of Word,
With Your wings of light,
Wipe clean my brow
Of the visions that linger.
Clear my sight,
protect me from all evil,
Untie the knot I have dreamed;
Set me free from this nighttime vision.

After reciting the prayer, wipe your face in a piece of bread dipped in beer and myrrh. This is an odd combination to our modern ears, but beer has a purifying, stimulating influence when applied to the skin and will cleanse the face, which is often contaminated with the sweat of fear after a nightmare. Isis was also known as the inventress of beer, and was sometimes considered identical to Hathor, the Lady of Beer. Myrrh has both scientifically documented antibacterial properties and is also a dynamic spiritual cleanser. Its stimulating, acrid odor will stimulate a return to full normal consciousness. The bread, aside from being a convenient sponge, was also sacred to Isis as Lady of Bread.

Simply washing the face with cool water can also help to clear away traces of a nightmare.

If you do have a bad dream, eating a small, carbohydrate-rich meal will help to restore you to peaceful sleep. The reasons for this effect are mainly physiological: food in the stomach draws blood away from the brain and into the digestive tract, making it harder to stay awake.

AN ONEIROCRIT'S HANDBOOK

The *oneirocrit* was a common member of the temple staff who was dedicated to the study and interpretation of dreams. Some of these priestesses and priests referred to handbooks, while others worked entirely from their own knowledge and experience. They focused primarily on "big" dreams in which the dreamer experienced a vision of a god or goddess or received instructions on how to heal an illness.

The Egyptians formalized the interpretation of dreams with numerous manuals on the subject, sometimes included with a daily almanac of favorable and unfavorable days. One of these almanacs included a "standard" dream interpretation text with an appendix, including the appropriate interpretations for the dreams of the followers of Set, who would interpret symbols very differently because of their faith.

While no "Dreambook for Followers of Isis" has survived, the priests and priestesses of Isis used dream interpretation according to their own beliefs and experiences. Several dream manuals containing material related to the worship of Serapis existed and were used widely. The following modern presentation is based on my interpretation of common dream symbols for those who follow Isis. You may find it useful to refer to Chapter Twenty-Two, "The Oracles of Isis," for more examples of Isian interpretations of common symbols. Until your interpretation skills are more practiced, some of the meanings given here may be of help in untangling your web of dreams.

The interpretations included here are for priestesses, priests, and other worshippers or "allies" of Isis. The meanings given here may not be accurate for you. Your own experiences will modify or even reverse some meanings. Never accept an interpretation that feels wrong to you. I have had frightening dreams which I have correctly interpreted in a positive way as well as bright dreams which have left me with a swiftly justified feeling of dread. For similar reasons, use caution in interpreting the dreams of others, and only attempt this when you are confident in your abilities to inter-

pret for yourself. Remind the person that you are interpreting for that you may be wrong, and that for each person dream language is different. If the snake curator at the zoo dreams of large snakes writhing about his bedroom, he will probably interpret it much differently from the same dream occurring to old Mrs. Smith who runs a bakery.

Dreams with strong religious or magical content may sometimes be connected with a festival or rite celebrated on the same date as the dream. Some of the known Egyptian and Isian holidays are found in Chapter Ten, "Festivals of Isis." Be generous in assigning festivals to dreams of different dates; the ancient calendars are so confused and contradictory that quite a bit of leeway is permissible.

When interpreting dreams, be aware that dream language is full of punning and plays on words. Odd or uncommon words or objects seen in a dream may yield a deeper meaning than their mere everyday reality. Dreams may also refrain from unfolding their influence or revealing their predictive quality for months or years from the initial date of their occurrence. Many people have reported dreaming of their future mate only to find a decade or more passes before they encounter the person defined in the dream. Sometimes, the dreamer will not yet have enough conscious knowledge to understand an important dream, which will be later validated when the dreamer is exposed to that knowledge.

Ultimately understanding a perplexing dream can be a powerful spiritual validation. Odd details of dreams of other places and times,

when encountered in the "real" world, support belief in reincarnation and past lives.

If you were fortunate enough to grow up in a family which passed along an active folklore, don't dismiss these symbols from your dream interpretation lexicon. Be aware of them, since dream interpretation manuals or other dream interpreters will probably be completely unaware of the meaning of these dream components. Your family or ethnic background will definitely influence the language of your dreams. For example, white is the color of mourning to many Asians. The Western world holds black as the color of death, and associates white with happier occasions, such as weddings. An identical dream could yield virtually opposite interpretations between a Westerner and an Asian.

BASIC DREAM ANALYSIS

When recording your dreams, pay special attention to their locations. Resist the temptation to ignore the setting because it seems so mundane —your workplace, a grocery store, a sports arena. All of these areas have particular associations, and nothing in a dream is really random.

Also pay attention to the people in your dream, even if they are part of the background, make minor contributions, or are only referred to by another person in the dream. Frequently individuals "stand in" for other persons. This type of substitution usually points out an important similarity between two otherwise unconnected people.

When going through your written dream records, it may help to underline the persons, places, and objects contained in your dream, and to interpret each item separately. Note your personal associations with each item. You may also find it helpful to read your notes aloud, speaking clearly and quickly. Often, you will find that words that seem to have no meaning may easily be misspoken and made into a word that has a meaning that fits the dream context more completely.

DREAM INTERPRETATIONS

Here are a few to help you begin. Your own interpretations will be the most important to you, and these are simply a guide.

Coffins, Tombs, Sarcophagi, Funeral Rites: Generally, once a person has embarked on a study of mystical or religious materials, death symbolism becomes in itself a symbol for initiation. Dreams pertaining to these areas, particularly if the dreamer is personally experiencing the rite, being shut in a coffin, etc., may be minor initiations in themselves, as an opportunity is provided to overcome the natural fear of these things.

In general, dreams of death or dreams in which the dreamer experiences morbid feelings usually indicate an area in life with which the dreamer is deeply unsatisfied, and which he or she may be "killing off" in the dreamtime. Dreams of accidents also usually symbolize existing problems which will cause further difficulties if not corrected.

Occasionally, a dream of an accident or illness is precognitive. It's important to remember that the fact that we are given the dream indicates that the potentially negative fate is avoidable if we take appropriate action.

Sexual Union: Dreams of sexual union, particularly if they culminate in orgasm, may be a metaphor for the *coniunctio mystis* or *hieros gamos*, the sacred union with a god or goddess. However, sometimes orgasm in dreams is not so much sexual in nature but ecstatic.

Boats, Ships, Ferries, Rivers: These items are associated with passage through the Underworld or astral world. They share the same meanings given for funerary items. They can also indicate sickness or departure.

Sun, Moon, and Stars: Dreaming of celestial objects can give clues to the timing of important events, particularly if their position or influence does not follow the present real condition of the moon or planet. Generally, dreams of the sun and moon are positive and favorable, but an excess of either energy, such as searing heat from the sun or chill from the moon, can indicate that the forces symbolized by these are out of balance.

Temples, Houses, Other Buildings: Any building in a dream may have aspects of a temple or enclosed sacred space. The path taken through a structure may be significant. If you enter by the back door, it may mean that your are exploring areas to which you do not yet have official access.

Gods, Goddesses, Other Luminous Beings: Dreams of a goddess or god most often reveal crucial information, and should be paid close attention when they occur. Dreams of the

gods, even by their most devout followers, are rare, and given at their will, not invoked by ours.

Relatives: Since our relationships with our relatives, both those living and those not physically present, are so complex, dreams of relatives must be gently examined. It is not uncommon to dream of your father and to have the content actually refer to your mother. In some cases, it is also possible to have a dream "for" another family member, who perhaps will not be as open to receiving the dream information directly, or is simply not as well-trained a dreamer.

Dreaming of someone who is not related to you but appears in your dream as a relative indicates a similarity between you and the individual dreamed about. The similarity may be positive or negative. Question why this particular trait seems to be underlined for you. Examine how possessing this particular trait affects your life now. As always, the associated meanings of the name of the person may help you to more clearly understand what is being revealed to you.

Children and/or Infants: Dreams of children and infants often symbolize new beginnings or projects rather than actual children or babies.

Foods, Drinks (or other items eaten or consumed): Dreaming of consuming a substance can mean that you need what is symbolized by the substance. Perhaps you think of champagne as expensive; drinking it in a dream could mean that you need to bring in prosperity forces. Eating or drinking can also symbolize destroying an influence in your life.

Pets and Wild Animals: These appearing in a dream can represent an aspect of yourself which needs attention.

Communicating by Telephone, Computer, Letters: Sometimes entities, either living or dead friends, or deity forces, will communicate in dreams through these modes. Pay attention; the message may be important. See the following entry for memory retention methods.

Reading Books, Visiting Libraries, Museums, Galleries: These activities in the dreamtime are usually symbolic of gaining information, which may be spiritual or practical. Beware of "taking notes" in a dream; usually, your mind will believe that you have actually written everything down, and may not pay the necessary attention to what is being revealed. When you awaken, you may be left with nothing. If you are hearing important information, repeat it in your mind in the dream several times, and try to associate it with a specific image. This will act as a trigger when you awaken, and may let you recreate more of the dream material.

☽·◌·☾

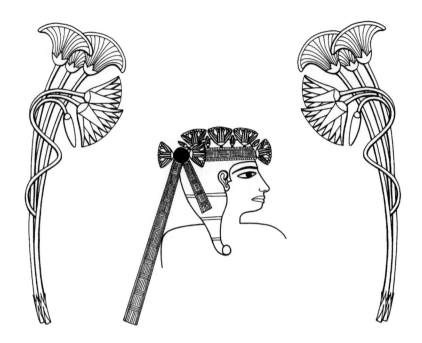

Chapter Twenty-Four
The Last Hour of Night

MYSTERIES OF ISIS

We do well ... to see her steadily and to see her whole—Isis, the great ruler of the Graeco-Roman world, ever active and magical with her gifts of knowledge, power, and wisdom, the eternal mainspring of men's deepest faith, hope, and love.

R. E. Witt, Isis in the Graeco-Roman World[1]

I SIS IS A GODDESS of mystery, of sacred secrets and initiation into the mechanisms of the universe, both physical and spiritual. Authors we suspect were initiated into her secrets torment modern readers with descriptions that break off suddenly: "But that is a secret of which I must not speak," or, more coyly, "I could tell more, but it is forbidden."

We can prepare for initiation, prepare to understand the mysteries, but at their heart, the divine secrets must be revealed;

understanding of them is a gift given by the grace of the Goddess, not by intellectual appreciation alone. For this reason, even if the ancient rites had been written down, true in every detail, the actual experience of the mystery would still remain unrevealed. The expression of the secrets changes with every season. The mystery is played through us; it is different for each of us as we are each different, and as the patterns of the gods this year are different from last year. Understanding of the mysteries floods us like a river, and may suddenly flood dry land at its banks. Yes, floods have happened before; perhaps eons ago the river flowed across the same land it now reclaims; perhaps that tall stone, dry for a million years, once parted the waters into two streams. But this time is not the same as any flood before; the time is different, circumstances altered.

So it is with the mysteries. The wash of insight and experience over an individual is the same, but every instance is different and unknowable

until the individuals have experienced it for themselves.

We can point to the mysteries; some eyes will be drawn to the pointing hand, but only a few will look beyond to the object pointed out. The inner mysteries will remain elusive. But the outer mysteries will prepare us for the inner, and perhaps hasten our understanding of them.

THE ORIGINS OF ISIS

Where did this ancient goddess first arise? She seems to spring up as suddenly as a lotus bud rising up from the moist dark earth of the Nile delta of Egypt, and blooming in the dawn of Egyptian civilization. She is a goddess without consort, without parentage, without child. All these would be associated with Her later.

For in the beginning, She is a lone goddess, sacred in Sebennytos, a delta city. The similarity of names between Isis, who in Egypt was called *Aset* and later, *Esa* or *Eset*, and those of Ishtar, Astarte, and Ashtoreth, suggests a distant common origin for these goddesses, who share many characteristics. And the stories that were to follow, of Isis' husband Osiris and of Isis' journey to find and regenerate him, find close parallels in the mysteries of those goddesses. In one tale the Queen of the palace where the coffin containing Osiris' body has been made into a pillar, has the name of Astarte.

Writers have offered many explanations for Isis' appearance in Egypt. Some, such as Budge, suggest that Isis and the rest of the Osirian pantheon were deified members of a human family. This

The goddess Ishtar.

deification of human beings was certainly not unknown in Egypt. It has been suggested then that the Osiris cycle of stories refers to the first king of united Egypt, making Isis the first queen. It is also very possible that certain events in the story of Isis and Osiris may have derived from events which occurred to a human royal pair named after or serving in the priesthoods of Isis and Osiris.

Other authors suggest that Isis came from the Libyan deserts, while some point to Her great and lasting popularity in the extreme far south of Egypt, and suggest a Nubian origin. Still others insist that the myths are just stories created from the observed cycle of natural events, where Isis is the fruitful earth of the field, and Osiris the grain which is cut and "killed," to resurrect the following year. Even as early as Plutarch these explanations were being offered for the origin of divine beings, although Plutarch strongly derided efforts to reduce all deities to mere manifestations of yearly fertility cycles.

Some authors have placed a common origin of the similar Middle Eastern religious mythologies in the heart of the culture of the Lost Continent of Atlantis. Whether this continent existed apart from the spiritual realm is the subject of much dispute. Those who favor its material existence point to the shallow Sargasso Sea in the midst of the Atlantic Ocean and the provocative undersea remains, apparently walls, off the coast of Bermuda. Historians, on the other hand, point to a possible "typographic error" dating back to Plato, and suggest that he had his distances

off by a factor of ten when he wrote of Atlantis, making the most likely candidate for the lost continent the small volcanic island of Thera, destroyed in a volcanic eruption which may have taken a good portion of Cretan culture along with it. Mystics disagree on many aspects of the Atlantis story. But some, including the eminent occultist Dion Fortune, maintain that the continent existed, its priesthood thrived, and that, on this planet at least, it was there that the worship of Isis first developed.

The phrase "on this planet" opens up the universe to speculation. Perhaps because ancient cultures were avid starwatchers, free from the glaze of light that veils the nighttime skies over our cities, virtually every deity became identified with one or more heavenly bodies and with various stellar phenomena. Modern interpretation of this information frequently results in claims of an extra-terrestrial yet non-divine origin for Isis and other Egyptian deities.

The most interesting "evidence" for this point of view is in the ancient detailed astronomical knowledge of invisible or undetectable stars, which the Egyptians may have possessed about the Sirius star system. They sometimes called this system the "Home of the Soul of Isis," consistent with one school of belief that deceased souls became stars circling the pole star in the hereafter. More recently, Whitley Streiber in his popular book *Communion*, claims that a female alien contacting him seemed to indicate that she personally was the ageless prototype of the all supreme-goddess beliefs of Earth.

Chapter
Twenty-
Four

Mysteries
of
Isis

255

So where did Isis come from? It doesn't matter. Not at all. Entertain whatever version you prefer: extraterrestrial, Atlantean, born from Nubia or Libya, delta mud or cosmic soup. The Goddess Isis did not arrive by spaceship; perhaps one of Her priestesses did. The Goddess Isis did not spring up from the earth of Egypt or Atlantis, but those who worshipped a version of Her energy were born in those lands. The Great Isis—the Cosmic Isis—is everywhere. She is a naming of a portion of the forces which created—and still are creating—our universe, and She is far beyond our ability to fully name. As we claim more of our own divinity, we recognize still more of Hers.

Isis, alone among the ancient goddesses, feeds a yearning that most of the ancient world did not even fully recognize as a human need. This was—and is—a yearning for divine love, for a Being who accepts, transmutes, and returns the emotions of Her worshippers. Acting out of Her own pain and passionate love, the manifestation of the "lesser" Isis is a deity who forgives because She knows what it was like to be condemned; who frees because She knows what it was like to be imprisoned; who loves deeply as a wife, mother, sister, and lover; who loves intimately even abstract concepts such as beauty, truth, knowledge, and mastery of the arts; who loves even warfare when it is required and honorably pursued. The loving passion of Isis for Her worshippers offers a beautiful contrast to the more aloof deities of Greece and Rome.

The Jesuit writer Andre-Jean Festugiére, commenting on Apuleius' religious fervor in *Personal Religion among the Greeks and Romans,* points out that Lucius was called by Isis to join Her followers and to consecrate his entire life to Her in return for the salvation She offered from his misguided, tragic life, which had resulted in his magical imprisonment in the body of an ass.[2] The entwinings of both Fortune and Destiny are untangled by the will of Isis, and Lucius repays Her benevolence to him with freely given devotion. He moves into the temple to be near the divine images, which he contemplates for many hours daily, "deriving an ineffable pleasure" from his nearness to the deity. At last instructed by Isis in a dream to return home, he can hardly bear to leave the temple, and dries "with my face the tears I shed on her feet." She called him to be initiated, an act which if undertaken without the express will of the Goddess was considered to be an offense warranting death for the over-eager or arrogant candidate.

Festugiére believes that the motivating force behind Lucius' devotions is simply that he feels loved by Isis. Festugiére writes:

He (Lucius) believes in the love of Isis. This faith of his is absolute. How could he not be loved by Isis, when she herself sought him out in his misery (let us recall that it was not to Isis but to whatever goddess showed herself in the moon, that he had addressed his prayer at Cenchreae) when she appeared to him in her own form, and, by a wondrous miracle, restored him to his man's shape, and thereafter, guided him every night by her counsel? … He felt himself loved. He loved in return. It was because of these things that he found in the contemplation of the Goddess an ineffable joy.

It is interesting that Festugiére seems himself to have fallen under the spell of Isis, as his writings on other pagan deities are often harsh and condemning.

Wherever human passions lead, Isis is there waiting; on the prows of ships exploring new trading; in the embrace of lovers; in the tender worry of parents over children; in the halls of the great Library at Alexandria where the scholars pursued their crafts; in the priests and priestesses keeping the holiness of the temples; in the cockpits of airplanes, capsules of space shuttles, and in the laboratories of researchers fighting disease.

Isis is not cowed by strength; She does not fear the knowledge or experience or skill of Her worshippers. Not burdened by canonical writings, reforming Her message anew to each worshipper, She does not fear exposure nor examination. Secure in Her own divinity, other deities are free to share Her temples, and She obliges by taking a chapel within their own sacred precincts. Although Her worship was universal throughout Egypt, the number of temples exclusive to Isis is very small. She is found everywhere.

ANCIENT PRACTICES

In Egypt, the mysteries of Isis and Osiris may have included the shutting-up of the initiate in a sarcophagus for an extended period of time. Many temples have underground crypts which may have been used as the "underworld" through which the initiates must pass on their

journey. During the Greco-Roman period, there is evidence from some temples that part of the initiation procedures may have included a ritual near-drowning where the candidate entered a subterranean crypt which was then flooded. This may have been associated with the very ancient belief that Osiris died by drowning, either accidentally or by the hand of Set (whose hot, dry nature seems to make it unlikely he would have chosen a watery means of death for his rival).

The Pyramids, several of which appear not to have been intended for use as tombs, may have been employed for some initiations. Earlyne Chaney gives an interesting account of an initiation she believes to have occurred during a past life, which included temporary entombment of the potential initiate in the innermost compartment of the pyramid, inside a sealed sarcophagus.[3] Joyce Verrette, in her novel *Winged Priestess*, also describes a pyramid initiation for a queen and priestess of Isis. The queen is shut into a sarcophagus of black marble, and for the next four days and nights proceeds through the other worlds, encountering the power which manifests as Isis in a grotto, and that which animates Osiris on a sunny plain. She encounters Tahuti (Thoth), the ibis-headed God of Wisdom, and jackal-headed Anupu, before coming into the presence of Amon-Ra. At last returning to her body, she has succeeded in becoming a "winged priestess," one who has survived the hazardous journey through the Underworld.[4]

Although evidence is scanty and ambiguous, it is possible that a "sacred marriage" or rite of sexual

The pyramid field of Gizeh.

union between the initiate and a priest or priestess may have formed part of some initiations, perhaps after the initiate was "resurrected" as Osiris reborn, though clear evidence remains elusive. Aside from the sexual content of the story of Isis and Osiris, there are only a few ambiguous inscriptions which may point to sexual union within the context of the Isian mystery rites. It is possible that sexual relations may have occurred between initiated and ordained priestesses and priests in the course of performing various ceremonies, particularly those related to the fertility of the land. However, these rites may not apply to the mysteries themselves, which when performed for the relatively undedicated (i.e., not a potential member of the priesthood) may have omitted any sexual content. For a recounting of how these traditions have been applied in modern times, Dion Fortune's novels *Moon Magic* and *The Sea Priestess* provide an interesting introduction.

Most, though not all, of the Mysteries of Isis are inextricably entwined with the Mysteries of Osiris. Ancient initiates often went through the rites of both, and of the two, the rites of Osiris were considered to be the more challenging. The worship by an initiate of the Lord of the Dead rather than the bright All-Goddess may be one reason for this feeling. Plutarch has an interesting comment on how the nature of Osiris was misunderstood even in his times:

There is a doctrine which modern priests hint at to satisfy their conscience, but only in veiled terms and with caution: namely, that this god (Osiris) rules and reigns over the dead, being none other than he whom the Greeks call Hades and Pluto. The truth of this statement is misunderstood and confuses the masses, who suppose that the sacred and holy one, who is in truth Osiris, lives in the earth and under the earth, where are concealed the bodies of those who appear to have reached their goal. He is actually very far removed from the earth, being undefiled, unspotted, and uncorrupted by any being which is subject to decay and death. The souls of men here, hedged in as they are by the body and its emotions, have no association with the god save for the dim vision of his presence which they achieve by the understanding gained through philosophy; but whenever they are freed and pass over the formless, invisible, dispassionate and holy kingdom, then is this their god their leader and king, for depending on him, they behold insatiably and desire the beauty which is, to men, ineffable and unutterable. This beauty, as the ancient story shows, Isis ever loves, and she pursues it and unites with it, filling this our world with all the beautiful and good qualities which have a part in creation. Such is the interpretation of these matters which is most becoming to the gods.

ISIS AND INITIATION

Initiation. The word means to begin as well as to have attained; it is a recognition of a starting-point rather than a completion. Standing alone, perhaps blindfolded or in darkness, alone or in a group, the initiate confronts his or her own strengths or inadequacies, debates his or her worthiness, devotion, and knowledge. Long months or years of intense study may have preceded this moment, with dozens of documents memorized, many rituals faithfully performed, much dedicated and unquestioning service to the gods and goddesses.

GUIDED INITIATIONS

Isis is a personally imminent, interactive goddess who does not require the intercession of a trained priestess or priest to contact a worshipper. The presence or counsel of others who have been initiated by Isis can be immensely helpful and bring great joy and confidence to the potential initiate, but these are not essential. Isis may choose to bring a worshipper through initiation in a working temple or other group, or initiation may occur in the course of everyday life, stripped of mystical decorations but carrying equal spiritual power.

Or, by the grace of Isis, it may occur while walking a dog.

Not all initiations occur in temples, nor are all the end result of careful study. One of the most

Chapter
Twenty-
Four

*Mysteries
of
Isis*

259

Thoth, ibis-headed god of wisdom.

ultimately meaningful and effective initiations I have experienced arose from a seemingly trivial incident.

One night while I was drinking coffee at a neighborhood cafe, a loose dog wandered up. He was a beautiful golden retriever, on his own and not too terribly smart about streets and cars. He had no tags. I took control of him because I felt obliged to help an animal in trouble, and hoped that someone else would do the same for my dogs if they were in the same situation. It was the first day of a three-day weekend, and I thought it was unlikely I could find his owner before the following Tuesday. Still, I didn't feel I could simply leave him loose to meet whatever fate arose. I took him home, where, in quick order, he terrorized my cats, attacked my male dog, and provided me with the unwelcome present of a dead baby possum from the backyard.

The next day I leashed him up and took him back to the area where I suspected he had come from, armed with fliers. As I walked along the neighborhood streets, I asked everyone where the dog might belong. Finally one woman sweeping her porch told me that the church would let out soon, and that someone there might recognize the dog. So I went and stood on the church steps until the service let out and a man thought he recognized the retriever as belonging some distance away. He gave me general directions and I set off, walking along streets that grew increasingly quieter until they were absolutely silent —no cars, no cries of children, no hum of lawnmowers, a complete lack of Sunday sounds. It was almost ominous, the lack of sound, but then I grew accustomed to it and my mind welcomed the rare silence and the slow rhythm of myself and the dog, walking in search. I carried the leash loosely, hoping he would lead me to his home.

As I walked, my thoughts ran over many areas of my life, and I came to some new conclusions and clarifications. I thought casually on the theme of Isis in Search, guided by Anubis, looking for the pieces of Osiris so that She could restore him to wholeness. The Osirian portion of the Isis mythos had always seemed sterile to me. Despite efforts, I had never connected meaningfully with Osiris as a God— as a god of mine—other than simply as the object of my goddess' love and sorrow, filtered through Her. Beneath the palm-lined streets, under clear warm sunshine, I thought of the palm groves once sacred to Osiris and picked up an orange palm nut to put on my altar.

Finally I met a man who also thought he knew the dog, and who went with me to another house, this one abundant with three or four golden retrievers. From there I was sent on again to a house at the edge of a canyon. As I walked up, I heard children cry out "Star's home!" and I smiled over the very Egyptian-style pun. I had brought home the Dog Star, another name for Sirius, Isis' sacred home in the heavens.

All this might have stayed a con-templative walk with a pun at the end of it but I decided, after walking back, to stop at a bookstore, feeling as if I had earned a reward for my efforts. I checked my usual sections but found nothing. Then a bright turquoise and gilt binding caught my eye on the Philosophy shelf and

I reached up for it, realizing the title of the book I was reaching for was simply one word: Isis. I looked twice, certain I had misread it. As I pulled the book down, on the cover was not a picture of Isis but of Osiris. I purchased it from the bookseller, who commented that he had never noticed that book on the shelf before.

When I returned home, the book was too charming to confine to a bookshelf. I propped it up on my altar. Despite Osiris' intimate relationship to Isis, I had never felt terribly comfortable with the somewhat dreary aspects of his role as God of the Dead. I had been bound up with a very one-sided conception of his Underworld aspects and entirely neglected his golden aspects of Osiris-As-Ra, Osiris the Perpetually Living, never to be enclosed in tomb or Underworld.

This book, seen daily, reflecting the altar light in the gilded image, gently prodded my mind. For the first time, I was giving altar space—and attention—to Osiris. Before long I felt myself awakening to a new conception of Osiris, dynamic and powerful, a worthy complement to vibrant Isis, not a mere weak shadow, brought temporarily to life and then consigned to the Underworld and life of the tomb. My conceptions of Isis and Osiris, and my own spirituality, changed positively as a result of a long walk with a lost dog.

The initiatory benefits and effects have been far more powerful than many more formal rituals have offered.

Initiations may come slowly or quickly, or may not seem to be coming at all. One priestess had

scarcely encountered the name of Isis when she was suddenly receiving complex initiatory visions and dreams. But for most, the process will be gradual and may seem under the control of the initiate or initiating group rather than the Goddess Herself. In some cases of being initiated into an organization rather than into the worship of a specific deity, this may actually be the case.

The number of possible varieties of initiation is infinite. Some of the more common types of Isian initiation include initiations into the Earth, Solar, Lunar, and Stellar aspects of Isis and into different explorations of the many aspects of Isis, such as Isis In Search, Isis the mother, Isis the Alchemist, and so on. Initiations may also occur involving related deities, such as initiations into aspects of Osiris, Anubis, Nepthys, and Khepera. These initiations, of which only a few are mentioned here, may occur one at a time or, more rarely, as a combined initiation, such as a Stellar experience of the Isis in Search aspect, which would differ from an Earth-oriented initiation into the same aspect.

A note on group initiations, initiations into lodges, and similar situations. The initiation rites performed or required by a group may be absolutely essential for membership and complete ability to operate within that particular group. However, these initiations may or may not coincide with the divine initiations offered by the deities to whom we ally ourselves. It is difficult, for example, to expect that twelve or fourteen individuals are all perfectly "ripe" for initiation on a

specific single day, or when the schedules of the members seem to continuously override the schedules of the heavens and the celebrations of the gods.

If there is a particular type of initiation that you want to pursue, several general techniques are useful. First of all, it is very important to keep accurate and complete records of your dreams, visions, and intuitions. See Chapter Twenty-Three, "Isis and Dreaming," for more information on this subject.

It is also helpful to master a divination skill and to develop psychic awareness in general. We are unconscious of most of what happens to us and within us spiritually. The rich nighttime hours we spend in sleep are often lost to our conscious minds. Even during the day, while the rest of our consciousness is occupied with mundane tasks, our subconscious, spiritual mind is functioning and may briefly burst into our awareness with a warning or unexpected insight. As unlikely as it may seem, it is possible to experience a genuine initiation and then bury it under the debris of everyday life, so that its effect is forced to lie dormant until one is willing to acknowledge it (or is forced to do so).

Finally, taking regular and frequent breaks from the crowded physical and mental conditions of modern life will make the mind and body more receptive to initiation. Many ills of modern society are brought on by the lack of "empty time," time which is productive for nothing but random thought and contemplation. One prominent magical group of the early part of this century refused to accept

members who were not already financially independent, as they believed that anyone who had to actually work for a living could never attain the personal insight necessary for magical work. While this approach is extreme and elitist, the basic premise—that being "of the world" makes it more challenging to advance spiritually—is all too true.

If you do decide to pursue a particular aspect of initiation, and you feel that Isis is in alliance with your choice, surround yourself with objects and images that remind you of the aspect of your initiation. Perform related activities. The "Meditations" in the chapters on the solar, lunar, earth, sea, and cosmic Isis are good starting points to explore these potential initiations. Your own experience will be unique, a gift to you by the grace of the Goddess Isis.

RECOGNIZING INITIATION

Initiation goes on forever; it is an unending spiral propelling us into new areas and new abilities. We may mark certain segments as beginnings or endings, or a special ceremony may lead us to assign a specific date to a process that is non-linear. As you progress, new insights may come to you on material you thought had been covered long ago. You may find yourself spiralling through the initiations mentioned here many times, each time travelling on a higher arc of the spiral.

You will know that you have completed a particular initiation when you feel comfortable and free about the subject. If you do not genuinely feel that you understand one or another aspect of Isis, there will be a telltale clutch in the stomach when someone asks you to explain your experiences in that area, or to guide them through it. There may always be areas that are not your specialty, but you should gain enough familiarity with them that you feel comfortable discussing them.

Please also be aware that experiencing an initiation does not automatically give you either the right or the responsibility to train others in that initiatory area. If Isis confirms to you that teaching is your calling, then by all means, teach. But you may also be experiencing initiations solely for your personal development. How to apply what is experienced will be different for everyone.

ORDINATION

At some point you may feel that the time has come to assume "official" duties, and that the time of pure study and devotion to your personal initiations is over. You feel competent enough in a number of areas of the worship of Isis to offer guidance to others, and to willingly and knowingly take on the responsibilities that ordination as a member of the clergy requires. This often corresponds to a desire to obtain formal recognition as a member of the clergy.

Seeking ordination is not to be undertaken lightly. You can lead a happy and fulfilling life in the worship of Isis and never seek "official" priest or priesthood.

Please don't seek ordination as a priest or priestess of Isis if:

- you feel you need more time for yourself, your family, or your

career. Becoming ordained is a new career. The payoffs are spiritual, and even then may be largely deferred until another lifetime.

- you had a vision of a really pleasant past life in a temple someplace.
- you think it's the only thing left that may give you a real spiritual or magical experience, so you may as well try it.
- you think that so-and-so will finally shut up, recognize you as a "real" priest or priestess, and give you the respect you deserve.
- you think it will get you a better

Chapter
Twenty-
Four

*Mysteries
of
Isis*

263

An Isis icon painted by Olivia Robertson, Archpriestess and founder of The Fellowship of Isis, presented to the author after her ordination. (By permission of the artist.)

- you think it will prove to your family that you are serious about this alternative religion thing.
- you believe that you have the one right, true, and only path to Isis, and you want the opportunity to make everyone conform for the glory of the Goddess.
- you believe that the Goddess will reward your devotion and hard work by giving you an easy life.

Please *do* seek ordination if you believe:

- that there is nothing else that will satisfy your longing to devote yourself to the work of Isis.
- that you can make a valid contribution to life, both within the faith and outside of it.
- you want to encourage others to explore the faith and you strive to make your own life a worthy example.
- though other aspects of worship and other deities may attract you at times, the allure of Isis remains constant.
- a dream or vision of Isis which feels true to your heart tells you to seek ordination.
- you recognize and accept that major demands may sometimes be made on your time and emotions.
- that even the threat of death could not make you recant your alliance with Isis in your heart.
- that even active opposition of persons whom you respect and whose opinions matter to you will not make you abandon your resolve.
- that you are willing to take on unexpected responsibilities.

If after this self-quizzing, you do believe you want the "official" title, you will then want to seek a group or individual who can ordain you and grant you recognition. Whatever group or individual grants this privilege will normally have their own curriculum of materials that they regard as essential for you to master prior to ordination. Although you may be initiated into many aspects of Isis, and consider yourself ready to be ordained, don't be surprised if this merely opens the door to a period of "graduate study" before ordination. If you believe that Isis means for your ordination to be an exception to these requirements, look again at your motives. If Isis does want you to receive special consideration in these areas, She will make that clear to the ordaining group Herself, or clear to you that the time is not yet right.

Above all, be alert to your own initiations and ordinations. The temple is not really a place where we *go*. It is all around us. The rites and rituals that truly add to the glory of the gods are the ones that only *we* can do. We offer our individuality as our highest gift to the gods. We can choose to see everything as initiation, and everything will *be* initiation. We can choose to see everything as worship, and everything will *be* worship. We are all already empowered as priestesses and priests, and only our heartfelt word of acceptance is necessary to enter into communion with Isis.

☽·✧·☾

Now we are in the hour between darkness and dawn. Twenty-four hours have passed, each with its lessons,

Chapter
Twenty-
Four

*Mysteries
of
Isis*

265

The Temple of Isis on the Island of Elephantine.

challenges, pleasures and pains. A day in the worship of Isis is passing, while a new one waits to flow in. And so the days and nights have followed, one after another, year after year. Isis has endured. And the yearning in human hearts for the touch of this Goddess' wings has also endured.

The rays of the sun reach out to us like Her gentle hands. The distant clouds on the horizon take grey light and transform it to golden pink. Listen. It is the sound from without or within that says, softly then growing into power,

Awake, awake, awake,
Awake in peace,

Lady of peace,
Rise thou in peace,
Rise thou in beauty,
Goddess of Life
Beautiful in heaven.
Heaven is in peace.
Earth is in peace.
O Goddess,
Daughter of Nut,
Daughter of Geb,
Beloved of Osiris,
Goddess rich in names!
All praise to You
All praise to You,
I adore You
I adore You
Lady Isis!

Appendix A

PLUTARCH'S ACCOUNT —— OF THE STORY OF ISIS —— AND OSIRIS

ALTHOUGH THE MYTH OF Isis and Osiris was known throughout Egypt, no single Egyptian source provides us with all of the details of the essential story. To find this in ancient sources it is necessary to go to Plutarch, an initiate and writer of the second century of the current era. In *On Isis and Osiris*, which was dedicated to Klea, a priestess of Isis and Osiris, he gives the following account of the mystery. To avoid confusion, please note that Plutarch calls Set "Typhon" and Horus "Aroueris." He also refers to Thoth/Tahuti as "Hermes."

This excerpt is from Plutarch's *Moralia* (translated by Frederick Cole Babbitt). London; William Heineman Ltd., 1936.

"HERE FOLLOWS THE STORY related in the briefest possible words with the omission of everything that is merely unprofitable or superfluous:

They say that the Sun, when he became aware of Rhea's intercourse with Kronos, invoked a curse upon her that she should not give birth to a child in any month or any year; but Hermes, being enamored of the goddess, consorted with her. Later, playing at draughts with the moon, he won from her the seventieth part of each of her periods of illumination, and from all the winnings he composed five days, and intercalated them as an addition to the three hundred and sixty days. The Egyptians even now call these five days intercalated and celebrate them as the birthdays of the gods. They relate that on the first of these days Osiris was born, and at the hour of his birth a voice issued forth saying, 'The Lord of All advances to the light.' But some relate

that a certain Pamyles, while he was drawing water in Thebes, heard a voice issuing from the shrine of Zeus, which bade him proclaim with a loud voice that a mighty and beneficent king, Osiris, had been born; and for this Kronos entrusted to him the child Osiris, which he brought up. It is in his honor that the festival of Pamylia is celebrated, a festival which resembles the phallic processions. On the second of these days Aroueris was born whom they call Apollo, and some call him also the elder Horus. On the third day Typhon was born, but not in due season or manner, but with a blow he broke through his mother's side and leapt forth. On the fourth day Isis was born in the regions that are ever moist; and on the fifth Nepthys, to whom they give the name of Finality and the name of Aphrodite, and some also the name of Victory. There is also a tradition that Osiris and Aroueris were sprung from the Sun, Isis from Hermes, and Typhon and Nepthys from Kronos. For this reason the kings considered the third of the intercalated days as inauspicious, and transacted no business on that day, nor did they give any attention to their bodies until nightfall. They relate, moreover, that Nepthys became the wife of Typhon; but Isis and Osiris were enamored of each other and consorted together in the darkness of the womb before their birth. Some say that Aroueris came from this union and was called the elder Horus by the Egyptians, but Apollo by the Greeks.

One of the first acts related of Osiris in his reign was to deliver the Egyptians from their destitute and brutish manner of living. This he did by showing them the fruits of cultivation, by giving them laws, and by teaching them to honor the gods. Later he traveled over the whole earth, civilizing it without the slightest need of arms, but most of the peoples he won over to his way by the charm of his persuasive discourse combined with song and all manner of music. Hence the Greeks came to identify him with Dionysos.

During his absence the tradition is that Typhon attempted nothing revolutionary because Isis, who was in control, was vigilant and alert; but when he returned home Typhon contrived a treacherous plot against him and formed a group of conspirators, seventy-two in number. He had also the cooperation of a queen from Ethiopia who was there at the time and whose name they report as Aso. Typhon, having secretly measured Osiris's body and having made ready a beautiful chest of corresponding size artistically ornamented, caused it to be brought into the room where the festivity was in progress. The company was much pleased at the sight of it and admired it greatly, whereupon Typhon jestingly promised to present it to the man who should find the chest to be exactly his length when he lay down in it. They all tried it in turn, but no one fitted it; then Osiris got into it and lay down, and those who were in the plot ran to it and slammed down the lid, which they fastened by nails from the outside and also by using molten lead. Then they carried the chest to the river and sent it on its way to the sea through the Tanitic Mouth. Wherefore the Egyptians even to this day name this mouth the hateful and execrable. Such is the tradition. They say also that the date on which this deed was done was the seventeenth day of Athyr, when the sun passes through Scorpion, and in the twenty-eighth year of the reign of Osiris; but some say that these are the years of his life and not of his reign.

The first to learn of the deed and to bring to men's knowledge an account of what had been done were the Pans and Satyrs who lived in the region around Chemmis, and so, even to this day, the sudden confusion and consternation of a crowd is called a panic. Isis, when the tidings reached her, at once cut off one of her tresses and put on a garment of mourning in a place where the city still bears the name of Kopto. Others think that the name means 'deprivation,' for they also express 'deprive' by means of *koptein*. But Isis wandered everywhere at her wit's end; no one whom she approached did she fail to address, and even when she met some little children she asked them about the chest. As it happened, they had seen it, and they told her the mouth of the river through which the friends of Typhon had launched the coffin into the sea. Wherefore the Egyptians think that little children possess the power of prophecy, and they try to divine the future from the portents which they find in children's words, especially when children are playing about in holy places and crying out whatever chances to come into their minds.

They relate also that Isis, learning that Osiris in his love had consorted with her sister through ignorance, in the belief that she was Isis, and seeing the proof of this in

the garland of melilote which he had left with Nepthys, sought to find the child; for the mother, immediately after its birth, had exposed it because of her fear of Typhon. And when the child had been found, after great toil and trouble, with the help of dogs which led Isis to it, it was brought up and became her guardian and attendant, receiving the name of Anubis, and it is said to protect the gods just as dogs protect men.

Thereafter Isis, as they relate, learned that the chest had been cast up by the sea near the land of Byblos and that the waves had gently set it down in the midst of a clump of heather. The heather in a short time ran up into a very beautiful and massive stock, and enfolded and embraced the chest with its growth and concealed it within its trunk. The king of the country admired the great size of the plant, and cut off the portion that enfolded the chest, which was now hidden from sight, and used it as a pillar to support the roof of his house. These facts, they say, Isis ascertained by the divine inspiration of Rumor, and came to Byblos and sat down by a spring, all defection and tears; she exchanged no word with anybody, save only that she welcomed the queen's maidservants and treated them with great amiability, plaiting their hair for them and imparting to their persons a wondrous fragrance from her own body. But when the queen observed her maidservants, a longing came upon her for the unknown woman and for such hairdressing and for a body fragrant with ambrosia. Thus it happened that Isis was sent for and became so intimate with the

queen that the queen made her the nurse of her baby. They say that the king's name was Malcander; the queen's name some say was Astarte, others Saosis, and still others Nemanus, which the Greeks would call Athenais.

They relate that Isis nursed the child by giving it her finger to suck instead of her breast, and in the night she would burn away the mortal portions of its body. She herself would turn into a swallow and flit about the pillar with a wailing lament, until the queen who had been watching, when she saw her babe on fire, gave forth a loud cry and thus deprived it of immortality. Then the goddess disclosed herself and asked for the pillar which served to support the roof. She removed it with the greatest ease and cut away the wood of the heather which surrounded the chest; then, when she had wrapped up the wood in a linen cloth and had poured perfume upon it, she entrusted it to the care of the kings; and even to this day the people of Byblos venerate this wood which is preserved in the shrine of Isis. Then the goddess threw herself down upon the coffin with such a dreadful wailing that the younger of the king's sons expired on the spot. The elder son she kept with her, and, having placed the coffin on board a boat, she put out from land. Since the Phaedrus river toward the early morning fostered a rather boisterous wind, the goddess grew angry and dried up its stream.

In the first place where she found seclusion, when she was quite by herself, they relate that she opened the chest and laid her face upon the face within and caressed it and wept. The child came quietly up behind her and saw what was there, and when the goddess became aware of his presence, she turned about and gave him one awful look of anger. The child could not endure the fright, and died. Others will have it so, but assert that he fell overboard into the sea from the boat that was mentioned above. He also is the recipient of honors because of the goddess; for they say that the Maneros of whom the Egyptians sing at their convivial gatherings is this very child. Some say, however, that his name was Palaestinus or Pelusius, and that the city founded by the goddess was named in his honor. They also recount that this Maneros who is the theme of their songs was the first to invent music. But some say that the word is not the name of any person, but an expression belonging to the vocabulary of drinking and feasting: 'Good luck be ours in things like this!' and that this is really the idea expressed by the exclamation 'maneros' whenever the Egyptians use it. In the same way we may be sure that the likeness of a corpse which, as it is exhibited to them, is carried around in a chest, is not a reminder of what happened to Osiris, as some assume; but it is to urge them, as they contemplate it, to use and to enjoy the present, since all very soon must be what it is now and this is their purpose in introducing it into the midst of merry-making.

As they relate, Isis proceeded to her son Horus, who was being reared in Buto, and bestowed the chest in a place well out of the way; but Typhon,[1] who was hunting by night in the light of the moon, happened upon it. Recognizing the body he divided it into fourteen parts and scattered them, each in a different place. Isis learned of this and sought for them again, sailing through the swamps in a boat of papyrus. This is the reasons why people sailing in such boats are not harmed by the crocodiles, since these creatures in their own way show either their fear or their reverence for the goddess.

The traditional result of Osiris's dismemberment is that there are many so-called tombs of Osiris in Egypt; for Isis held a funeral for each part when she had found it. Others deny this and assert that she cause effigies of him to be made and these she distributed among the several cities, pretending that she was giving them his body, in order that he might receive divine honors in a greater number of cities, and also that, if Typhon should succeed in overpowering Horus, he might despair of ever finding the true tomb when so many were pointed out to him, all of them called the tomb of Osiris.

Of the parts of Osiris's body the only one which Isis did not find was the male member, for the reason that this had been at once tossed into the river, and the lepidotus, the sea-bream, and the pike had fed upon it; and it is from these very fishes the Egyptians are most scrupulous in abstaining. But Isis made a replica of the member to take its place, and consecrated the phallus, in honor of which the Egyptians even at the present day celebrate a festival.

Later, as they relate, Osiris came to Horus from the other world and exercised and trained him for the battle. After a time Osiris asked Horus what he held to be the most noble of all things. When Horus replied, 'To avenge one's father and mother for evil done to them,' Osiris then asked him what animal he considered the most useful for them who go forth to battle; and when Horus said, 'A horse,' Osiris was surprised and raised the question why it was that he had not rather said a lion than a horse. Horus answered that a lion was a useful thing for a man in need of assistance, but that a horse served best for cutting off the flight of an enemy and annihilating him. When Osiris heard this he was much pleased, since he felt that Horus had now an adequate preparation. It is said that, as many were continually transferring their allegiance to Horus, Typhon's concubine, Thoueris, also came over to him; and a serpent which pursued her was cut to pieces by Horus's men, and now, in memory of this, the people throw down a rope in their midst and chop it up.

Now the battle, as they relate, lasted many days and Horus prevailed. Isis, however, to whom Typhon was delivered in chains, did not cause him to be put to death, but released him and let him go. Horus could not endure this with equanimity, but laid hands upon his mother and wrested the royal diadem from her head; but Hermes put upon her a helmet like unto the head of a cow.

Typhon formally accused Horus of being an illegitimate child, but with the help of Hermes to plead his cause it was decided by the gods that he also was legitimate. Typhon was then overcome in two other battles.

Osiris consorted with Isis after his death, and she became the mother of Harpocrates, untimely born and weak in his lower limbs.

Stories akin to these and to others like them they say are related about Typhon; how that, prompted by jealousy and hostility, he wrought terrible deeds and, by bringing utter confusion upon the things, filled the whole Earth, and the ocean as well, with ills, and later paid the penalty therefor. But the avenger, the sister and wife of Osiris, after she had quenched and suppressed the madness of fury of Typhon, was not indifferent to the contests and struggles which she had endured, nor to her own wanderings nor to her manifold deeds of wisdom and many feats of bravery, nor would she accept oblivion and silence for them, but she intermingled in the most holy rites portrayals and suggestions and representations of her experiences at that time, and sanctified them, both as a lesson in godliness and an encouragement for men and women who find themselves in the clutch of like calamities. She herself and Osiris, translated for their virtues from good demigods (daimones) into gods, as were Heracles and Dionysos later, not incongruously enjoy double honors, both those of gods and those of demigods, and their powers extend everywhere, but are greatest in the regions above the earth and beneath the earth."

☽ · ◠⊙◡ · ☾

Plutarch's Account of the Origin of Sarapis

PLUTARCH GIVES AN ACCOUNT of how the worship of Sarapis began.

This excerpt is from Plutarch's *Moralia* (translated by Frederick Cole Babbitt). London; William Heineman Ltd., 1936.

" . . . **m**EN ASSERT THAT Plouton is none other than Sarapis and that Persephone is Isis, even as Archemachus of Euboea has said, and also Heracleides Ponticus who holds the oracle in Canopus to be an oracle of Plouton.

Ptolemy Soter saw in a dream the colossal statue of Plouton in Sinope, not knowing nor having ever seen how it looked, and in his dream the statue bade him convey it with all speed to Alexandria. He had no information and no means of knowing where the statue was situated, but as he related the vision to his friends there was discovered for him a much trav-

eled man by the name of Sosibius, who said that he had seen in Sinope just such a great statue as the king thought he saw. Ptolemy, therefore, sent Soteles and Dionysius, who, after a considerable time and with great difficulty, and not without the help of divine providence, succeeded in stealing the statue and bringing it away. When it had been conveyed to Egypt and exposed to view, Timotehus, the expositor of sacred law, and Manetho of Sebennytys, and their associates, conjectured that it was the statue of Plouton, basing their conjecture on the Cerberus and the serpent with it, and they convinced Ptolemy that it was the statue of none other of the gods but Sarapis. It certainly did not bear this name when it came from

Sinope, but, after it had been conveyed to Alexandria, it took to itself the name which Plouton bears among the Egyptians, that of Sarapis. Moveover, since Herecleius the physical philosopher says, 'The same are Hades and Dionysos, to honor whom they rage and rave,' people are inclined to come to this opinion. In fact, those who insist that the body is called Hades, since the soul is, as it were, deranged and inebriate when it is in the body, are too frivolous in their use of allegory. It is better to identify Osiris with Dionysos and Sarapis with Osiris, who received this appellation at the time when he changed his nature. For this reason Sarapis is a god of all peoples in common, even as Osiris is; and this they who have par-ticipated in the holy rites well know.

It is not worthwhile to pay any attention to the Phrygian writings, in which it is said that Serapis was the son of Heracles, and Isis was his daughter, and Typhon was the son of Alcaeus, who also was a son of Heracles; nor must we fail to condemn Phylarchus, who writes that Dionysos was the first to bring from India into Egypt two bulls, and that the name of one was Apis and of the other Osiris. But Sarapis is the name of him who sets the universe in order, and it is derived 'sweep' (sairein) which some say means 'to beautify' and 'to put in order.' As a matter of fact, these statements of Phylarchus are absurd, but even more absurd are those put forth by those who say that Sarapis is no god at all, but the name of the coffin of Apis; and that there are in Memphis certain bronze gates called the Gates of Oblivion and Lamentation, which are opened when the burial of Apis takes place, and they give out a deep and harsh sound; and it is because of this that we lay hand upon anything of bronze that gives out a sound. More moderate is the statement of those who say that the derivation is from 'shoot' (seuesthai) or 'scoot' (sousthai), meaning the general movement of the universe. Most of the priests say that Osiris and Apis are conjoined into one, thus explaining to us and informing us that we must regard Apis as the bodily image of the soul of Osiris. But it is my opinion that, if the name Sarapis is Egyptian, it denotes cheerfulness and rejoicing, and I base this opinion on the fact that the Egyptians call their festival of rejoicing sairei."

Appendix C

APULEIUS' ACCOUNT
OF THE PLOIAPHESIA

THIS IS VIRTUALLY THE only full account we have of any of the Isian rituals performed in Greco-Roman times. The translation used here is J. Gwyn Griffith's, from Apuleius of Madaura's *The Isis Book* (*Metamorphoses, Book XI*), E.J. Brill Publishing Company, Leiden, The Netherlands.

"NOW THERE GRADUALLY APPEARED the forerunners of the great procession, each finely decked out with the fancy dress of his choice. One man girded with a belt played the part of a soldier; another with cloak tucked up was shown by his boots and spears to be a huntsman, while another, wearing gilded shoes, a silk gown, and expensive ornaments, pretended to be a woman by attaching a wig to his head and walking with a wanton gait. Another again, distinguished by his greaves, shield, helmet and sword, you would think had just emerged from a gladiatorial school. Then there was one acting a magistrate, complete with torches and purple; and another with cloak, staff, woven sandals and goat-beard played a philosopher.

There were two with different kinds of reed rods, one acting a fowler with bird-lime, the other a fisherman with hooks. I saw too a tame she-bear dressed like a matron and carried in a sedan-chair; a monkey with a plaited cap and clothes of Phrygian saffron carrying a gold cup like the shepherd Ganymede; an ass with wings glued on his back walking beside a decrepit old man, so that one suggested Bellerophon, the other Pegasus, but both were equally comic.

While these amusing delights of the people were appearing all over the place, the procession proper of the Saviour Goddess was on its way. Women radiant in white garments, rejoicing in different kinds of emblems, which they carried, and garlanded with flowers of spring, were strewing the ground with blossoms from their bosoms along the road where the sacred company proceeded. Other women had reversed shining mirrors behind their backs to show respect to the goddess as she moved after them; others carrying ivory combs represented with waving arms and bending fingers the adornment and combing of the queen's hair; others again bespattered the streets with various perfumes and a delightful balm shaken out in drops. A large number of people, besides, of both sexes were seeking the blessing of Her who is the creator of the stars of heaven with lanterns, torches, wax tapers, and other kinds of artificial light. Then came the charming music of many instruments, and the sound of pipe and flute in the sweeetest melodies. They were followed by a delightful choir of the most select youths, radiant in snow-white festal tunics; they repeated a captivating song which a skilled poet had written for music with the aid of the Goddesses of Song, and the theme of this from time to time contained musical preludes to the solemn vows to come. There came also flautists dedicated to great Sarapis, who repeated through a reed, held sideways towards the right ear, a tune traditional to the temple and its deity; and there were many shouting out, 'Keep the way clear for the holy procession!'

Then surged on the throngs of those initiated into the divine mysteries, men and women of every rank and age, shining in the immaculate whiteness of linen raiment. The women had wrapped a transparent veil round their locks, that were moist with perfume, and the

men had gleaming pates after shaving their heads completely. Together they produced a shrill tinkling noise with sistrums that were of bronze or silver, or indeed of gold. With them were the terrestrial stars of the great faith, those noble leaders, the priests of the ritual, who, clad in white linen that was fitted tightly round the breasts and reached to their feet, bore forward the distinguished emblems of the mightiest gods. The first of them stretched out a lantern which gleamed out with a bright light, not indeed like those that illumines our night banquets, but a golden vessel that kindled a quite big flame in its central orifice. A second priest was dressed similarly but with both his hands he carried a high altar, that is a 'source of help,' a distinctive name derived from the helping providence of the eminent goddess. A third walked holding up a palm-branch with leaves delicately wrought of gold, and also a herald's staff such as Mercury has. The fourth displayed an emblem of justice, a deformed left hand with the palm outstretched; this seemed, because of its innate slowness, and lack of all cunning and skill, to represent justice better than the right hand. The same man carried too a small golden vessel rounded in the shape of a female breast, from which he poured libations of milk. A fifth priest carried a golden winnowing-basket made of laurel twigs, and another bore a two-handled pitcher.

There was no delay when the gods then came forward, deigning to tread with human feet. First came that dread messenger of both celestial and infernal beings, Anubis, of lofty stature and with a face now black, now golden, holding high his dog's neck; in his left hand he bore a herald's staff and with his right hand he shook a green palm-branch. Hard on his steps followed a cow in upright posture; that cow was the fertile image of the goddess who is the creator of all, and one of the blessed priesthood carried the image on his shoulders with proud steps. Another carried a box holding secret things and concealing within it the hidden attributes of the sublime faith. Another bore in his happy bosom the revered image of the highest deity, in a likeness not of an ox or bird or wild animal, nor even of a man, but inspiring reverence both through its skilled workmanship and by its very strangeness, it was an unutterable witness to a faith ever lofty which claimed to be hidden in a vast silence. It was fashioned of gleaming gold in the following form: a small vase it was, most cunningly hollowed out, with a base finely rounded, while outside it was adorned with wondrous Egyptian figures. Its mouth was not so high and stretched to a channel, standing out in a long spout; on its other side was a handle turning well away and joined in a sweeping curve. On top of the handle was set an asp in a coiled knot, its scaly neck rearing itself with a streaked swelling.

And behold! here come to me the promised blessings of the most helpful goddess and a priest approaches bringing with him my destiny and my very salvation. He was equipped as the divine promise had foretold, carrying in his right hand a sistrum intended for the goddess, and a crown for me—and assuredly the crown was most

fitting, since after enduring so many and so great toils and passing through so many dangers, by the providence of the mighty goddess I was now overcoming Fortune that had buffeted me so cruelly. Yet I did not push forward impetuously disturbed by sudden joy, for I was naturally afraid that the orderly sequence of the sacred rite would be upset by the precipitous rush of a four-footed beast. But slowly with quiet steps, such as a man might make, I gradually edged my way through the crowd, that gave before me, clearly by the guidance of the goddess, and I gently crept inwards.

But the priest, as in fact I was able to find out, remembered his vision by night, and marvelled how well everything agreed with the instructions received. He instantly stopped, and raising his right hand without any prompting, held the crown of roses up to my very mouth. Then I in my agitation, with my heart throbbing wildly, took up with greedy mouth the crown which was bright with the bloom of lovely inwoven roses, and eagerly hoping for fulfillment of the promise, I most eagerly munched through it all. Nor was I disappointed in the heavenly promise: at once my ugly animal form left me.

First my scruffy bristles fell off, then my rough hide became thin and the fat belly subsided, while the soles of my feet now ended in toes instead of hoofs and the hands were no longer feet, doing their work now in my upright posture. My lofty neck contracted, my mouth and head became round; my huge ears regained their former slenderness and my rock-like molars returned to human scale; and my

Appendix C

*Apuleius'
Account of
the
Ploiaphesia*

277

tail, my chief torment of old, was non-existent! The people marvelled; and the devotees expressed their adoration of such a manifest token of the highest deity's power and of the glory which had conformed to the visions of the night, as well as her easy skill in achieving my transformation. This they did with clear voices in unison, raising their hands to heaven and acclaiming the radiant blessing bestowed by the goddess.

But I was smitten with profound amazement and stood rooted to the spot in silence for my mind could not take in so sudden and so mighty a joy. What would be best for me to say first? How should I first use my restored voice? With what conversation could I most aptly inaugurate my reborn power of speech? In what words and at what length was I to thank so great a goddess? But the priest, who had by divine communication, as ever, become acquainted with all my misfortunes from the start, although he himself had been deeply moved by the wondrous miracle, first gave orders with a meaningful nod that a linen garment should be given to cover me; for as soon as the ass had removed its loathsome skin from me, I pressed my thighs closely together and applied my hands carefully, so that as far as my nakedness allowed, I had decently covered myself up with a veil given by nature. Then one of the band of devotees smartly took off his outer cloak and quickly put it over me. This done, the priest, with a benign expression, looked in astonishment at my form which was now indeed thoroughly human and spoke thus:

'After enduring many different troubles and after being driven by the wildest storms of Fortune and her heaviest gales, at last, Lucius, you have come to the haven of Rest and the altar of Mercy. Your high birth was of no avail to you nor even your position in society, nor yet the learning in which you are so rich, but on the slippery path of your hot-headed youth you fell into low pleasures and your have gained a grim reward for your ill-starred curiosity. Nevertheless the blindness of Fortune, while it tortured you with the worst of dangers, yet led you in its unforeseeing evil to your state of religious bliss. Let her quit now and rage in her wildest frenzy and seek another object for her cruelty. For hostile fate has no power over those whose lives have been claimed by the majesty of our goddess. What avail to wicked Fortune were the robbers, the wild beasts, the slavery, the hardships of journeys that winded on and back, and the daily fear of death? Now you have been received into the protection of a Fortune who is not blind but sees, and who illumines the other gods too with the radiance of her light.

'Show, then, a happier face in keeping with the white cloak you have assumed. Follow the procession of the Saviour Goddess with triumphant step. Let the unbelievers take note and acknowledge their mistake: behold, here is Lucius! He has been freed from his former sufferings and, rejoicing in the providence of mighty Isis, he is victorious over his Fortune. But to be safer and better equipped, enrol your name in this holy military service, whose solemn oath you were asked to take not long ago, and vow yourself from this moment to the ministry of our religious. Accept of your own free will the yoke of service. For when you have begun to serve the goddess, then will you better realize the result of your freedom.'

After prophesying in this manner the excellent priest took several gasping weary breaths and was silent. Then I mingled with the sacred procession and went forward, accompanying the shrine, so that I was plain and prominent for the whole populace to see. Men pointed to me with their fingers and nodded their heads. All the people were talking about me: 'This is the man who has been today restored to human shape through the splendid divinity of the all-powerful goddess. Happy is he, by heaven, and thrice blessed, to have clearly deserved, by the purity of his former life and his pious loyalty, such a wondrous favour from heaven that he is, as it were, born again and has at once pledged himself to service in the sacred rites.'

In the meantime, amid the clamour of vows made in festive spirit, we gradually passed onwards and now, approaching the sea-shore, we reached the very spot where my double the ass had lain the day before. When the images of the gods had been duly set down there, from reverent lips the chief priest first uttered the most exalted prayers over a ship that had been built with exquisite skill and decorated round about with wonderful Egyptian paintings. With a bright torch, with an egg and with sulphur he purified the ship so well that it was purity itself. Then he publicly named it and dedicated it to the goddess. The gleaming sail of this auspicious barque bore golden letters woven into its texture. These signified the inaugural prayer for fortunate sailing in the new year's commerce. A rounded pine rose as its mast, lofty in its radiance and with a finely resplendent top. The stern had a curving beak and shone with a covering of gold leaf. In short the whole ship was aglow with the polish of smooth citrus-wood. Thereupon all the people, both the devotees and the unattached alike, vied in loading the ship with baskets heaped with spices and similar offerings and they poured on the waves libations of meal mixed with milk, until the ship, laden full with generous gifts and votive tokens of good omen, was freed from its anchor cables and launched to sea with a favourable breeze that blew especially for it. When by reason of its movement it had faded from our sight, the bearers of the images took up again their respective loads and with a will made their way back to the temple, observing the same dignified order of procession.

But when we had arrived at the temple itself, the chief priest and the bearers of the divine images together with those who had already been initiated into the mysteries of the awful sanctuary, were received into the chamber of the goddess and there set down in order the breathing effigies. Then one of them, whom they called the Lector, stood near the entrance and after summoning a gathering of the pastophori—that is the name of a sacred college—as though to a public meeting, in the same place he pronounced from a high pedestal, using the writings in a book, prayers

Appendix
C

*Apuleius'
Account of
the
Ploiaphesia*

279

for the prosperity of our great emperor, the senate, the knights, and the whole Roman people, as well as of sailors and ships and the entire domain of our rule. Then he proclaimed the Launching of the Ships in Greek and after the Greek ritual. That this speech brought pleasure to everyone was clear from the subsequent applause of the people. Thereupon, elated with joy, members of the populace presented boughs, greenery and garlands, kissing the while the feet of the goddess, her silver-wrought statue being on the temple steps. After this they departed to their homes. As for me, however, my mind did not allow me to budge an inch from the spot; I was wrapt in my gaze on the image of the goddess and I began to ponder my previous misfortunes."

Appendix D

RESOURCES

This list, as with all else in this book, is only a small selection of the many fine Isis-oriented goods and services available. It is not meant to be exhaustive, and consists only of vendors and organizations I can personally recommend.

TEMPLE STOCK

Dream Merchants
3316 Adams Ave.
San Diego, CA 92116
(619) 563-5591

Isiscraft
Box K-43305
Adams Ave.
San Diego, CA 92116

Incense, oils, scarabs, statuary, Egyptian rubber stamps, and other Isis-oriented gifts and supplies. Send $1.00 for catalog and free lucky scarab.

Mermade Magickal Arts
850 S. Rancho Dr. #2-297
Las Vegas, NV 89106

Katlyn provides incense, books, icons, and other temple furnishings, all of outstanding quality and beauty.

Renée Sabri
4847 Schuyler Ave.
La Mesa, CA
(619) 469-2493
FAX (619) 226-4761

Papyri, scarabs, Egyptian oils, jewelry, and other tempting items.

BOOKS

E.J. Brill
P.O. Box 9000 2300 PA
Leiden, The Netherlands
telephone: 0 71-31 2624

Expensive, scholarly texts in various languages dealing with the spread of the worship of Isis and Serapis, as well as other religious matters.
Better university libraries also often have some of these volumes.

MAGAZINES

Padiusiri
2977 S. Marvin Ave.
Tucson, AZ 85730
(520) 790-2699

Padiusiri is a Priest of Isis and very knowledgeable in a variety of Isian traditions. He has published a series of newsletters on various aspects of Isian worship in Egypt and the Greco-Roman world. Inquire for subscription rates and availability.

RETREATS

The Isis Oasis
20889 Geyserville Ave.
Geyserville, CA 95441
(707) 857-3524
(800) 228-8015

Run by Lorian Vigne, a Priestess of the Fellowship of Isis, this lovely retreat provides a calm setting for meetings or even just a holiday. The Egyptian stained glass windows in the chapel/theater are worth a visit alone. A small Egyptian temple is also on the grounds, along with many exotic cats.

RELIGIOUS ORGANIZATIONS

Membership Secretary
The Fellowship of Isis
Huntington Castle
Clonegal
Enniscorthy
Eire

The Fellowship of Isis unites followers of Isis (as well as of many other deities) in a non-restrictive union devoted to the well-being of all. Founded by the Honorable Olivia Robertson and her late brother, Lord Strathloch, the foundation headquarters are in the family castle. Their permanent Temple to Isis is in the crypt. The Fellowship presently has over ten thousand members worldwide. Membership is free, and can be applied for by writing to the secretary of the Foundation. Subscription to their quarterly Isian Newsletter costs about ten dollars a year.

ESSENTIAL OILS

Starfire Herb Company
P.O. Box 20606
Oakland, CA 94620
(510) 835-4033

Marilee Bigelow, the proprietor, offers fine, reliable, quality essential oils and other products.

MUSIC

Melissa Morgan
P.O. Box 4024
San Diego, CA 92104

Melissa is a harpist who collaborated with flutist Diane Clarke on the album *Invocation to Isis*. Some music stores carry her tapes, all of which are beautiful. They can also be ordered directly from Melissa.

Ali Jihad Racy
Lyrichord Disc, Inc.
141 Perry St.
New York, N.Y. 10014

Ali Jihad Racy's *Ancient Egypt* offers an instrumental version of the "Lamentations of Isis" and a "Hymn to Osiris," among others. This tape can usually be found in the ethnic or world music sections of larger or specialty music stores.

Georgia Kelly

I've used Georgia Kelly's *Tarashanti* as ritual music for many years. All of her tapes are excellent for use in meditation and ritual. She has also collaborated with Steven Halpern. Both of these artists can be found in the New Age sections of large music stores, or at metaphysical bookstores.

Steven McDonald
1030 S. Main, Ste. E
Burbank, CA 91506

Steven McDonald is the official composer for the rites of the Church of the Eternal Source. He offers a number of tapes from various festival celebrations. These can be ordered directly from him.

INCESES

Auroshika Agarbathies
Sri Aurobindo Ashram
Pondicherry
605-002
South India

A fine morning incense based on solar-oriented geraniums is provided by Auroshika. This incense used to be called "Joie du Soleil," or "Joy of the Sun." It is now marketed under the name "Geranium." The tangy fragrance is ideal for morning rites, and will help to awaken the priestess or priest as well as the Goddess. This particular scent seems to be becoming harder to find, but is worth the effort. Auroshika incenses are available through many metaphysical bookstores and New Age shops.

Spiritual Sky
P.O. Box 3068
Visalia, CA 93278
(209) 625-0565

Also recommended as an alternative to kyphi for evening rites is the "Lotus" incense put out by Spiritual Sky. While no true essential oil of lotus is available, this blend of ingredients is very pleasant and evocative. My experiences with other brands of incense labelled "lotus" have not been good. This incense, unfortunately, is also difficult to find.

Haridas Madhavdas Primo
    Incense
Primo Incense Distributing Co.
19231 36th Ave. West, Ste. H
Lynnwood, WA 98036

Haridas Madhavdas Primo Incense, packaged in triangular boxes, is generally very good. They offer a variety of scents. Their jasmine is particularly good, in either the standard or premium forms.

Devonshire Apothecary
P.O. Box 160215
Austin, TX 78716-0215
(512) 442-0019

Devonshire Apothecary offers several incenses that I prefer for temple use. The first of these is a copper-colored incense called "Temple," which I used to buy from a repackager who called it "Temple of Isis." This is an excellent purification incense. Their lotus incense is a light lavender in color and has a lovely, soft scent, less strong than the other lotus incense recommended. Call or write for a catalog.

The Crystal Cave
777 S. Main St., Ste. 2
Orange, CA 92668
(714) 543-0551

A particularly pleasant oil blend called "Isis" is available through The Crystal Cave. This was the first oil I ever used in rites to Isis, and the slightest whiff of it always reminds me of my early attempts to join with the Goddess. They also offer an excellent kyphi oil.

ENDNOTES

Chapter One

    p. 4, 1. Provided by the kind permission of Padiusiri.

Chapter Two

    p. 13, 1. And it's still being promised. There's now a men's aftershave called "Cool Water."

    p. 16, 2. de Pisan, Christine. *Les Cent Histoires de Troye 1499/1500.*

Chapter Four

    p. 38, 1. This temple can be seen in the film *Indiana Jones and the Last Crusade*, where it was used as the exterior of the cavern containing the Grail.

Chapter Five

    p. 49, 1. Budge, E. A. Wallis. *Egyptian Magic.* Secaucus, NJ: University Books, no publication date. Reprint of 1899 edition.

    p. 49, 2. Ellis, Normandi. *Awakening Osiris.* Grand Rapids, MI: Phanes Press, 1988.

    p. 51, 3. Budge, E. A. Wallis. *Egyptian Magic.* Ibid.

Chapter Six

    p. 67, 1. I use the term "priestess" here, as it is more common for a woman to successfully invoke a goddess than for a man to do so. However, it can be done, just as women are capable of bringing through the energy of a god. In these situations, it is important to connect with those aspects of the self which the priest or priestess feels are of the same nature as the deity being invoked. This has nothing to do with "passive" or "active" aspects of deity; it is a matter of the points of identification between the priest or priestess and the deity. It may be easier for some men, for example, to invoke Isis by speaking through their *anima* image—a visualization of their perfected woman partner (who is actually an aspect of their own selves).

        This pertains only to invoking, which is a bringing-within of the divine energy. Evoking, or calling forth the deity, can be done readily by persons of either sex for deities of either sex.

    p. 68, 2. Fortune, Dion. *The Sea Priestess.* London: privately printed, 1938.

    p. 71, 3. Apuleius of Madaura's *The Isis Book* (*Metamorphoses, Book XI*), translated and with a commentary by J. Gwyn Griffiths. Leiden, The Netherlands: E. J. Brill Publishing Company.

    p. 72, 4. Vanderlip, Vera Frederika. *The Four Greek Hymns of Isidorus and the Cult of Isis.* Toronto, Canada: A. M. Hakkert, 1972.

    p. 73, 5. "Lawgiver," an epithet also applied to Demeter.

p. 73, 6. Isis is given the male title here.

p. 73, 7. Grant, Frederick C. *Hellenistic Religions: The Age of Syncretism.* Bobbs-Merrill, Liberal Arts Press, 1953.

Chapter Seven

p. 84, 1. Isis may have had justification, however. In one of the spells of *The Book of Coming Forth By Day*, where the deceased is made to name the different parts of a boat to be used in the transport of the soul across the celestial Nile, the boat asks the deceased to reveal its name. The deceased answers, "That leg of Isis which Ra cut off in order to bring blood to the Night-barque." This obviously refers to another mythological tale, such as the one we have in the Turin Papyrus, but it has been lost to us.

p. 85, 2. For another explanation of the Isis-Ra myth as an alchemical allegory, see Chapter Eighteen, "Isis and Alchemy."

Chapter Eight

p. 89, 1. While this book was going to press, I gained access to Zabkar's translation of the hymns of Isis at Philae. Had I seen this resource before, this chapter would have been much different. For a much more detailed description and explanation of Isis as a war goddess, I urge my readers to consult *Hymns to Isis in Her Temple at Philae* by Louis V. Zabkar, published by University Press of New England at Hanover and London for Brandeis University Press, 1988.

Curiously enough, the hymns of Isis at Philae, that serene, beautiful island parting the waters of the Nile, show her at her most "bellicose," as Zabkar puts it. Nor is her warlike nature only revealed in words; one panel at Philae shows Isis brandishing a curved scimitar. Hymn 5 shows she intended to use it:

> *...(Isis)*
> *Who attacks the powerful ones,*
> *Mightier than the mighty, stronger than the strong;*
> *who smites millions (by) cutting off (their) heads,*
> *Great of massacre against her Enemy.*

The titles revealed in the inscriptions at Philae, Assuan, and Abydos also emphasize her passionately warlike character:

> *Isis, The Vanguard of the Army*
> *Isis, More Effective than a Million Soldiers*
> *Mistress of Flame who Assaults the Rebels*
> *Mistress of Battle*
> *(Who) Fought on the River of the Two Lands to Overthrow all Your Enemies*

Philae's special role as a depository of texts emphasizing Isis' warlike nature is better understood when we realize that Philae was essentially a border outpost, a temple on the frontier of Egypt. There is some evidence that Ptolemy VI's pylon on Philae was intended as a functioning magical barrier against aggression from the unstable south. It is also significant that the original founder of the temple on Philae was Nekhhnebf, the last native pharaoh of Egypt who would have been aware of the delicate state of peace in his empire.

Perhaps it is small wonder, then, that her worship remained strong here long after the other temples had been shut down. And even the conquest by Christian forces was short-lived: the island was under undiluted Christian control from only about 575 (some sources give 595) to 641, scarcely the span of a single life, when it was taken over by conquering Muslims. Flooded by the Aswan dam, when it reemerged through a miracle of modern technology and surprising cooperation between nations, there is no doubt under whose aegis the stones were reconstructed. Isis has retrieved her sanctuary, though she had to bring it out from the waters as the Egyptians believed the world was first made, a mound rising from the waters of chaos.

The symbology is also interesting: the island of Biggeh was Osiris's territory, where in his passive form he waited for the visits of Isis every ten days to bring him offerings. Biggeh is the island which was separated into two sections by the floodwaters, and which also had a temple of Isis, probably for her to "visit" when bringing the offerings for Osiris. The temple of Isis of Philae now stands on the island of Biggeh; Isis and Osiris are no longer parted. Has he risen up from the waters of the Underworld as well?

p. 94, 2. From a letter written by Aurelian to the Roman Senate. Quoted by Edward Wright in his article, "Palmyra, Queen City of the Desert," in *Wonders of the Past, Vol. I,* William H. Wise & Co., New York, N.Y., 1933, p. 235.

p. 94, 3. Lichtheim, Miriam. *Ancient Egyptian Literature: Volume III: The Late Period.* Berkeley, CA: University of California Press, 1980.

Chapter Nine

p. 97, 1. Fortune, Dion. *The Sea Priestess.* Ibid.

p. 98, 2. Fortune, Dion. *The Sea Priestess.* Ibid.

Chapter Ten

p. 102, 1. Ebers, Georg. *An Egyptian Princess.* A. L. Burt Co., English version of the second German edition, 1868.

p. 105, 2. Fortune, Dion. *The Sea Priestess.* Ibid.

Chapter Eleven

p. 116, 1. Medical compounds under the name of Isis are still produced, most notably by Isis Pharmaceuticals Inc., a Carlsbad, California company. An article in the April 30, 1994, edition of the *San Diego Union-Tribune* states that "Isis Pharmaceuticals Inc. this week reported the first positive results from a new type of treatment that attacks diseases at a cellular level.

"The Isis treatment uses so called anti-sense technology. In a small, preliminary test, it appeared to halt a typically intractable disease that causes blindness in AIDS patients and others with weakened immune systems.

"Carlsbad-based Isis reported that its Isis 2922 compound stopped the progression of cytomegalovirus-induced retinitis in all but one of the patients treated with medium to high doses.

" '... We feel confident that the responses of the patients in our study were the result of Isis 2922 therapy,' Dr. Daniel Kisner said.

"Isis said some side effects were noted and that further study was needed ... 'Isis has gone a long way in demonstrating that this problem can be solved,' said James McCamant, editor of the *Medical Technology Stock Letter* in Berkeley. 'Are these test results absolute proof? No,' McCamant said, 'But it does remove most of the doubt about anti-sense technology.'

"Isis plans to launch a broader study by this summer one several hundred patients with CMV retinitis."

Obviously, the naming of the company Isis does not mean that the scientists and managers are Isis-worshippers. However, the ancients did believe in the Power of Her name, and this, although possibly unintentional, is an interesting example of a survival of a tradition of naming medicines for this Goddess.

p. 117, 2. An Egyptian-French underwater archaeological expedition recently rescued an apparently Isian statue fragment and other relics from the submerged ruins of the Pharos Lighthouse. Hundreds of other relics will remain submerged, to be permanently buried by the erection of a seawall which will protect the remains of a nearby historic fort. The expedition, headed by Jean-Yves Empereur of the French Center of Alexandrian Studies, may succeed in bringing up a few more pieces before the construction resumes.

p. 117, 3. Additional information on dreams is included in Chapter Twenty-Three, "Isis and Dreaming."

p. 119, 4. Fortune, Dion. *Aspects of Occultism.* York Beach, ME: Samuel Weiser, Inc., 1973.

p. 122, 5. Majno, Guido. *Healing Hand: Man and Wound in the Ancient World.* Cambridge, MA: Harvard University Press, 1974.

p. 122, 6. Jayne, Walter, M.D. *The Healing Gods of Ancient Civilizatons.* Yale University Press, 1925. Reprinted by University Books, Inc., New Hyde Park, NY, 1962, pp. 66–67.

Chapter Twelve

p. 131, 1. Temple, Robert. *The Sirius Mystery.* Rochester, VT: Inner Traditions, 1987.

p. 141, 2. For Plutarch's account of the origin of the worship of Serapis, please see Appendix B.

p. 148, 3. For an extensive discussion of the Black Virgin, see Ean Begg's *The Cult of the Black Virgin.* New York, NY: Penguin, 1989.

p. 148, 4. Stein, Diane. *The Goddess Book of Days.* St. Paul, MN: Llewellyn Publications, 1988.

Chapter Fourteen

p. 159, 1. I feel obliged to acknowledge that most of the recipes included here are of Asian, specifically Chinese, origin. This may appear strange in a book on Isis. However, I've wanted to include only recipes that I have actually had experience in preparing for feasts, and my cooking skills are primarily limited to Chinese dishes. As the Chinese still celebrate lunar feasts on a regular basis, and because of the similarity between Isis and Kuan Yin, I don't believe I offend my gods with this menu; I hope I don't offend the reader.

p. 166, 2. I am indebted to Scott Cunningham for providing this incantation, which he noted from a translation from an ancient source.

p. 166, 3. Mnevis was another sacred bull-deity of Egypt.

Chapter Fifteen

p. 168, 1. Gioseffi, Daniela. *Earth Dancing.*

p. 168, 2. Spence, Lewis. *The Myths of Ancient Egypt.* London: George G. Harrap & Co., 1917.

p. 170, 3. See *The Search for Omm Sety: Reincarnation and Eternal Love,* by Jonathan Cott and Hanny El Zeini, for more information on this remarkable modern priestess of Isis (New York, NY: Doubleday & Company, Inc., 1987).

p. 175, 4. Buonaventure, Wendy. *Serpent of the Nile: Women and Dance in the Arab World.* London: Saqi Books, 1989.

p. 176, 5. For instructions on creating your own sistrum, please see Chapter Twenty-One, "Isis and the Worship of the Hands."

Chapter Sixteen

p. 182, 1. Neumann, Erich. *Amor and Psyche: The Psychic Development of the Feminine.* Princeton, NJ: Princeton University Press, paperback ed., 1971.

p. 182, 2. Witt, R. E. *Isis in the Greco-Roman World.* Ithaca, NY: Cornell University Press, 1971, p. 249.

p. 182, 3. Lawrence, D. H. *St. Mawr and the Man Who Died.* New York, NY: Vintage Books, a reprint of 1953 paperback edition.

p. 183, 4. Kinstler, Clysta. *The Moon under Her Feet: The Story of Mary Magdalene in the Service of the Great Mother.* San Francisco: Harper, 1991.

p. 183, 5. Fortune, Dion. *Moon Magic.* The Aquarian Press, 1956. Reprinted by Samuel Weiser Inc., New York, 1978.
_____. *The Sea Priestess.* Ibid.
_____. *The Winged Bull.* UK: The Aquarian Press, 1990.

Chapter Seventeen

p. 189, 1. I am indebted to Paula Morgan for inspiring this rite and the parenting dedication which follows.

Chapter Eighteen

p. 194, 1. For a detailed examination of this text and the questions it presents, see Marie-Louise Von Franz' book, *Alchemy: An Introduction to the Symbolism and the Psychology.* Irving, TX: Spring Publications, Inc., 1980.

p. 195, 2. Fortune, Dion. *Moon Magic.* Ibid.

p. 195, 3. Manniche, Lise. *An Ancient Egyptian Herbal.* Austin, TX: University of Texas Press, 1989.

Chapter Twenty

p. 203, 1. Giordano Bruno was an Italian philosopher. His pantheistic views, which included a fondness for Egyptian deities, along with other heresies, led to his imprisonment during the Inquisition and burning at the stake on February 17, 1600.

p. 204, 2. The "Station of Isis," referring to one of the rest-stations visited by processions in Her honor. The priests, carrying a shrine, would go among the populace, stopping at different pre-arranged spots to perform ceremonies and blessings.

p. 205, 3. Krupp, E. C. *Echoes of the Ancient Skies: The Astronomy of Lost Civilizations.* New York, NY: Harper & Row, 1978.

p. 205, 4. Temple, Robert. *The Sirius Mystery.* Ibid.

Chapter Twenty-One

p. 211, 1. Shah, Indries. *Oriental Magic.* New York, NY: Philosophical Library, 1957.

p. 213, 2. Many thanks to Jeff Schröter.

Chapter Twenty-Four

p. 253, 1. Witt, R. E. *Isis in the Greco-Roman World.* Ibid.

p. 256, 2. Festugiére, Andre-Jean. *Personal Religion among the Greeks and Romans.* Reprint of 1954 ed., Westport, CT: Greenwood Press, 1984.

p. 257, 3. Chaney, Earlyne. *Initiation in the Great Pyramid.* Upland, CA: Astara, 1978.

p. 257, 4. Verrette, Joyce. *Winged Priestess.* New York, NY: Fawcett, 1980.

Selected

BIBLIOGRAPHY
——— AND OTHER BOOKS ———
OF INTEREST

Allen, Richard Hinckley. *Star Names, Their Lore and Meaning.* New York: Dover Publications, 1963. Reprint of 1899 edition entitled *Star Names and Their Meanings.*
   A handy guide to ancient star lore.

Angus, S. *The Mystery-Religions and Christianity: A Study in the Religious Background of Early Christianity.* New York: Charles Scribner's Sons, 1925.

Apuleius of Madaura. *The Isis Book* (*Metamorphoses, Book XI*). Translated and with a commentary by J. Gwyn Griffiths. Leiden, The Netherlands: E. J. Brill Publishing Co., 1975.

Ashcroft-Nowicki, Dolores. *First Steps in Ritual: Safe, Effective Techniques for Experiencing the Inner Worlds.* Foreword by Gareth Knight. Wellingborough, Northamptonshire, England: The Aquarian Press, 1982.
   Although all of the exercises offered here are of use to a serious explorer of the mysteries, the chapter entitled "The Egyptian Tradition" offers a simple but powerful rite for exploring the mysteries of Isis. Recommended.

——————————————, ed. *The Forgotten Mage: The Magical Lectures of Colonel C. R. F. Seymour.* Wellingborough, Northamptonshire, England: The Aquarian Press, 1986.

Baring, Anne, and Jules Cashford. *The Myth of the Goddess: Evolution of an Image.* London: Viking Arkana, 1991.
   This wide-ranging book has a substantial section on Isis, and is an excellent reference work on many other goddesses as well. Recommended.

Begg, Ean. *The Cult of the Black Virgin.* New York, NY: Penguin, 1989.

Budge, E. A. Wallis. *Gods of the Egyptians, Vols. I & II.* New York, NY: Dover Publications, 1969 (reprint of 1903 edition).

——————————. *Osiris, Vols. I & II.* New York, NY: Dover Publications, 1973 (reprint of 1911 edition).

——————————. *Egyptian Magic.* Secaucus, NJ: University Books, no publication date. Reprint of 1899 edition.

_____. *From Fetish to God in Ancient Egypt.* New York, NY: Benjamin Blom, Inc., 1972.

    Budge is frequently outdated in his analyses, but his books often include material hard to find in more recent sources.

Budichovsky, Marie-Christine. *La Diffusion des Cultes Isiaques Autour de la Mer Adriatique Vol I. Etudes Preliminaires aux Religions Orientales dans L'Empire Romain.* Leiden, The Netherlands: E. J. Brill Publishing Co., 1977.

Buonaventura, Wendy. *Serpent of the Nile.* London: Saqi Books, 1989.

    A beautifully illustrated examination of the art of dance in the Arab world.

Chaney, Earlyne. *Initiation in the Great Pyramid.* Upland, CA: Astara, 1978.

    The author's evocative memories of a past life in Egypt.

Chuvin, Pierre. *A Chronicle of the Last Pagans.* Translated by B. A. Archer. Cambridge, MA: Harvard University Press, 1990.

Cott, Jonathan, and Hanny El Zeini. *The Search for Omm Sety: Reincarnation and Eternal Love.* New York, NY: Doubleday & Company, Inc., 1987.

    An interesting account of a real-life priestess of Isis, Omm Sety, who believed she had lived in ancient Egypt, and who could guide modern archeologists by her memories. She lived alone for several decades near the Osireion at Abydos, keeping the festivals and serving the gods.

Cumont, Franz. *The Oriental Religions in Roman Paganism.* New York, NY: Dover Publications, 1956.

    Good basic chronology of the spread of the worship of Isis and Serapis.

Cunningham, Scott. *Cunningham's Encyclopedia of Crystal, Gem, and Metal Magic.* St. Paul, MN: Llewellyn Publications, 1988.

_____. *The Complete Book of Incense, Oils, & Brews.* St. Paul, MN: Llewellyn Publications, 1989.

Dill, Samuel. *Roman Society from Nero to Marcus Aurelius.* New York, NY: Meridian Library, 1956 (reprint of 1904 edition).

    Includes an interesting chapter on the worship of Isis and Serapis.

Dunand, Francoise. *Le Culte d'Isis dans le Bassin Oriental de la Mediterran Çe. Etudes Preliminaires aux Religions Orientales dans L'Empire Romain.* Vols. I-III. Leiden, The Netherlands: E. J. Brill Publishing Co., 1973.

Ebers, Georg. *An Egyptian Princess.* A. L. Burt Co., English version of the second German edition, 1868.

Ellis, Normandi. *Awakening Osiris.* Grand Rapids, MI: Phanes Press, 1988.

    This beautiful liturgy is well worth the time and attention of any seeker after the Egyptian deities. Ellis' mastery of sacred imagery is delightful and inspiring to read.

Farrar, Janet and Stewart Farrar. *The Witches Goddess: The Feminine Principle of Divinity*. WA: Phoenix, 1987.

Festugiére, Andre-Jean. *Personal Religion among the Greeks*. Reprint of 1954 ed. Westport, CT: Greenwood Press, 1984.

Fortune, Dion. *Aspects of Occultism*. York Beach, ME: Samuel Weiser Inc., 1973.

——————. *Moon Magic: Being the Memoirs of a Mistress of that Art*. The Aquarian Press, 1956. Reprinted by Samuel Weiser Inc., 1978.

——————. *The Sea Priestess*. The Aquarian Press, 1957. Reprinted by Samuel Weiser Inc., New York, 1978.

——————. *The Winged Bull*. UK: The Aquarian Press, 1990.
    Classic magical novels describing a priestess of Isis. Dion Fortune wrote these books to try to provide a method of "literary initiation" whereby the reader would be connected with the powers behind the books; she succeeded.

Frankfort, Henri. *Ancient Egyptian Religion*. New York, NY: Columbia University Press, 1948.

Grant, Frederick C. *Hellenistic Religions: The Age of Syncretism*. Bobbs-Merrill, Liberal Arts Press, 1953.

Graves, Robert. *Difficult Questions, Easy Answers: A Collection of Essays*. Garden City, NY: Doubleday & Co., 1973.

Griffiths — See Apuleius.

Heyob, Sharon Kelly. *The Cult of Isis among Women in the Greco-Roman World*. Leiden, The Netherlands: E. J. Brill Publishing Co., 1975.

Jayne, Walter Addison, M.D. *The Healing Gods of Ancient Civilizations*. Yale University Press, 1925. Reprinted by University Books, Inc. New Hyde Park, NY, 1962.
    A detailed look at healing deities worldwide.

Kees, Herman. *Ancient Egypt: A Cultural Topography*. Edited by T. G. H. James. Chicago: University of Chicago Press, 1961.
    A detailed, scholarly look at Egyptian society and religious practices.

Kinstler, Clysta. *The Moon under Her Feet: The Story of Mary Magdalene in the Service of the Great Mother*. San Francisco: Harper, 1991.
    This novel casts Mary Magdalene as a Priestess of Isis.

Krupp, E. C. *Echoes of the Ancient Skies: The Astronomy of Lost Civilizations*. New York, NY: Harper & Row, 1978.
    Particularly useful in understanding the ancient Egyptian associations of stars and deities, particularly Isis, Osiris, and Anubis.

Lawrence, D. H. *St. Mawr and The Man Who Died*. Vintage Books, a division of Random House, New York. Reprint of 1953 paperback edition.

The Man Who Died (originally published as *The Escaped Cock*) tells the story of a Christ who did not die on the cross and who took refuge with a priestess of Isis.

Lichtheim, Miriam. *Ancient Egyptian Literature.* 3 vols. Berkeley, CA: University of California Press, 1980.
Excellent translations of both common and uncommon texts.

MacQuitty, William. *Island of Isis: Philae, Temple of the Nile.* New York, NY: Charles Scribner's Sons, 1976.
A beautifully photographed document of the island temple and its history, through the transfer of the temple to higher ground to avoid the floodwaters caused by the Aswan Dam.

Majno, Guido. *Healing Hand: Man and Wound in the Ancient World.* Cambridge, MA: Harvard University Press, 1974.

Manniche, Lise. *An Ancient Egyptian Herbal.* Austin, TX: University of Texas Press, 1989.

Maspero, Gaston. *Popular Stories of Ancient Egypt.* New Hyde Park, NY: University Books, 1967.

Mercatante, Anthony S. *Who's Who in Egyptian Mythology.* New York, NY: Clarkson N. Potter, Inc., 1978.
An excellent guide to Egyptian culture and religious beliefs.

Meyer, Marvin W., ed. *The Ancient Mysteries: A Sourcebook. Sacred Texts of the Mystery Religions of the Ancient Mediterranean World.* San Francisco: Harper & Row, 1987.
Highly useful compendium of some of the more important mystery texts of the ancient world. Contains several documents pertaining to Isis.

Morenz, Siegfried. *Egyptian Religion.* Translated by Ann E. Keep. Ithaca, NY: Cornell University Press, 1973.

Neumann, Erich. *Amor and Psyche: The Psychic Development of the Feminine.* Princeton, NJ: Princeton University Press, paperback ed., 1971.

O'Regan, Vivienne. *The Pillar of Isis.* London: Aquarian/Thorsons, 1992.
An excellent volume, written by a Hierophant-Priestess of the Fellowship of Isis. The Temple Meditations are especially useful and valuable to all seekers after Isis.

Plutarch. *De Iside et Osiride.* Translated and edited by J. Gwyn Griffiths. Cambridge: University Printing House, University of Wales Press, 1970.
A thoroughly annotated translation of Plutarch's examination of the Egyptian faiths in the Greco-Roman world.

Richardson, Alan. *Dancers to the Gods.* Wellingborough, Northamptonshire, England: Aquarian Press, 1985

_____. *Priestess: The Life and Magic of Dion Fortune.* Wellingborough, Northamptonshire, England: Aquarian Press, 1987.

Robertson, Olivia. *The Call of Isis.* Huntington Castle, Clonegal, Enniscorthy, Eire: Cesara Publications.

    The personal account of the co-founder of the Fellowship of Isis describes her methods of healing and trance work.

Rufus, Anneli S. and Kristan Lawson. *Goddess Sites: Europe.* San Francisco: HarperSanFranciso, 1991.

    This bright, delightful book gives information on numerous Goddess sites, including visiting information, hours, costs, routes, and so on. Who could resist staying at the "Hotel Isis," across from the Temple of Isis in Szombathely, Hungary, if only to collect the matchbooks?

Sauneron, Serge. *The Priests of Ancient Egypt.* New York, NY: Grove Press, Inc., 1980.

    A detailed look at the duties of the clergy in the ancient Egyptian temples.

Schwaller De Lubicz, Isha. *Her-Bak.* Vols. I & II. New York, NY: Inner Traditions International Ltd., 1978 (1st American edition).

Solmsen, Friedrich. *Isis among the Greeks and Romans.* Cambridge, MA: Harvard University Press, 1979.

Stambaugh, John E. *Sarapis under the Early Ptolemies.* Leiden, The Netherlands: E. J. Brill Publishing Co., 1972.

Temple, Robert. *The Sirius Mystery.* Rochester, VT: Inner Traditions, 1987.

Tran Tam Tinh, V. *Le Culte des Divinites Orientales à Herculanum.* Leiden, The Netherlands: E. J. Brill Publishing Co., 1971.

Verrette, Joyce. *Winged Priestess.* New York, NY: Fawcett, 1980.

Von Franz, Marie-Louise. *A Psychological Interpretation of* The Golden Ass *of Apuleius.* Irving, TX: Spring Publications, Inc., 1980.

_____. *Alchemy: An Introduction to the Symbolism and the Psychology.* Toronto, Canada: Inner City Books, 1980.

Warner, Marina. *Alone of All Her Sex: The Myth & the Cult of the Virgin Mary.* New York, NY: Knopf, 1983.

Wild, Robert A. *Water in the Cultic Worship of Isis and Sarapis.* Leiden, The Netherlands: E. J. Brill Publishing Co., 1981.

    Detailed descriptions of many temples of Isis and Serapis.

Witt, R. E. *Isis in the Greco-Roman World.* Ithaca, NY: Cornell University Press, 1971.

    Witt's beautifully written book is essential reading for anyone interested in the spread of the faith of Isis during the Greek and Roman periods.

Zabkar, Louis V. *Hymns to Isis in Her Temple at Philae.* University Press of New England at Hanover and London for Brandeis University Press, 1988.

INDEX

A

Abydos, 7-8, 13, 35, 112, 132
Aegean Sea, 23, 159
Agathetyche, 71
AIDS, 123-124
Aion, 130
Al-Khem, 192, 201
Al-Uzza, 37, 53
alchemist(s), 191-193, 197, 261
alchemy, 9, 22, 52, 84, 135, 191-195
Alexander the Great, 2, 140
Alexandria, 2, 22, 35-36, 73-74, 77-78, 91, 97-98, 116-118, 147, 166, 173, 191, 198, 228, 257, 273-274
amethyst, 56
Amnael, 193-194
Amon-Ra, 240, 257
amulets, 50, 210, 212
anchor, 58, 279
ankh, 4, 6, 15, 25, 52, 58, 164, 171, 217, 237
ankham flower water, 49
anoint(ing), 2, 7, 13, 16-17, 43, 111, 196, 211
Anpu (see also "Anubis"), 29, 239
Antares, 204
Antonius, Marcus, 53, 79, 91-92
Anubis, 3, 29, 34, 53, 104, 113, 116, 126, 128, 130-132, 206, 222, 227, 239, 260-261, 269, 276
Anubophores, 131
Anupu (see also "Anubis"), 29-30, 131, 239, 257
Aphrodite (see also "Venus"), 37, 44, 68, 75, 98, 138, 141, 145, 179, 181, 200, 204, 268
Apis Bull, 52-53, 145
Apuleius, 63, 68, 99, 115, 165, 172, 181, 183, 222, 256, 275, 277, 279
aquamarine, 57
Arrow Star, 132
Arsinoe (sister of Cleopatra), 79, 90
Artemis (see also "Diana"), 142-143, 182
"As above, so below," 57, 135
Asclepius, 116-117
Ashteshyt (sister of Zenobia), 94
Ashtoreth, 98, 254
asperge(ing), 12, 164
Astarte, 59, 98, 147, 254, 270
Atlantic, 98, 255
Atlantis, 98, 255-256
Aurelian (Roman Emperor), 93-94
Avalokitesvara, 140
Azekheramun (Meroitic King), 39

B

Barque of Ra, 59, 87, 240
Base of the Most Perfect Triangle, 60
Bast, 52, 137-139, 169, 188, 237
Becoming Weak boat, 83
beer, 8, 76, 113, 138-139, 158, 248
beetles (see also "scarab"), 52-53, 137, 210-211, 233-234
belly dancing, 169
Belona, 70
Bembine Table of Isis (*Mensa Isiaca*), 40
beryl, 57
Binah, 68, 97-98
birth-house(s), 34
Black Isis, 54, 133, 199-201
Black Land, 24, 192, 202
Black Madonna, 139
Black Sea, 28
Black Virgin, 148
Bodhisattva, 140
Boubastis, 72, 138
bread, 58, 76, 157, 159, 161-163, 194, 197, 211-212, 248
Brier, Dr. Robert, 102
Bright Isis, 141, 199-201
bronze, 54-56, 70, 274, 276
Buddhism, 140
Budge, E. Wallis, 51-52, 254, 280
Buonaventure, Wendy, 174

Byblos, 59, 98-99, 226, 269-270

C

Caesar, Julius, 90-91
Caesarea, 91
calendar(s), 31, 101-104, 106, 112, 148, 206, 249
Cancer (constellation), 206
Canis Major, 207
carnelian, 57
Cecropeian Minerva, 70
cedar, 61, 195-196
censing, 18
Ceres (see also "Demeter"), 47, 68, 70
Cernunnos, 145
chakras, 113, 120
chant(s), 17, 73-74, 110, 124
children, 40, 44, 52, 72-73, 87, 103, 107, 119, 141, 147, 161, 168, 185, 187-190, 240, 251, 257, 260, 269
China, 23, 46
Christ, 47, 182-183
Christianity, 216
citrus wood, 61, 165, 214
Cleopatra (the Seventh), 90-92
Cleopatra Selene, 91-92
cobra, 79, 240
Codex Marcianus, 193
Cologne, Germany, 28
color, 5, 29, 51, 55, 58, 61-66, 122, 152, 161, 163, 212, 234, 250
Constantine (Roman Emperor), 23
copal, 19, 166
copper, 54-55, 58, 96, 213-214
Coptos, 36
coral, 57, 63
cornucopia, 47, 58, 75, 217
crescent moon, 58-59, 78, 147, 150, 168, 222, 240
Crowley, Aliester, 57-59

crystal(s), 9, 18-19, 57, 82, 87, 96, 185, 195, 203, 212
Cunningham, Scott, 16
Cybele, 177-178
Cyme, 72

D

dance, 105, 167, 169-170, 172, 174-176, 207, 236, 239
Dark Isis (see also "Black Isis"), 200, 225, 243
Daughter of Isis, 79, 138, 188
de Lubicz, Isha Schwaller, 74
de Pisan, Christine, 16
Delphinus, 53, 206
Demeter (see also "Ceres" and "Persephone"), 47, 60, 69, 141-142, 144
Denderah, 32-34, 75, 113, 132, 203, 205, 207
Devil, 227
Diana, 68, 70, 142-143
Diana Dictynna, 70
Dionysos, 268, 272, 274
Dionysus, 128, 144-145, 159, 165, 169
divination, 56, 137, 210, 212-213, 219-221, 232-234, 262
Divine Midwife, 61, 187, 189
Djed (Backbone, or Pillar, of Osiris), 45, 50, 216, 226
dog(s), 29, 53, 121, 132, 134, 194, 207, 222, 259-261, 269, 277
Dog-Star, 53
dolphin(s), 53, 206
Domitian (Roman Emperor), 131
dream incubation, 117, 247
dreams, 3, 9, 67, 152, 190, 196-198, 229, 238-239, 243-252, 261-262
Duncan, Isadora, 172

E

Ea, 97-98
Eady, Dorothy, 13
eagle(s), 53
Ebers, Georg, 101
Ebers Papyrus, 122
eclipse(s), 86
Egypt, 7, 14, 21-26, 28, 33-35, 38-39, 41, 47, 52-57, 59-61, 64, 71, 73, 77, 89-93, 97-102, 104, 106, 113, 124, 127-131, 134, 137-138, 141-142, 144-148, 155-156, 158, 165, 167-170, 172, 192, 210-211, 217-218, 223, 225-227, 233-234, 237-238, 240, 254-257, 267, 271, 273-274
Eleusis, 68, 165
Ellis, Normandi, 49
embalming, 25, 131, 227
emerald, 44, 57, 135, 211
Emerald Tablet (Smaragadene Tablet), 57, 135
Ennead (Company of the Gods), 137
epagomenal day(s), 103-104, 113
equinox, 82, 106, 112
Eros, 180-182
essential oil, 9, 104, 166, 195-196
Ethiopia, 28, 268
Europa, 143
Eye(s) of Horus, 75, 98-99, 166

F

faience, 51, 211-212
Fayoum Oasis, 71
festivals, 13, 16, 33-34, 38, 99, 101-105, 107, 109, 111-113, 159, 217, 249
Festugiére, Andre-Jean, 256-257
Fifteenth-Day Feast, 104
Flesh of Isis, 7
fluorescent lighting, 17, 64

food, 29, 47, 83, 111, 121, 130, 137, 155-158, 162-163, 244, 248

Fortuna, 204

Fortune, Dion, 62, 67, 97-98, 105, 118, 183, 195, 201, 223, 255, 258

France, 23, 159, 174

frankincense, 9, 18, 92, 99, 166, 195-196

Freya, 145-146

Fu Xi, 141

full moon, 18, 98, 103-104, 152, 164, 232

G

galabayah, 47, 62

Galactrophousa (Isis Lactans), 47

Galen, 115

Gallienus (Roman Emperor), 93

Ganga, 140

gardenia, 49, 194, 196

Garfield, Dr. Patricia, 245-247

Gateway of Life, 61

gazelle(s), 53

Ge, 68, 97-98

Geb, 4, 75, 102-103, 134, 137, 265

Germany, 23, 159

ghawaji dancers, 170

Gioseffi, Daniela, 168

Goddess Above Fate, 225

Goddess of Brightness, 73

Goddess of Healing, 73, 133

Goddess of Love and Magic, 21

Goddess of Magic, 73

Goddess of Ten Thousand Names, 73-74, 89, 205

Goddess of the Air, 3

Goddess of the Moon, 3, 57

Goddess of the Throne, 21, 128

going-forth of Isis, 110-111

gold, 37, 44, 49, 51, 54-57, 59, 72, 77, 113, 137, 151, 191, 193-194, 211, 216-217, 275-277, 279

grain measure (see also "*modius*"), 58

granite, 57, 100

Graves, Robert, 59, 102, 229

Great Cow, 53

Great Mother, 61, 78, 140, 190

Great of Magic, 121

Great Physician, 14, 50, 57, 112, 115, 117, 119, 121, 123, 125

Great Sorceress Who Heals, 21, 76, 121

Griffith, J. Gwyn, 68, 275

griffon(s), 53

Gypsies, 139, 220

H

Hades, 258, 274

Hair of Isis, 63

Hapi (god of the Nile), 108-109

Harita, 140

Harpocrates, 34, 79, 130, 188, 272

harpoon, 55, 58, 96

Harran, 23

Hathor, 34, 55, 58, 113, 130, 138-139, 165, 169, 200, 207, 213, 215, 239, 241, 248

hawk(s), 38, 53, 94, 128-130, 240

healing, 12-18, 23-24, 35-37, 50, 55-57, 60, 65, 73-74, 77, 115-124, 126, 131, 133, 141-142, 159, 235, 243, 247

Hecate, 68, 70, 98

Heget, 241

Hera (see also "Juno"), 76, 98, 141-144, 166

Hermes, 57, 72, 166, 267-268, 271

Hermouthis, 71

Herne, 145

Hidden Goddess, 23

hieros gamos, 36, 251

Hilaria, 126, 230

Hipparchus, 198

hippopotamus, 55, 134, 163, 204, 206, 224

Holy of Holies, 33

horn and crescent head-dress, 58

Horns of the Moon, 58

Horus, 12, 23, 25-26, 34, 38, 47, 51, 55, 58-59, 75, 77, 83-84, 86, 96, 98-99, 102-104, 106, 110, 112, 122, 128-130, 133-138, 146-147, 159, 166, 169, 178, 187-189, 191, 193-194, 204, 216, 225-227, 229-230, 239-240, 267-268, 270-271

hyacinth (jacinth), 57

hymn(s), 1, 5-6, 71-74, 104, 133, 210

hyssop, 15-16, 111

I

Ihy, 152

Imperial Rome, 53

Inanna, 204-205, 226

incandescent lighting, 64

incense, 7, 9, 12, 19, 40-41, 50, 62, 80-81, 92, 99, 107, 151, 163, 165-166, 171, 180, 190, 193-196, 212, 242

initiation, 5-6, 38, 56, 63, 87, 100, 102, 152-153, 181, 183, 185, 208, 227, 231, 234-235, 239, 243, 245, 250, 253, 257, 259, 261-264

Inventrix of Medicines, 121

Io, 142-144

Iseum, 34

Ishtar, 204, 228, 254

Isidis Navigium, 60-61, 98-99, 113, 206, 218

Isidorus, 71, 73, 79

Isis Amenti, 23

Isis and Asian Deities, 139

Isis and Celtic-Scandina-
vian Deities, 145

Isis and Christian Deities,
147

Isis and Egyptian Deities,
128

Isis and Greco-Roman
Deities, 141

Isis as Sea Goddess, 97, 99

Isis Euploia (Isis of Good
Sailing), 97

Isis Hathor, 207

Isis Lactans (Galactrop-
housa), 47

Isis Medica, 121

Isis Myrionymous (Isis of
the Myriad of Names),
73

Isis of Alexandria, 73

Isis of Memphis, 73

Isis of Philae, 73

Isis of the Myriad of
Names (Isis Myriony-
mous), 73, 77

Isis of Victory, 89

Isis Pelagia (Isis of the Sea),
97

Isis Pharia, 98

Isis Satit, 207

Isis Sophia, 54

Isis Sothis, 207

Isis Victrix, 54, 89, 96, 124

Isis-Astarte (see also
"Astarte"), 76, 177

Isis-Inanna (see also
"Inanna"), 76, 177, 179

Isis-Nekhebet, 54

Isis-Renenet, 51

Isis-Sothis, 59, 78, 206, 230

Isopo, 16

ithyphallic (see also "penis"
and "phallus"), 129

J

jacinth (hyacinth), 57

jasmine, 49, 166, 195-196

jasper, 57

Jesus, 147, 226

Juno (see also "Hera"), 70

Jupiter (see also "Zeus"),
182

K

Ka'aba, 37

Kali, 139-140

Keeper of the Robes
(stolist-priestess or
priest), 43

Khemi (the Black Land),
24

Khepra, 137, 202, 211, 239

khereb, 9

Khonsu, 152

King Juba of Mauritania,
91

Kinstler, Clystra, 183

Klea (priestess of Isis and
Osiris), 26, 79, 267

Knot of Isis, 48-49, 55, 60,
140-141, 161

Koiak, Sacred Rites of, 103,
106, 111-112

Kore, 144

Kronos, 72, 267-268

Krupp, E. C., 204

Kuan Yin, 140-141, 161

kundalini, 240

kyphi (incense), 19, 195-
196, 211

L

Lady of Books (see also
"Seshet"), 133

Lady of Green Plants, 73

Lady of Life, 73, 76

Lady of Light, 3, 61, 73, 76

Lady of Light and Flame, 3

Lady of the Green Plants,
3

Lame Year, 102

lamentations, 124, 133

Land of the Sun, 24

lapis lazuli, 57

Lawgiver, 73

Lawrence, D. H., 182-183

Lebanon, 61

Leiden, Netherlands, 39,
275

Leiden Museum, 39

Leo, 206

Library of Alexandria, 2, 22

light, cleansing with, 15,
17-18, 248

Lilith, 195, 224

lingam, 58

lion(s), 53, 194, 225, 237,
242, 271

London, 23, 35-36, 267,
273

Lord of Rainstorms, 73

love, 9, 21-22, 26, 41, 57,
61, 69, 72, 75-76, 86,
89, 94, 96, 123, 128,
132, 134, 140, 145, 150-
152, 161-162, 164-165,
169, 177-183, 185, 190,
192, 196, 200, 224, 230,
233-241, 243, 253, 256,
260, 269

Lucius, 69-70, 79, 97, 99,
256, 278

Lunar Goddess, 18, 54

M

Ma'at, 7, 226

Madinet Madi, 71

Madrid, 39

Majno, Guido, 121-122

malachite, 57, 63

mammisseums, 34

marble, 1, 35, 40, 57, 257

Mardi Gras, 113-114, 216

Maria the Egyptian, 192

Mary, 23, 47, 59, 74, 147-
148, 183

Masonic (philosophy), 24

Matet ("Becoming Strong"
solar boat), 83, 136

Mauritania, 91-92

Mecca, 37

Mediterranean, 12, 21, 59,
98, 141, 158, 165

Melanophores (Wearers of
Black), 61

Menouthis, 36, 77

Mensa Isiaca (Bembine Table of Isis), 40, 221

Meroe, 2, 13, 39

Merul, 130, 188

meryt box, 7, 43

Metamorphoses, 68, 115, 275

Metternich Stele, 136

Middle East, 23, 28, 36, 137

milk, 8, 53, 60, 75, 99, 159, 162-163, 187-188, 276, 279

Milk of Isis, 159, 162, 187-188

Min, 36, 133, 150, 241

Mistress of the Dawn, 3

Mithraism, 216

modius (see also "grain measure"), 58, 142

moon, crescent, 58-59, 78, 87, 140, 147, 150, 159, 168, 171, 222, 240

moon, full, 18, 59, 68, 98, 103-104, 152, 164, 232

Moon Magic, 62, 183, 195, 258

moonstone, 57

Morgan, Vivien Le Fay, 62, 195

Morning Rite, 1-2, 5, 8-9, 81

Mother of the Apis Bull, 53

Mother of the Gods, 70, 77

Mount Anzin, 23

Mozart, Wolfgang Amadeus, 173-174

Murchison Waterfall, 10

music, 9, 98, 110-111, 138, 167-175, 177, 232, 236, 239, 268, 270, 276

music, classical, 173

Mut, 51, 78

myrrh, 9, 19, 81, 166, 195-196, 211, 248

mystery plays, 32, 106, 187

N

names, 4, 20, 24, 52, 57, 70, 73-74, 77-80, 89, 96, 113, 134, 139-140, 143, 165, 172, 183, 202, 205, 207, 227, 254, 265

Naming of the Places, 73-74

naos, 7

Napoleon, 37

natron water, 14-15

Nebthet, 133

Nehallenia, 146

Nekhebet, 51, 236

Nepthys, 86-87, 102-104, 124, 126, 129, 131-134, 137, 149-150, 178, 206, 224, 227, 238-239, 261, 268-269

Neumann, Erich, 182

Night of the Drop, 112

Nike, 60

Nile, 1-2, 10, 12-13, 24, 35, 38-39, 41, 75, 78, 98, 102-103, 106, 108-113, 137, 140, 144, 150, 163, 165-166, 172, 174, 182, 185, 192, 203, 228, 232, 235, 237-238, 254

nilometer(s), 34-35

Noontime Rite, 81-83, 85, 87, 229

Notre Dame, 37, 206

Nu Kua, 141

Nubia, 28, 39, 106, 130, 256

Nut, 4, 57, 75, 83, 103, 108-110, 128-130, 132, 134-135, 137, 188, 239, 260, 265

O

Odenathus, 93-94

Odin, 146-147, 226

offerings, 2, 7-9, 34, 71, 81, 97, 100, 111, 154-157, 197, 206, 279

olivine, 58

oloi, 173-174

Olympus, 71, 181

Omm Sety, see "Sety, Omm"

One Above Fate, 90

oneirocrit, 248

opopanax resin, 19

ordination, 107, 233, 263-264

Orion, 206

orison, 1, 151

Ortygian Proserpine, 70

Osar-Apis, 116, 141

Osireion at Abydos, 13

Osiris, 3-4, 7-8, 13, 21-22, 24-26, 33, 35-36, 45, 47, 49-50, 52-54, 59-62, 72, 79, 89-92, 97-100, 102-106, 108, 111-112, 116, 122-124, 126-129, 131-137, 141-142, 144-150, 157-158, 164-166, 169, 177-178, 181-183, 187-188, 191, 193, 202-203, 206-207, 212, 216, 220, 223-228, 230, 233, 235-236, 238-241, 254-255, 257-261, 265, 267-272, 274

Ouroboros, 192

Oxyrhynchus Papyrus, 140

P

Padiusiri, 1, 198

paeanistai, 172

palm(s), 15, 63, 70, 74, 93, 99, 102, 120, 123, 150, 156-157, 164-165, 213, 216-218, 220, 232, 234-235, 260, 276-277

Palmyra, 93

Paphian Venus, 70

Paphos, 69

parenting, 189-190

Paris, 28, 37, 206

pastophors, 117-118

peacock(s), 53

pearl(s), 44, 57, 63, 151

Pedesi and Pehor, 39

Pedikhons, Prince, 94-95

penis (see also "ithyphallic" and "phallus"), 129

pentagram, 59

peret Sopdet, 102

perfect year, 102

perfume(s), 196, 270, 276

peridot, 58

Persephone, 68, 78, 98, 141, 144, 181, 273

Pessinuntia, 70

Petra, 37-38, 53, 92-93

phallus (see also "ithy-phallic" and "penis"), 58-59, 271

Pharaoh's Treasury, 37

Pharos at Alexandria, 36, 77-78, 100, 116, 228

Philae, Island of, 23, 31, 38-39, 73, 108, 113, 130, 157, 188

Phoebus, 69

Pietà, 147

pig(s), 53

pine cones, 61, 165

plants, 3, 56, 73, 108, 119-120, 164, 166, 194, 201

Plato, 255

Pleiades, 206

plexuses, 120

Pliny, 204

Ploiaphesia, 98-99, 106, 112, 165, 172, 206, 275, 277, 279

Plutarch, 26, 62, 131, 133, 141, 195, 255, 258, 267, 269, 271, 273

PMS, 184

polarity, 129, 184-185, 227, 241

praisesongs, 67, 71

Proserpine (see also "Persephone"), 69-70

Psyche, 180-182

Ptolemy (astronomer), 203

Ptolemy (brother of Cleoptra), 90

purification, 4, 10-16, 18, 32, 96, 99, 121, 174-176, 227

Pythagoras, 60, 68

Q

Queen Astarte, 59, 147

Queen Isis, 70

Queen of Rivers and Winds and Sea, 72

Queen of Seamanship, 73

Queen of the Thunderbolt, 72

Queen of the Underworld, 2-3

Queen of War, 72

R

Ra, 25, 55, 59, 75, 79, 83-85, 87, 94, 97, 100, 105, 108, 122, 129, 135, 137-139, 142, 146, 168-169, 191, 202, 240

ram(s), 53

rayon, 65

red hawk, 38

renpit geb, see "Lame Year"

renpit nofert, see "perfect year"

Rhamnusia, 70

Rhea, 68, 267

Rhodophoria, 165

ritual clothing, 44, 47, 60, 64

ritual(s), 2, 5-7, 9, 12-13, 16-18, 43-45, 47-48, 50-51, 56, 59-66, 80, 84, 102, 106-107, 111, 121, 132, 157, 165, 175, 182, 214, 220-222, 224, 248, 257, 259, 261, 264, 275-276, 280

robe(s), 2, 12, 43-44, 47-48, 59, 61-63, 70, 80, 93, 102, 107, 131, 146, 206, 223, 233, 263

Robes of Concealment, 59

Roman Legions, 23, 141

Rome, 1, 20, 39, 53, 56, 90-91, 93-94, 97, 131, 142, 256

ruby, 58

rudder, 47, 59

S

Sacred House, 27

sacred marriage, 36, 224, 257

sail, 59, 98-100, 279

sapphire, 58

Sarapis [sic], see also "Serapis," 12, 173, 223, 273-274, 276

Satit, 207

scarab (see also "beetles"), 52-53, 210-211, 233

sceptre, 51, 59

School of Medicine at Alexandria, 22, 116

Scorpion Goddesses, 53, 136

Sekhmet, 139, 237

Selkit, 136, 204

Semket ("Becoming Weak" solar boat), 83

Serapis, 2, 12, 22, 34-36, 58, 80, 116, 131, 141-142, 158, 188, 204, 220, 228, 244, 249, 274

serpent(s), 52, 54, 60, 70, 94, 174, 271, 273

Serpot, Queen, 94-95

Seshet (see also "Lady of Books"), 133, 236

Set, 4, 14-15, 22, 26, 30, 48, 51, 53-55, 58-60, 65, 71, 73, 75, 83-84, 91, 99-100, 102-104, 112, 122-123, 127, 130-138, 145, 149-151, 157-158, 160, 162-164, 169-171, 173, 178, 184, 187, 193, 210-211, 217, 219-220, 224, 226-227, 230, 232, 236, 238-239, 244, 247-249, 257, 260, 267, 269, 277, 279

Set knot, 60, 134

Set-headed scepter, 29, 230

Set-headed staff, 51

Sety, Omm, 13, 35, 169

Seven Scorpion Goddesses, 53, 136

Severus (Roman Emperor), 93

Shaddai el Chai, 68

shaman(s), 18, 145, 175, 210, 216, 222

Shen, 151, 164, 217, 236

shrine box, 7, 35, 41

Shu, 137

Silk Road, 2, 46

silver, 36, 54, 56-57, 72, 105, 159, 164, 193-194, 217-218, 276

Siq, 37

Sirius, 53, 79, 87, 102-103, 132, 202-203, 206-208, 218, 228, 240-241, 255, 260

sistrum, 2, 4, 28, 47, 60, 96, 137, 144, 167, 171, 175-176, 213-216, 239, 277

situla, 60, 158-159, 188

Smaragadene Tablet (Emerald Tablet), 135

Sobek, 127, 150, 165, 235

Socnaipou Nesos, 101, 127, 220

Sothis, 24, 79, 102, 108-110, 206-207, 218, 228

spells, 79, 122, 124, 178

Spence, Lewis, 168

Sphinx, 35, 242

sponge, 60, 248

St. Denis, Ruth, 172

stolist-priestess or priest (Keeper of the Robes), 43

stone(s), 13, 18-19, 30, 34, 37, 40, 48-49, 51, 55-58, 60, 101, 163-164, 185, 194-195, 200, 211, 233, 254

Sun Goddess, 3, 54, 82, 87, 229

symbols, 12, 50, 52-54, 58-59, 61, 91, 98, 129, 138, 146, 159-160, 162, 213, 217-218, 221, 234, 249-250

T

T'ang Dynasty, 23

Tacitus, 59, 145

Tahuti (see also "Thoth"), 103, 106, 135, 228, 236, 257, 267

Tamera, 24

Tara, 140

tarot, 219-221, 231, 234

Taurus, 204

Tefnut, 8, 137

Temple, Robert, 131, 206

Temple of Debod, 39

Temple of Dendur, 39

Temple of Taffa, 39

temple(s), 1-4, 6-9, 11-14, 19, 21-24, 27-41, 43-46, 52-54, 56-57, 62, 67, 69, 71-73, 79, 81-82, 91-93, 98-102, 106, 108, 110-113, 115, 117-118, 121, 124, 127, 131-132, 135, 137, 139, 141-143, 147, 150, 155-159, 163-165, 167, 169-170, 172-176, 178, 183, 185-187, 193, 195, 197-198, 203-208, 210-211, 213, 216-217, 220, 222-224, 226-227, 230, 232, 237, 244-245, 247-248, 251, 256-257, 259, 263-265, 276, 279-280

Thames, 35

The Golden Ass, 99, 183

Theosophic (philosophy), 24

Thet knot, 48-49, 140

Thor, 146

Thoth (see also "Tahuti"), 12, 25-26, 57, 71, 75, 82-83, 103, 117, 130, 135-136, 152, 165, 192-193, 211, 226-227, 236-237, 257, 259, 267

throne, 15, 21, 25-26, 46, 59-60, 79, 90-91, 93, 128-129, 132-134, 146, 169, 188, 205, 223, 230, 235, 238

triangle, 60, 75, 206, 213

Turin Papyrus, 84

turquoise, 58, 66, 212, 260

Tutankhamen, 45, 56

Typhon, 267-272, 274

U

ueb ("washed ones"), 12

ueb (Set-headed staff), 51

Upper Egypt, 23, 38

Upper Nile, 10

uraeus, 47, 52, 60

uraeus-snake, 52

Ursa Major, 204

ushabti, 242

V

Veiled Isis, 68

Venus (see also "Aphrodite"), 44, 68, 70, 145, 179, 181-182, 204

Versluis, Arthur, 84

Vesuvius, 158

Virgin Mary, 23, 47, 59

Virgo, 204-205

Voltaire, 220

W

wand, 9, 60, 96

Wearers of Black (Melanophores), 61

Wepawet, 130

wheat, 58, 60, 144, 146, 194, 204, 223

Wicca, 28

Wild, Robert, 12

wine, 8, 99, 144, 158-159, 161-162, 195-196, 232

Winged Isis, 46-47, 60, 78

winter solstice, 54, 106, 216-217

Witt, R. E., 182, 253

Wolinski, Arelene, 113

X

Xenophon, 143, 182

Y

Yemaja, 97

yoni, 60-61

Ysis, Ladye of Herbs, 16

Yssop, 16

Z

Zenobia, 92-94

Zeus (see also "Jupiter"), 142-144, 166, 268

On the following pages you will find listed, with their current prices, some of the books now available on related subjects. Your book dealer stocks most of these and will stock new titles in the Llewellyn series as they become available. We urge your patronage.

TO GET A FREE CATALOG

You are invited to write for our bi-monthly news magazine/catalog, *Llewellyn's New Worlds of Mind and Spirit*. A sample copy is free, and it will continue coming to you at no cost as long as you are an active mail customer. Or you may subscribe for just $10 in the United States and Canada ($20 overseas, first class mail). Many bookstores also have *New Worlds* available to their customers. Ask for it.

In *New Worlds* you will find news and features about new books, tapes and services; announcements of meetings and seminars; helpful articles; author interviews and much more. Write to:

Llewellyn's New Worlds of Mind and Spirit
P.O. Box 64383-560, St. Paul, MN 55164-0383, U.S.A.

TO ORDER BOOKS AND TAPES

If your book store does not carry the titles described on the following pages, you may order them directly from Llewellyn by sending the full price in U.S. funds, plus postage and handling (see below).

Credit card orders: VISA, MasterCard, American Express are accepted. Call us toll-free within the United States and Canada at 1-800-THE-MOON.

Special Group Discount: Because there is a great deal of interest in group discussion and study of the subject matter of this book, we offer a 20% quantity discount to group leaders or agents. Our Special Quantity Price for a minimum order of five copies of *Mysteries of Isis* is $79.80 cash-with-order. Include postage and handling charges noted below.

Postage and Handling: Include $4 postage and handling for orders $15 and under; $5 for orders over $15. There are no postage and handling charges for orders over $100. Postage and handling rates are subject to change. We ship UPS whenever possible within the continental United States; delivery is guaranteed. Please provide your street address as UPS does not deliver to P.O. boxes. Orders shipped to Alaska, Hawaii, Canada, Mexico and Puerto Rico will be sent via first class mail. Allow 4-6 weeks for delivery. **International orders:** Airmail – add retail price of each book and $5 for each non-book item (audiotapes, etc.); Surface mail – add $1 per item.

Minnesota residents add 7% sales tax.

Mail orders to:
Llewellyn Worldwide, P.O. Box 64383-560, St. Paul, MN 55164-0383, U.S.A.

For customer service, call (612) 291-1970.

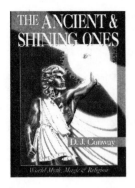

THE ANCIENT & SHINING ONES

World Myth, Magic & Religion

by D.J. Conway

The Ancient & Shining Ones is a handy, comprehensive reference guide to the myths and deities from ancient religions around the world. Now you can easily find the information you need to develop your own rituals and worship using the Gods/Goddesses with which you resonate most strongly. More than just a mythological dictionary, *The Ancient & Shining Ones* explains the magickal aspects of each deity and explores such practices as Witchcraft, Ceremonial Magick, Shamanism and the Qabala. It also discusses the importance of ritual and magick, and what makes magick work.

Most people are too vague in appealing for help from the Cosmic Beings—they either end up contacting the wrong energy source, or they are unable to make any contact at all, and their petitions go unanswered. In order to touch the power of the universe, we must re-educate ourselves about the Ancient Ones. The ancient pools of energy created and fed by centuries of belief and worship in the deities still exist. Today these energies can bring peace of mind, spiritual illumination and contentment. On a very earthy level, they can produce love, good health, money, protection, and success.

0–87542–170–9, 448 pgs., 7 x 10, 300 illus., softcover **$17.95**

EGYPTIAN MAGICK

Enter the Body of Light & Travel the Magickal Universe

by Gerald & Betty Schueler

(Formerly *Coming Into the Light*.) The ancient Egyptians taught a highly complex philosophy which rivals the magickal doctrine taught today. Clearly documented is a major element of the system, the Magickal Universe—the invisible realm that exists all around us but is hidden from our physical senses. Through rituals (which are provided in *Egyptian Magick*), the Egyptian magician would enter his Body of Light, or auric body, and shift his consciousness; he could then see and converse with the gods, goddesses and other beings who are found in these regions.

This book reveals Egyptian magick in a way that has never been done before. It provides modern translations of the famous magickal texts known as *The Book of the Dead*, and shows that they are not simply religious prayers or spells to be spoken over the body of a dead king. Rather, they are powerful and highly effective rituals to be performed by living magicians who seek to know the truth about themselves and their world.

1-56718-604-1, 432 pgs., 6 x 9, 24 color plates, softcover **$19.95**

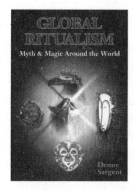

GLOBAL RITUALISM

Myth & Magic Around the World

by Denny Sargent

The concept of ritual and spirituality is common to all peoples, as the same archetypal powers dwell in the psyches of people everywhere. From Haiti to Egypt, *Global Ritualism* analyzes the common themes and archetypal symbols of higher ritual so that you can define how these archetypes play out in your own life. As you build a "global vocabulary" of such spiritual and magical symbols, you will be able to construct your own vibrant, living rituals—actively following a mythos that you create rather than one that has been given to you.

Let the subconscious language of human archetypes become your path to spiritual evolution and meaning. Become an "eclectic ritualist" and dare to live a more fulfilling life! Includes 300 photos of actual rituals as they are enacted around the world, including 16 pages of color photos.

0-87542-700-6, 256 pgs., 271 photos, 16 color pgs., 7 x 10, softcover..............$19.95

MAIDEN, MOTHER, CRONE

The Myth and Reality of the Triple Goddess

by D.J. Conway

The Triple Goddess is with every one of us each day of our lives. In our inner journeys toward spiritual evolution, each woman and man goes through the stages of Maiden (infant to puberty), Mother (adult and parent) and Crone (aging elder). *Maiden, Mother, Crone* is a guide to the myths and interpretations of the Great Goddess archetype and her three faces, so that we may better understand and more peacefully accept the cycle of birth and death.

Learning to interpret the symbolic language of the myths is important to spiritual growth, for the symbols are part of the map that guides each of us to the Divine Center. Through learning the true meaning of the ancient symbols, through facing the cycles of life, and by following the meditations and simple rituals provided in this book, women and men alike can translate these ancient teachings into personal revelations.

Not all goddesses can be conveniently divided into the clear aspects of Maiden, Mother and Crone. This book covers these as well, including the Fates, the Muses, Valkyries and others.

0-87542-171-7, 240 pgs., 6 x 9, softcover...$12.95

MYTHIC ASTROLOGY

Archetypal Powers in the Horoscope

by Ariel Guttman & Kenneth Johnson

Here is an entirely new dimension of self-discovery based on understanding the mythic archetypes represented in the astrological birth chart. Myth has always been closely linked with astrology; all our planets are named for the Graeco-Roman deities and derive their interpretative meanings from them. To richly experience the myths which lie at the heart of astrology is to gain a deeper and more spiritual perspective on the art of astrology and on life itself.

Mythic Astrology is unique because it allows the reader to explore the connection between astrology and the spirituality of myth in depth, without the necessity of a background in astrology, anthropology or the classics. This book is an important contribution to the continuing study of mythology as a form of New Age spirituality and is also a reference work of enduring value. Students of mythology, the Goddess, art, history, Jungian psychological symbolism and literature—as well as lovers of astrology—will all enjoy the text and numerous illustrations.

0-87542-248-9, 382 pgs., 7 x 10, 100 illus., softcover **$17.95**

WHISPERS OF THE MOON

The Life & Work of Scott Cunningham, Pagan Prophet

by David Harrington & deTraci Regula

Scott Cunningham (b. 1956–d. 1993) authored more than 50 books in his lifetime, 15 of which lay the foundation for the non-institutional growth of modern Wicca. For tens of thousands of new Wiccans, their first magic circle was cast using his words of power. In addition, Scott also opened up a new understanding of positive, nature-based magics such as herb, gem and elemental magic.

Whispers of the Moon combines Scott's unfinished autobiography with the added efforts of two of his closest friends. While the book traces his life and growth as a writer as well as a philosopher-magician, it also includes some of Scott's poetry, portions of letters, exposition of his personal philosophy and religion, and the complete text of his self-published pamphlet from 1982, *A Formula Book of Magical Incenses & Oils*.

With remembrances of Scott from many people, this book answers questions about his life, illness, and death at age 37; his involvement in various Wiccan traditions; and his methods of research and discipline as a writer. What's more, it clearly demonstrates his importance as a leader of modern-day nature religion.

ISBN: 1-56718-559-2, 6 x 9, 272 pp., photos, softcover **$15.00**